ActsofFaith

AdamFaith

THE AUTOBIOGRAPHY

ActsofFaith

BANTAM PRESS

LONDON · NEW YORK · TORONTO · SYDNEY · AUCKLAND

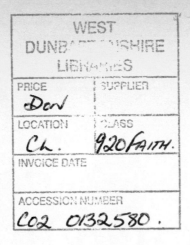
TRANSWORLD PUBLISHERS LTD
61–63 Uxbridge Road, London W5 5SA

TRANSWORLD PUBLISHERS (AUSTRALIA) PTY LTD
15–25 Helles Avenue, Moorebank, NSW 2170

TRANSWORLD PUBLISHERS (NZ) LTD
3 William Pickering Drive, Albany, Auckland

Published 1996 by Bantam Press
a division of Transworld Publishers Ltd
Copyright © Adam Faith 1996

Reprinted 1996

A catalogue record for this book is available from the British Library
ISBN 0593 039416

Printed and bound in Great Britain by
Mackays of Chatham PLC, Chatham, Kent

For
Jacqueline
and
Katya

Acknowledgements

My thanks to:

Jack Martin, for his friendship to me and my family, and for introducing me to David Hockney and his work; Andrew Tribe, my old friend who has saved me from myself on many occasions, and made me laugh like a drain while he was doing it; Ravi Tikoo, who has given me the benefit of his great wisdom; Rodney Milne-Day (minor), a kind and patient man, a true gentleman and friend; Dave Courtney, who forgave me when I forgot about friendship; Lord (Bernard) Donahue, who, in times of trouble, was one of the first to offer me his support, for which I'll always be grateful.

Ross, Mara and Lorenzo and the kids, who made me, Jackie and Katya feel as if San Lorenzo's was like a second home.

Terry O'Neill, my first true friend – I hope it lasts for ever.

Bill Bowman, for his support and sensitivity in moments of dire need; Mickey Towner – a family couldn't have a more concerned and loyal friend; Paul and Karen Killik – good friends and my best audience; the 'Kelly' family from Henfield – a very great thank-you for helping Katya and Jackie get through my car crash; Mario, who makes it impossible to be miserable in his wonderful restaurant Signor Sassi.

Alan Field for rekindling my interest in acting.

Helena (Helly) Sykes, Katya's surrogate sister, and a wonderful friend to Jackie and me, for keeping us laughing round the camp-fires of Africa with her readings of Mills and Boon.

And Sir Harry and Judy Solomon, my newest friends, who so often seem like my oldest.

And thanks to:

Will Pearson for his contribution to this book. And a big thank-you to Emma Tremlett whose editing skills helped to get this book into a shape fit to put before the publishers. A very special thanks to my literary agent, Ed Victor.

Roy Wilson and Ian Hodgson (and dear Wally) who are more family than friends.

There's nothing I could do, or say, about Alan Shalet, to repay him for his friendship over the years. And also Minnie Irving, the most wonderful mother-in-law a man could have.

And of course, thank you to Jacqueline, for putting up with me, and loving me more than I deserve; and Katya, for making her dad feel loved and important.

ListofIllustrations

A rare early sighting: Pamela and me watching over the twins, Roger and Christine.

Acton Vale flats, still lurking. Ours was the top one. *Terry O'Neill.*

Mean, moody and magnificent, James Dean, *East of Eden. Kobal Collection.*

Me as James Dean – East of Acton. *Victoria & Albert Museum/Harry Hammond.*

The place that launched a thousand hips – the 2i's coffee bar. *Topham Picture Library.*

Six-Five Special, BBC TV, November 1957 with my best mate Hurgy on the washboard, far right. *British Film Institute.*

Eat your heart out, Elvis – *Drum Beat*, BBC TV, 3 April 1959. *BBC.*

Recording 'Someone Else's Baby' in Abbey Road No. 2 studio with John Barry, October 1959. *Rex Features.*

Adam and Eve – Eve Taylor, the Agent from Hell. *Rex Features.*

X-rated stuff – my first film role. *The Vintage Magazine Co.*

'What Do You Want?' hits number one in the NME charts. *British Library Newspaper Library.*

A Rank Studios bash – so many women, so little time. *Victoria & Albert Museum/Harry Hammond.*

Live at Wembley – the 1960 NME Poll Winners concert. *Victoria & Albert Museum/Harry Hammond*.

This is why I went into show business? September 1960. *John Frost*.

Pan-Galactic line-up, 1960. From left to right: Billy Fury, Jess Conrad, Gene Vincent, Joe Brown, Eddie Cochran, me, Marty Wilde.

'Poor me' – my second No. 1.

Cliff Richard and me rehearsing for the Royal Command Variety Performance, May 1960 (Cliff is on the left!). *Popperfoto*.

Who's that woman standing next to Lonnie Donegan? *Popperfoto*.

Getting sketched by Feliks Topolski, for the BBC's flagship chat show, *Face to Face*, December 1960. *BBC*.

Tudor Court, Esher – my own little home in the west. *Victoria & Albert Museum/Harry Hammond*.

My 21st, with Mum and Dad. *Popperfoto*.

I get my first (BBC) TV series, September 1962. Backing by the Roulettes. From left to right: John Rogers, me, Peter Thorpe. *Popperfoto*.

Worse than words can say – John Rogers (left) is killed in a crash on the way to a gig in Sunderland. *British Library Newspaper Library*.

Mandy Rice-Davies leaves the smoke of scandal behind at Heathrow, 1963. *Hulton Getty*.

Jackie, my wife, before we met.

The gang's all here – the Faith team at work. Clockwise from me: Janice Sherbourne (secretary); The Roulettes – Bob Henrit (drums), Peter Thorpe (rhythm guitar), Mod Rogan (bass) and Russ Ballard (lead guitar); Doris Askham (fan club helper); Eve Taylor (manager); Alan Shalet (accountant); Maurice Press (agent); Dennis Nelhams (PA); Bert Harris (roadie); Angela Miall (fan club secretary); Vincente Catala (butler); Angelina Catala (cook) and Lesley Miall (fan club helper). *Rex Features*.

Following in the footsteps – Sandie Shaw on piano, Chris Andrews playing it. *Rex Features*.

The Beatles and The Rolling Stones head the December 1964 chart – just a little bit of competition.

Taking an early bath from the horrendous South Africa tour. *John Frost*.

£55,000 poorer, but I was so glad to be home. *Syndication International*.

Jackie: one look and I was in love. *Syndication International*.

'Take good care of your baby . . .' I think we got engaged around this time. *Terry O'Neill*.

We wanted a quiet little wedding. Caxton Hall, 19 August 1967. *Hulton Getty*.

Icons of our times – Dame Sybil Thorndike with Noël Coward – two of my life's greatest influences. *Hulton Getty*.

Jack looks great but what *was* I thinking of? *Terry O'Neill.*

As Feste, in *Twelfth Night* at Northampton Rep, February 1970. *Popperfoto.*

Hands up! Birth of our daughter and only child, Katya, in 1970. *Terry O'Neill.*

Budgie hits the unsuspecting airwaves, April 1971. *London Weekend Television.*

On location with Charlie Endell, aka Ian Cuthbertson, 1972. *London Weekend Television.*

About to get duffed up on *Budgie* (note the 'Budgie Jacket'). *London Weekend Television.*

Getting duffed up . . . by John Rhys Davies. *London Weekend Television.*

And getting told off by Ian Cuthbertson. *London Weekend Television.*

Now get out of that . . . 14 August 1973. The Granada's engine block is on the back seat. *Hulton Getty.*

Crawling from the wreckage – in ward G4 of Crawley hospital. *Terry O'Neill.*

Rising like Lazarus from my day bed – the one where I discovered I had a daughter. *Terry O'Neill.*

Don't mess with me, kid . . . Katya, tender in age, but not in will.

Katya with Jackie in bed.

I survived the cemetery – just. Post-crash, 1974. *Terry O'Neill.*

On the set of *Stardust* with David Essex. That's me sitting right at the back. *British Film Institute.*

A scene from *Stardust*: Mike Menary rolling up with Jim Maclaine between takes. *British Film Institute.*

This hurts me more than it hurts you . . . more *Stardust* memories. *British Film Institute.*

Leo Sayer, 1974. *Rex Features.*

Tommy Yeardye's wife, Tommy, Michael Medwin, Michael Parkinson, me and Florence, my darling fur coat – Beverly Hills Hotel, Los Angeles, 1975. *Terry O'Neill.*

Seventies Man – there's Florence again. *Rex Features.*

Crowhurst Place, 1979.

At home with Paul and Linda McCartney plus children, Michael Jackson, Jackie, Angelina and Katya and the boys from Blackpool – Wally Walker, Roy Wilson and Ian Hodgson.

With Paul McCartney, 1980.

Jackie's riding instructor, Paul Redmond, with Jackie, Katya and me, 1980.

Working hard at my desk in Fortnum & Mason's, 1980. *M & M Management/David Montgomery.*

This is what the helicopter looked like before I bent it. *M & M Management/David Montgomery.*

With Roger Daltrey and John McVicar, Cannes 1980. *Syndication International.*

Rehearsing *Alfie* with director Alan Parker, Liverpool Playhouse, October 1983.

No such thing as a private life? *British Library Newspaper Library.*

Chris Evert, 1984. *Rex Features.*

With Elton John, 1985. *Rex Features.*

The *Sun* breaks the news of a 'broken' heart. *John Frost.*

Budgie the Musical first-night party, with Seb Coe, 1988. *Syndication International.*

With Don Black, Ronnie Corbett and Jimmy Tarbuck at the same bash. *Syndication International.*

Linda Agram, me and Helly (Helena Sykes, Kat's best friend) in the Serengetti, 1988.

Morning ablutions, Jackie and Katya, Sand River, Masai Mara, 1988.

En famille, *Budgie the Musical*, first night. *Rex Features.*

With the then chancellor, Nigel Lawson, his wife, Thérèse, and Jackie, after a party in aid of Great Ormond Street Children's Hospital.

The *Daily Mail* heralds the 'Faith in Money' column, 25 November 1988. *British Library Newspaper Library.*

The old proverbial hits the fan – and I come out covered in it. The Levitt débâcle, January 1991. *British Library Newspaper Library.*

Well, it seemed like a really good idea to start with . . . The fateful 'I can make you into a millionaire' headline. *British Library Newspaper Library.*

With my oldest friend Terry O'Neill in 1991. *Rex Features.*

Love Hurts, Zoë Wanamaker and 'our' baby, 1992. *BBC.*

Hard at it filming *Love Hurts* in Israel. *BBC.*

A *Working Lunch* lunch, on the BBC business programme, 1994. *Rex Features.*

How to make something out of nothing – the art of tabloid news. *British Library Newspaper Library.*

Just good friends . . . with Louise Lombard. *Rex Features.*

Katya graduates from Harvard University – I broke through security to sit behind her, hence the astonished look on her face.

My all-time favourite photograph of Katya and me.

ActsofFaith

'Goodbye,' said the fox. 'And now here is my secret, a very simple secret: it is only with the heart that one can see rightly; what is essential is invisible to the eye.'

Antoine de Saint-Exupéry
The Little Prince

ChapterOne

MY GRANDMOTHER WAS A PROSTITUTE! I DON'T REMEMBER being in the least bit surprised by this startling news. I can't exactly say why, but it seemed perfectly normal to me that my mum's old lady should have earned her daily bread by working the pubs in Acton High Street. It sort of fitted in with what little I'd picked up, over the years, about my 'maternal' grandmother. 'A little' was exactly what I did know about my mum's family. Nell – I can't remember when I called my mum anything else other than her Christian name – wasn't the sort of person that sat around with the brood at her feet, regaling us with family folklore. Most of what I know about my family history is more from osmosis.

Come to think of it, I have never known a flipping thing about my mum's dad. Where, what, who was Grandad? There was a rumour that the old boy had slunk off to serve in the Great War and had never come back. 'The Old Cow', as my mum called her, was left stranded with three young children and a reef of debt, so she had to fend for her family in any way she could.

1

Now don't get me wrong! I'm not, in any way, standing in judgement on her. Times were hard and she had a family to raise, she did it the only way she knew how. But her choice of lifestyle didn't exactly make for a normal upbringing for my mum and her brother and sister.

Even though my Aunt Doll denies that her mum's extra-curricular activities included money changing hands for services rendered, it sort of fits in with my mum's view of it all. I remember well one night my mum, for some reason, breaking the rule of a lifetime and telling me a little bit about her childhood.

For grandma, business came first, and her children had better not get in the way of it. The last thing a punter wanted to see, when he came in through her front door with carnal pleasure on his mind, was three small examples of its consequence. God help the kids if he took fright and scarpered. The Old Cow would go ballistic.

By the fire she kept a hand-shovel. Her weapon.

Blinded by drink and rage she'd set about the kids. Laying into them until they were too black and blue to take any more, or her arm too tired to lift the flailing shovel.

By the time the armistice was signed, Ellen, the oldest, was eight. She'd developed the hearing of a bat. At the first scrape of the key in the lock she'd grab her younger brother and sister and bundle them into the cupboard under the stairs. They'd cower there in the dark until the grunting above stopped and the soft slow creaks on the staircase overhead told them it was safe to come back out. Blinking at the brightness from the stark, white light hanging uncovered from the hall ceiling, they'd cautiously creep out, like bunnies from their burrow, and play within easy sound of the front door; waiting, ears pricked, on the old girl coming back with fresh goods.

They knew neglect all right, and a terrible fear. But in one way the children were lucky: they had Ellen. She became the mother that they should have had; the one who saved them and cared for them. My Aunt Doll swears that Ellen saved her life. And Ellen Wright was my mother, Nell.

There's no doubt about it Ellen was an amazing woman. I can't say whether I've inherited any of her strength of mind, her will, or the overwhelming drive she had to care for people. Perhaps I've kept nothing more than the sharp jaw-line and cheekbones that are the last echo of my grandmother. But I do

2

know that for my mum, when she was small, life was all about survival; the practical business of getting through the days, one after another. That was what she'd learned from growing up. Her idea of loving was to provide for her children, and defend them to the death. But loving them? How, in a cupboard under the stairs, hiding for her very life, could she have learned about that?

Yes, Nell was something else, all right. But maybe more as a woman than a mum.

In Nell's home, we were fed, we were clothed, we got on with it. Life was that simple, that direct. Yet I can't remember ever feeling deprived of anything as a kid. It seemed to me that it was a normal, average, happy upbringing.

But something must have been missing, because I've grown up wanting to be loved by the wide world, and all the people in it. Especially the women. Maybe it's to do with having a strong woman as a mum.

I was born Terence Nelhams (or so I was led to believe), in the middle of an air raid, on 23 June 1940. It was the one time when my mum's blitz routine broke down. Instead of running for the park, where the shelter was, she got down under the kitchen table and gave birth to me.

Why does one memory stick in the mind's eye and not another? For me the past is like a darkened theatre with a spotlight highlighting the occasional memory. I never get to see the whole scene, but certain memories are ablaze with feeling, colour, texture and smell.

Here's one! Terry Nelhams, flat on his back, rattling down the road in a big old Silver Cross perambulator. Clothes, food and the washing-gear for the night piled up on top of him. Sister Pamela perched precariously on top of that lot, clinging on for grim death. Nell's at the back, the she-wolf protecting her brood, pushing as fast as she can. Coat-tails flapping and streaming out behind her, my big brother Dennis running alongside, his little legs pumping like pistons to keep up.

And my mother ran. She ran like the wind before the coming storm. She saw every day what the bombs could do. She'd seen her friends get torn apart, the odd limb hanging on the lampposts after a raid. She knew you had to be quick. Quick, run to the park, clatter down those huge wide wooden steps, down, down into

3

the vast warm belly of the brick-vaulted shelter where your kids might survive.

The night's black as tar, darker than it's been since the Middle Ages, with no moon to guide the bombers in the siren's dying wail. Quick, down the road, left over the bumpy level crossing, a quick right through the iron gate into the park. That pram rattled on like a runaway train. Mum pushed like our lives depended on it. Which, of course, they did.

Then, wham! Disaster! Straight into a park bench. Everyone arse-over-tit. Everything spilling out onto the path, a great heap of crashed humanity and scattered belongings. Unlike my dad, Nell had a good grasp of the less polite words in the English language. In those couple of hectic minutes of panic at that park bench, I probably learnt most of the swear words in common usage.

No time to cry. Time to laugh about it later, in the safety of the air-raid shelter. My mother frantically picking things up, hurry, hurry. Get up and run again. Beat the bombs, before they had a chance to take her flock from her.

I was no more than four, but I can still taste and feel and smell the atmosphere of that frightened running before the bombs. Such relief when at last we'd cascaded down the broad steps, into the overpoweringly smelly but safe warmth below.

The air-raid shelter was lined with narrow bunks along the walls, in tiers of three, like a prison camp. Even as a small child I noticed the smell – that warm fetid stink of hundreds of hot crowded sweating bodies, seething in the dim half-light.

The war brought out the best, and the worst, in people. Perhaps it was the thought that at any time they might die. For the most part they were cheerful, or pretended to be. They sang, played accordions and mouth-organs. Round the next corner there'd be a family eating and drinking. A group of men playing cards. Lovers cuddled up on a bunk, going as far as they dared under the blankets. To many, it was like a gigantic, subterranean holiday-camp, where no-one had a care in the world. I think most were simply glad to be alive and have this sanctuary. But there were some my childish eyes could not make sense of. Sitting, staring, far away in a brown study. Never speaking. Or escaping in a fog of alcohol. Trying not to think.

There was no privacy, at all, not anywhere. Once my dad, on the top bunk, in his sleepy stupor, ground his cigarette out on the bald scalp of my Uncle Sid sleeping underneath. As soon as everyone realized what had happened, our whole area burst out in hysterical laughter, with my poor uncle hopping around, holding his head and yodelling with the pain. Every time Sid was caught out feeling the burn, the neighbourhood fell about laughing uncontrollably again.

In the morning, when you came up from the shelter, it wasn't so funny. There was always the fear: will our home still be there? Has it been flattened? Where will they send us? People hurried back to their streets, filled with the dread of what they might see, yet desperate to know the truth. The awful scream of a woman neighbour crying out for a child, her home, a pet.

We lived in Goldsmith Road, near the level-crossing. At the bottom of the garden was the railway track, which ran straight from Napier's armaments factory in South Acton. The trains used to rumble by, laden with bombs and shells. Sometimes a troop-train would come past and we'd flap our handkerchiefs at the khaki soldiers leaning from the windows, waving at us, hoping they'd toss us a stick or two of chewing gum. Of course they didn't. Luxuries, like gum, were reserved for the Yanks. Our lads were lucky to get an edible meal, never mind sweets.

Perhaps the railway and the factory made us a target for the Heinkels and the Dorniers? We'd had a lot of raids, but stayed through them all. My parents – well Mum really – like many, resisting the orders to evacuate, wanting to see it through as a family.

And then a new weapon came that was even worse than the bombers. A terror-weapon. People tried to make light of it by calling it a 'doodlebug'. But Christ, it scared us all.

One morning, sitting at the kitchen table, we heard the familiar low rumbling noise up in the sky. We all prayed it wouldn't stop whirring before it passed over our house. Suddenly, silence. Today it was our turn. My mother moved fast. She swung me onto her lap, and folded the upper part of her body right down over mine, and prayed. There was the most god almighty blast, and then the whole kitchen window blew in towards us. We went over like a pack of cards, in a hot wave of disintegrating glass and wood. It was a V1.

We staggered to our feet, shaking and white beneath the coating of dust. My mum, the first, as usual, to get her act together, checked on her brood. There were red spots of blood across her face where the flying splinters had hit her. Cuts oozing little scarlet rivulets through the grime. But we were alive.

After that escape, the instant the siren sounded, whatever we were doing – eating, sleeping, having a bath – it was drop the lot and Action Stations.

One morning when we came back up out of our safe smelly burrow under the municipal park there was a big smoking hole where the houses next door had been. Bits of their innards snaked up out of the wreckage like a row of enormous rotted dragon's teeth. Time to go.

And so began a gypsy-like round of make-shift living, starting with a walk down the Uxbridge Road to Uncle Sid's place.

Sid had a dismal basement flat in Shepherd's Bush and it was here that I acquired my life-long terror of rats. I only discovered why years later, in the Fifties, when Orwell's *1984* was shown on television. I watched the little screen in horror as these rats ran along the glass tube towards the helmet, scrabbling and squeaking on their way to torture Winston. I was transfixed, sweating like a pig on a spit.

'No wonder you're scared of rats,' said Nell, noticing my panic.

'What? What?' The words were strangled as I tried to tear my eyes away from the box. 'What?'

'One night, when we were at Uncle Sid's,' she explained, 'we heard you and Pamela screaming in your cots. When we got to you, there were rats climbing over your faces, licking the dried milk off your mouths.'

I stared up at her.

'We moved out the next day,' she said.

Yuk! It still makes me shudder to think of those dirty, horrible creatures licking their lips and then licking our mouths. For someone who doesn't exactly empathize with rodents I seemed to bump into them at every turn. There were a lot of rats around when I was a kid. When a building they'd been occupying was bombed out, the rats just moved on to the next one.

Once a mate and I were riding our bikes on a North Acton industrial estate. It was early evening. Suddenly, up in front of us a dark river flowed across the road. A mass of brown things jumping from the middle of it. We stood and watched, unsure of what we were looking at. Whatever it was, we didn't like it. Then it came into focus. An army of rats, a great tide moving in a pack from a blackened shell.

6

* * *

After the V1 hit, we started living like the rats, scurrying here, there and everywhere about the country, looking for a safe place to lay our heads. We were always on the move. My other uncle, Ernie, drove us in his truck all the way up the A1 to a little village called Bathley, just outside Newark-on-Trent. Mum in the front, my grandmother, Pamela, myself and a hotchpotch of aunts and cousins snuggled up together, higgledy-piggledy under a tarpaulin, trying to keep the biting night air from freezing us to death. What a laugh. There was a lot of laughing during the war. I'm sure that afterwards grown-ups missed the war just because of the laughs.

My uncle had a mate who offered us his cottage in the country. What an adventure. An orchard, a swing on one of the trees, fields. Wonderful! It was the first time I'd seen a cow or a pig, vegetables and real eggs. Us kids would troop into the milking-shed with our jugs for the creamy, foamy, fresh milk, still warm. Bliss, after the food queues and the bleak danger of the city.

It was happiness, for a while, then on again. We never knew why it was time to leave our little utopia, but leave we did. Maybe Mum knew. If she did she never let us in on it.

It was the start of the unhappiest period of the war for me. Somehow or other, I don't remember why, Pam and I got packed off on our own and ended up in a horrible place in Bradford. Me chewing chalk by the handful in the nursery school, even swallowing it, to draw attention to my abject misery. But to no avail.

When the worst of the V1 flying bombs was supposedly over, we moved back to Acton, near the railway track again, sharing a house with Aunt Doll. Although the Heinkels and Dorniers had almost gone, and the V1s were gradually tailing off, there was a new wave of terror on its way, the V2. Like the V1s, the V2s came at you without warning, but they were bigger and deadlier. As the bomb ran out of steam, all that remained was to pray it wouldn't be you. Then, with a sound like a huge iron safe slamming shut, half the next street would disappear in a hurricane of blast and heat.

Chapter Two

MY DAD, ALF, ON ACCOUNT OF HIS FLAT FEET, HAD BEEN PUT TO driving trucks to and from the London docks. When the war ended they kept him on. That meant that he was in pole position to take advantage of the mountain of stuff that happened to find itself falling off the back of lorries. Little luxury items – like meat.

The black market was booming. No-one saw it as crime, more as just rewards for putting up with the war. No-one, that is, except my dad. My old man just didn't have the temperament to be 'public enemy number one'. To him, right was right, and wrong was wrong.

One time Pam and I pinched a couple of tuppenny paper diaries from Woolworths in Ruislip Town. When we got home we hid our spoils in our rooms. Mum found them that evening and made the fateful error of telling Alf who totally lost his rag and ordered Mum to sort it out. Next day, Pam and I were on the first bus to Woolworths. The bus fare was more than the diaries were worth. We shame-facedly went to the shop assistant on the diary counter, apologized, and returned our loot. Why on earth didn't we just lob the diaries into the canal and go and share a bottle of Tizer? It didn't even occur to us. The old lady gave the command and we followed orders.

So that was the sort of moral high ground the old lady had to deal with. But Nell was relentless and the more Alf regaled us with tales of that day's spoils, the more our mouths watered and tums ached for a crumb or two from the wonderful-sounding goodies, until Nell wasn't having any more of it. 'We've won the bloody war, haven't we? Aren't we due some of the victor's rewards?' she argued. 'Or have the Germans defeated us, after all?'

It certainly seemed like that to Mum. No butter, no fruit, no eggs, scraps of gristly meat fit for a dog: nothing had changed. Her patience was wearing thin. Within a matter of weeks, Alf gave in to the inevitable.

A few days later, at the crack of dawn, he turned up with a mate of his. The pair of them looked about as innocent as a couple of body-snatchers. Between them they were carrying a piece of wood roughly the size of a door. In the middle was a huge chunk of butter, about a yard square. A gigantic yellow cube, glistening with a light sheen – exactly like the sweat on their nervous faces.

As if by magic the word spread. It seemed like the whole neighbourhood passed through our kitchen that night, everyone leaving with their little half-pound blocks of luxury. This wonderful stuff they'd been deprived of for five years.

We kids looked on entranced, in silent wonder. The excitement. The danger. That night my dad took on the glamour of Al Capone. But for Alf it was all too much. He couldn't stand the strain: it was to be the only time he allowed himself to be talked into crime.

My parents seemed to keep an emotional distance from us, but that doesn't mean I grew up in an unhappy home. It was very free and easy-going. Mum never minded much what we got up to – as long as it didn't bring trouble to the front door.

All my mates loved coming to my place because there were so very few house rules. They could even swear, which Nell did all the time, only not, most definitely *not*, when Dad was around. He hated to hear swearing in front of kids and women.

Nell never worried if any of us missed a meal. She'd cook the stuff, and if we weren't there to eat it at the usual time, she'd just stick it in the oven. 'Oh, come on, Nell,' we'd moan, strolling in an hour or two late for tea, 'the gravy's gone all hard.' Her cooking wasn't exactly cordon bleu at the best of times, but if you got to her gravy after it had had time to set, you needed a pneumatic drill to get into it. 'Yes, well tough,' she'd say. 'You should have been here when it was ready.'

I don't remember much conventional family life. We'd rarely sit down for a meal together, even on Sundays; which was unusual for a working-class family in those days when Sunday lunch was an unmissable ritual for most homes. But Nell wasn't big on ritual and we all went our own ways in a kind of loosely connected gang. For all that, ours was a 'stick-together-if-there's-trouble' family.

After the war, Alf tired of the rough trade of lorry driving and went back to his more civilized civvy job as a coach driver. He was happier. Coach-drivers were the respected 'Kings' of the road. They were the élite. With their nice uniforms and their kid-leather gloves and shiny new coaches they lorded it up on the highways of postwar Britain. I suppose it was because so few people had cars. These plush buses lifted them out of their dreary war-torn towns to the exciting fun palaces on the coast. Places like Southend, Margate and Brighton. Very occasionally Dad would take me on one of these trips. I loved it. Up front with him in his coach, my bum getting roasted from sitting on the engine casing, I acted like his assistant. I'd fuss around at the halfway stop – toilet break for the mums and a quick pint for the dads – calling them back to the coach after the break. I was only knee-high to Ronnie Corbett, but I imagined every kid on that coach envied me my special status, and boy, did I feel important.

Dad was the most detached of us all. He practically lived in a separate universe. He'd set out early for work every morning and that was the last we'd see of him, most days, until late at night. Once the summer season started we didn't see him for weeks on end. We wouldn't be up when he left in the morning, and we'd be back in the land of nod by the time he got home. The only evidence of his presence was the pile of coins on the kitchen table every morning – the tips he made on his seaside outings. Mum kept them in a big jar on the mantelpiece.

Sometimes when things got a bit dull the old lady would shout for a 'count-up'. She'd fetch down the big glass sweet jar in which she'd squirrelled away all the cash. We'd all sit round the kitchen

10

table, goggle-eyed at this massive pile of coins that cascaded out. Pennies, threepenny bits, shiny sixpenny pieces sparkling in a sea of copper. One of us would take the pennies, the next would take the threepenny bits, a third take the sixpences, and so on until we'd added it all up. Those tips went towards buying us Christmas and birthday presents.

My dad worked hard to give his kids the odd treat. He'd hand over his wages at the end of the week, content for my mother to run things, and she'd give him back a few pounds in pocket-money. He was the kindest, most passive of men – and also the most distant. It wasn't that he didn't love us. He did. But as with my mother, I just wasn't aware that he did. He never made a show of it. I think he simply ran away from the emotion and grind of everyday family life. He worked hard but never particularly enjoyed it. Like most people, he had a lifelong dream of winning the football pools and retiring at an early age.

But at least in his cab he could be in his own little world. When he was up there, with a coach-load of strangers behind him, he was free. No responsibilities, other than the people he was driving.

I've made him sound like a kind of cipher, a blank in the family, and he was that; but I remember walking in on my parents one afternoon, in their bedroom. My mum was on her back, gazing up at my dad. She put her head to one side, smiled, and said calmly, 'Just close the door on your way out, would you, Bill!' (why she called me Bill is another story). Maybe that was where my Dad asserted himself – in bed.

Apart from cracking the pools, his other dream was to work out an infallible system for winning on the horses. He dedicated the best part of his life to it. Every spare minute was spent monitoring every horse-race run in Britain. He had mountains of notebooks, where he kept records of past form. All the wins, the placed horses, the ones that pulled up, the losers. He had complete lists of all the jockeys; whole volumes about the trainers. It was his life's work. And it led him nowhere.

What he got from my mother in pocket-money went on testing out this universal betting system. It didn't work very often – he usually came home with his pockets empty. It was his only vice, as far as I ever knew, and although it was an obsession, it was a modest one. He gambled with shillings. Harmless. Mind you, we were lucky my mum held the purse-strings, or we'd probably all have starved.

If my dad aspired to anything in life other than perfecting his system of gambling, it was to that nice, pleasant, safe little middle-class existence we saw in films like *The Titfield Thunderbolt*. A semi-detached half-timbered mock-Tudor house in Acacia Avenue, Ealing. The little half-timbered Morris car to go with it. A telephone, maybe a washing-machine for Mum. The children going off with a happy wave to their charming little school.

Not a lot to ask, but Dad was destined for disappointment. He harboured this small aspiration, without the where-for-all to achieve it. His problem was that he was born without an ounce of ambition.

I recall only one serious argument between my parents. Alf came home one night and put his lunch-box heavily down on the table. 'Hello,' we thought, 'something's up.'

Nell came over from the stove and stood in front of him, arms folded. He looked at her sheepishly.

Garners & Valiant (the coach firm he worked for in Hounslow) had asked him to become a foreman. Big move up the ladder. Mum had sent him off to work that morning to accept the job. It meant more money.

'Right,' she said firmly, 'you've taken the job?'

Alf's eyes dropped to the floor. He didn't need to answer.

'Look, Mum,' (us kids called her Nell, but Alf called her Mum), 'it's too much . . . I just want to drive the coach. It's all those unions, all that . . .' The word 'responsibility' hung in the air between them, unspoken.

My mother went for him. She lashed at him with her scorn; she tried persuasion, coaxing, all the techniques in her formidable armoury. But it was useless. He just sat there, while the storm broke around his head. Poor old Dad! All he wanted was his tea and an hour with *The Sporting Life*. He didn't take the job, and Mum never tried to push him up the ladder again.

Instead, she moved up the ladder herself. When I was born she had a part-time job as a charlady scrubbing a factory floor. By the time I was nineteen, she was managing one of the biggest office cleaning companies in London. Nell looked at the fences in her path, saw the notice saying 'Keep Out' – and then climbed over. Alf would stop at the first gate, read the sign, and that would be it: he'd be back on the public path, where he thought he belonged. I wanted him to be strong. I wanted him to teach me where the line was and what would happen if I overstepped it, but he never did. When I tried to test myself against him, he slipped away from me, elusively, like a ghost.

I think I missed not having a strong male role-model in my life; a man I could copy and fix my character on. But if it wasn't to be my dad, it had to be someone else. It was at the 'flicks', the picture palaces, that I found my heroes.

Before the invention of television, you went 'out' to dream. You went once a week to the movies, where for a handful of pennies you could plunge head first into a fantasy world, leaving the drudge of reality behind. Here the actors played out lives that were bigger than any of us could ever imagine. The very fact that these flickering gods were twenty feet tall, and way up above our heads, reinforced the notion of our smallness and their greatness. Humphrey Bogart, Cary Grant, James Cagney – they were all heroes.

The cinema was my first love – after girls, that is – and it re-inforced the dream that my mum had instilled into me as a kid. It gave me the notion that I could become someone, and live some-where else. Of course I never really believed, deep down, that I was ever going to be that new person. Or get to this better place. But every week the cinema sharpened the hunger I felt to get free of the Acton Vale flats. And in the end, the movies gave me the person I wanted to be.

Chapter Three

I F MY DAD TUGGED HIS FORELOCK AT LIFE, MY MUM WAS THE complete opposite. She didn't so much despise social conventions as utterly ignore them.

She thought all the bowing and scraping to the royal family was ridiculous, pervasive as it was then in British life. And I think that her independence of mind helped me believe in my own dream, which grew more ambitious as the years rolled by. I didn't just want out of a claustrophobic, crummy inner-city flat: I wanted a big house at the end of a long drive, with massive, curling, wrought-iron gates and green lawns rolling down to the sea, like the house in *Mrs Miniver*.

But as it was, 18 Goldsmith Road had an outside toilet, and we all took turns every Friday night in the tin bath that hung up on the back of the scullery door. This was done in a very strict pecking order according to age – Dad first, then Mum, then Dennis, then Pamela, then me. I'm sure that when it came to my turn I was dirtier after the bath than I was before I was chucked into it. Later when the twins arrived it got even worse. Because they were such a novelty and despite our protests, Nell put them at the top of the queue.

I hated bath night. It was always cold. Central heating was at least twenty years away. I'd sit there, pink from the chest down, in front of the kitchen stove, in water that varied between freezing and scalding. Nell was a big woman, and after a couple of minutes of rubbing away at me with a bristly scrubbing-brush that felt like a hedgehog's back and a block of some horrible carbolic, I'd be writhing about in a fit of pure unadulterated agony. It was like banging your head on a brick wall: lovely when you stopped. Then came the good bit. Scrubbed and packaged in our clean pyjamas, we'd be shoved between a pair of clean white sheets, warmed by a boiling hot-water bottle.

For a few years, I think it was when I was six or seven, we got away from Acton. The government had started building a new housing development in Ruislip, about six miles west of Acton, to re-house the likes of us. We were offered, and accepted, one of the very first houses on a new model estate.

The mayor of Ruislip came for the opening and had tea. This was the first step towards my dream home. It had an indoor bathroom and loo, an everyday room, and a best room. There were bedrooms upstairs and a garden front and back. I even had my own little vegetable garden: I grew runner beans up the back of the tool shed; tomatoes on the sunny side of the house, and lettuces under glass. I was a regular little Percy Thrower, and I loved it.

Ruislip was open countryside in those days and we were surrounded by fields and meadows – I thought I'd died and gone to heaven. A brook ran through the local farm. Pam and I, along with the Brown kids who lived next door, would spend entire days trying to jump this stream, or we'd dam it, or just paddle in it, cooling our heels. It was my second taste of the countryside and it felt as natural to me as if I'd lived there all my life.

But dear, oh dear! Poor old Nell. While us kids were in seventh heaven, she was in hell. She missed the concrete, the carbon monoxide, her mates. By the time I was about to hit puberty, she'd had enough of the 1950s proto-suburbs and decided to move us all back to town. She pestered the council until they'd found her a family who wanted out of Acton and we exchanged our beautiful little country estate for a box in Acton Vale flats built by German prisoners-of-war. I'm sure they built them as badly as they could, to pay us back for capturing them.

In a day or two Mum had all her cronies gathered round her again, and was back in her element, as happy as she'd ever been. Me? I was devastated.

My father's mother lived with us, having nowhere else to go. Somehow or other Nell squeezed us all into three bedrooms. Mum, Dad, Gran – a misery guts by nature – Dennis, Pamela, me and the twins. Dennis, Roger and I shared one room. Dennis and I had a divan between us. We were constantly fighting over whose side of the bed we were on. Eventually Dennis came up with a solution. He got hold of a plank of wood from a bomb site and we installed it down the middle of the bed, splitting it in two. It wasn't ideal. But at least it was better to snuggle up to a bit of wood than your brother's left leg. I can't remember where the rest slept, but Mum and Dad had a room of their own.

As I recall we never had a holiday. We never went on a family outing. Not even to the seaside, which was strange, considering my father's job. Now I hope I'm not giving the impression that life was hard. It wasn't like that at all: it was just normal. What we knew and accepted. Perhaps even the average 1950s childhood. My dad was in work, and I never, ever felt deprived in any way of any material thing.

Nell was the Donna Corleone of our flats. Her door was always open, and a constant tide of women and children ebbed and flowed around her in the middle of this teeming estate. She was a big heavy woman, on the short side, but broad and very strong, with a strength of mind even greater than the strength of her body. All these people came to her for that strength; and for the implacable truth of her advice on how to deal with their lives.

'What's for tea, Mum?' we'd shout as we came crashing into the kitchen from school.

'Sit down there and be quiet,' she'd say. 'Mrs Murphy's just telling me something.' And we'd sit down silently and listen to an endless stream of women with black eyes and broken teeth, often as not crying their eyes out, telling how the old man had been beating them up, how he'd gambled the rent away, or worse. Mum would bend her sharp chiselled face towards the woman and ask her for all the details, so that she could judge what they were to do for the best.

Mrs Murphy had a tale that was one of the very worst.

'What am I going to do, Nell? He keeps beating me up; and he's made Shelagh pregnant.'

The Murphy family lived just up the road from us, and I'd started going out with one of the girls. We were both about the same age, thirteen or fourteen. Opposite our long block of flats was a row of coal-sheds, where people kept all sorts of things, from motorbikes to racing-pigeons, and occasionally coal. One afternoon, I was playing doctors and nurses in our shed, with this girl, when I heard a roar from my mum on the top floor.

'Oi! Bill! Up here! I want you.'

Oh blimey! Now what have I done wrong? I trudged up the forty-nine steps, expecting an earful over something or other. I wasn't ready for what she told me.

'You stay away from that girl,' she warned me.

'Maria?' I asked. 'Why?'

'Because she's pregnant too.'

'What?'

'Yes,' said my mother, 'and I don't want you blamed for it. It's her father.' It was true, the old bastard had made all four girls in his family pregnant. Mrs Murphy was bringing her grand-children up as her own kids.

The good old days.

What was striking, looking back, was that even God-awful people like Mr Murphy were dealt with inside the community. It was unheard of for the police to intervene between husband and wife, unless it came to murder. There was no such thing as a social worker on our patch: the Social Services were still nothing more than a gleam in a bureaucrat's eye. There was only my mum, and people like her. She'd go round with a couple of her well-built mates. All washer-women's forearms and grim determination. Stare the bloke that was beating his missis up, or whatever, straight in the eye and give him 'what-for'.

'You leave her alone, d'you hear?' Nell would bark. 'Or you'll have us to deal with.' Sometimes, just occasionally, the beating would stop. All right, the beaten woman needed permanent pro-tection; but what she might not need was for her marriage to be broken up and for her children to be cast to the four winds, put into care or fostered.

My mother was only doing in adult life what she'd learned to do as a child: using her own strength to protect the people around her who were weaker, and innocent, and suffering horrible abuse.

The Sunday after we moved back to Acton, Mum made us all get dressed up in our best clothes, and we walked from the flat in the Vale right up to the top end of Acton High Street. She waltzed up the road like a lioness marking her territory. I must have been eleven or twelve by then, and I can't remember being more depressed in my entire life. That afternoon, on that walk, I found real ambition. My definition of ambition is not the question 'Where do you want to go in your life?' You never quite know where you want to go. It's 'What do you want to get away from?' And on that dismal, Sunday-best trudge up the street, past the grubby, sad little shops, my ambition flowered in a big way.

From that moment I knew I was going to get out. I didn't know how. But I was getting out.

ChapterFour

JUST BEFORE WE LEFT SCHOOL, I WENT WITH MY BEST FRIEND RAY Tibbles to see James Dean in *Rebel Without A Cause*. Ray knew he wanted to be a photographer when he started work. I envied him that certainty. I had absolutely no idea what I wanted to do. But by the time the last flickering image died on that cinema screen, I knew exactly who I wanted to be: James Dean, I wanted to be James Dean. I didn't want to look like him, or talk like him, or smoke like him – I actually wanted to *be* him. He was the model I'd been searching for. I went to see the film again and again, sucking in that gigantic act, soaking up the way he spoke, dressed and carried himself. So young, but what a man – and, I imagined, he looked like me.

My hero did what he liked. He had no regard for convention and he spoke my frustrations for me. The petty rules and regulations of 1950s life might gang up to thwart him, but he never accepted them. He kicked out against them with a raw energy. He stood up to the so-called adults who wanted to crush him, and exposed their emotional incompetence and their hypocrisy. He was honest. He broke all the rules. He strode through life with a manly swagger, and lesser men and women reeled away from him. He was the first teenager to say, 'Sod what's gone. *This* is how it's going to be, from now on.' He set alight a whole generation of kids silently screaming to break free from the left-overs of a repressive Victorian society.

He was a REBEL. And that's what I wanted to be.

I spent a small fortune on film magazines, scanning them feverishly for any and every little snippet I could glean about my new hero. I took in every fact I could find, ploughing it over and over into my memory, until it had really become a part of me. I read one day how Dean, as a raw new talent, had been hired to act opposite Elizabeth Taylor, the biggest female star the world had ever seen. They were on the set of *Giant*, in the desert of New Mexico. They were about to shoot the scene where Liz Taylor meets Dean at his small oil-rig. James Dean sat alone on the set for the whole morning, with his heart in his mouth. How, when he got out in front of that camera, was he ever going to match up to the Queen of Hollywood? How could he overcome his fear. If he didn't get on top of it, it would kill not only the scene, but his whole performance. If he didn't dredge up an act as big as Taylor's from somewhere, bang would go his confidence, and his acting career with it.

Eventually the boy-star stood up, walked a 150 yards out into the desert, until he was standing right in front of the vast crowd of people who'd come to watch the filming. When he was sure that he had everybody's undivided attention, he unbuttoned his 501s, and took a piss right there in the sand in front of them. Then he went right back and did the scene. He'd confronted a worse fear than working opposite Elizabeth Taylor, and overcome it.

That story struck a cord in me that branded itself across my very being. It became my motto for life: 'Always attack the thing you most fear.' Don't just sit there, in your armchair, letting life frighten you – go out and piss on your fear.

When Ray Connolly made a documentary on Dean in the Seventies he tagged him 'the first American teenager', but I think he was the first teenager ever. At least he was around our way. I'd been one for two years and hadn't even heard of the word. The animal was an undiscovered species in our manor until Jimmy Dean turned up.

In those days you left school on the Friday afternoon, and went to work on the Monday morning. You didn't have a year or a month or even a week off to think about it. Blimey, if I'd announced to Nell that I was taking a year off 'to find myself', she would have had me committed to the funny farm. No, the minute you were legally able to, you had to get out and earn your keep.

But who the hell wanted to get caught up in the daily grind of everyday life? Not me, that's for sure. What I wanted to be, what I longed to be when I looked up at that huge figure on the screen, was an actor.

An actor! Don't make me laugh. What a ridiculous ambition for a Fifties working-class boy from Acton to have. Working-class kids worked. They didn't play around at acting. In any case, why would I want to be an actor? Even if my fairy godmother did wave her wand and the impossible somehow came true, I was never going to get to play James Dean's brother in Hollywood. The kind of roles I'd have in the Britain of 1954 would at best be a dimwit corporal playing opposite the scathing, witty, debonair middle-class officer and gentleman (usually Kenneth More). No, not for me. Right from the start, it was all or nothing. If I couldn't be the officer, I didn't want to play the game.

I drove Dennis potty, keeping him awake all night boring him with my working-class chip. Den was great. He aspired. One night desperate, bleary eyed, from my ramblings, he came up with a compromise.

'If you can't *be* James Dean, go for second best. Direct him. Become a director.' Content that he'd solved my problem, he dismissed me from the other side of the plank, and happily snored his way through the night.

After breakfast, I got on my bike, and cycled round all the London studios. I hustled round Ealing, Twickenham, Shepperton with the idea of begging any job in the film world that would get me a foot on the bottom of the ladder. Tea-maker, chief bottle-washer, general dogsbody; I didn't care, as long as I could get a foot in the door.

There was only one problem – I never once got past the commissioner on the gate. Those commissioners were all ex-army types; they'd been little tin gods during the war, with their sergeant's stripes, and they were even bigger little tin gods now, only in dafter uniforms. Still, they had the power and I didn't. Each and every one of them told me to 'Bugger off out of it.'

If I couldn't get past the so-and-so's on the gates, in my quest to break into film business, I could still dress like my hero.

Cowboy hats were thin on the ground in Acton High Street. So I got myself a second-hand Australian Army bush-hat in Shepherds Bush market – I went there every Saturday to buy my Hank Janson paperbacks. By the time I'd had a go with the scissors and the Sellotape I had myself a fair copy of the hat Jimmy wore in *Giant*. Did I feel the business swanning about the Vale flats, with my cowboy hat and the pair of Levi blue-jeans my dad's mate brought me back from America. Levi's were rarer than money – and in some ways more valuable. When I wore my Jimmy Dean rig-up, I was him. I wasn't little Terry Nelhams from the Vale flats, I was twenty feet tall, I was the man. Blue jeans! How cool. What a lad, what a rebel I thought I was. Looking back now, it's a wonder I didn't get filled in by some of the Teddy boys who were always hanging around. With their velvet-collared drape coats and long whiskers they looked back to the Edwardian past instead of to the American future.

I did have a go at the old Teddy boy look for a while. But I was too short for the long draped jackets. I looked even sadder than I did in my cowboy outfit. Anyway, I never could get the hang of those bike-chains. It was no good just swinging one around, you had to know how to use it.

The first big test of my 'rebellion' came when I wore my Jimmy Dean outfit to school one day. Jeans were strictly forbidden at John Perring School. We were supposed to wear grey flannel trousers. Which I couldn't stand. Not least because they itched. Before I got my Levi's I used to wear my pyjamas under the flannels.

I strutted through the gates in my new gear. I was coming straight off the set of *Giant*. Mr Foxman, the headmaster, spotted me from his office window. The sly old bugger didn't say anything then, but right in the middle of morning assembly, he stopped the proceedings dead and dragged me up onto the stage. The hall fell silent. I stood there, in front of the whole school, with my knees knocking. All the rebellion draining out of me.

'Right,' barked the headmaster, grabbing me by the arm and shaking me, 'I want you all to look at Terence Nelhams here. Can everybody see him?' Three hundred heads nodded in silent confirmation. 'Good,' continued Foxman, 'because this is how you are not to dress at my school. Not ever. Understand?' Again the silent nodding heads. The headmaster gave a grunt of satisfaction, and me a push towards the edge of the stage. 'Get yourself home, boy,' he thundered, 'and come back when you're properly dressed.'

When I got home, Nell was surprised to see me. 'What the hell you doing here? Why aren't you in school?'

'Mr Foxman sent me home for wearing jeans,' I told her. 'I've got to put on a pair of trousers.' My mother looked at me. A gleam came into her eye and her shoulders stiffened. My heart sank slowly into my boots. I'd seen that look before.

'Is that what he did?' said my mother grimly. 'Right, you come with me.' She dragged me back to school. I had that terrible feeling you have as a kid, when you've done something that's made the adults who control your life want to fight. Please, let the ground open up and swallow me.

When we reached the school, the old lady marched me straight into the secretary's office. The woman's head snapped up as we burst in, and she made an 'Oh!' of surprise. My mother glared at her.

'Is he in?' my mother barked at her.

'Er, it's Mrs Nelhams, isn't it? Can I do something for you?'

'Is he in?' repeated my mother.

'The headmaster is in, yes,' replied the school secretary stiffly, recovering a little from her initial shock. 'Have you got an appointment?'

'Never mind all that,' said my mother. She strode forward, brushed the protesting secretary to one side, flung open the door to the headmaster's study and hauled me in. Mr Foxman looked up from his paper-shuffling. He was not a happy man. He wasn't used to unannounced intrusions into his little domain.

'Did you send him home?' bellowed my mother, with a furious nod of her head sideways and downwards at me.

'I . . . Yes, I did,' stammered the headmaster.

'For wearing those?' snapped Nell, pointing at the offending jeans.

'Yes.'

'Why?'

'Because I won't have those garments in my school,' Foxman replied, climbing slowly to his feet. 'They're work trousers.'

'They're very strong,' my mother told him. 'And they'll last four times longer than flannels. If you'd like to buy him four pairs of flannel trousers he'll come to school in flannel trousers. But until you do that, don't you ever, ever, send my son home again. Is that clear?'

And she glared at Mr Foxman in the same way that she'd glared at me, with pretty much the same effect. Old Foxman opened his mouth to speak, closed it again, looked down at the floor, and was beaten. I was allowed to stay, dressed as I was – the only boy in the school with a pair of Levi's.

But it was a hollow victory. Would Jimmy Dean have needed his mum to fight his battles for him?

Maybe it's because I'm small in build myself, but I've always hated bullying. At school I was pretty titchy, and not very sporty. Even so, there was a boy there even smaller than myself, and even less sporty. He wore thick glasses and was picked on by all and sundry. This kid's chief tormentor was a very big, very nasty piece of work whose name, as I recall it, was Chilton.

Standing in the dinner-queue one day, Chilton started having a go at this little boy in front of everyone. Barging in front of him, sneering at him, and generally humiliating him. Nobody would stand up to Chilton.

I should have kept my mouth shut; but against all the small stock of my common sense, I found it opening and the words 'Why don't you pick on somebody else?' coming out of it.

Chilton spun on his heel and glowered down at me.

'What about you?' he snarled.

'Yeah, what about me?' I growled back, trying to hold his gaze without wavering, which was quite difficult, because all I wanted to do was flop on the floor and pretend to be dead. We exchanged a few more pleasantries, and before I knew where I was I'd challenged Chilton, the school bully, to a fight.

That whole afternoon passed in a haze of fear. I had no idea what lessons I was doing, what people said to me, what the time was: nothing. The real world had ceased to exist. All I could feel was this big lump of fright down inside of me, churning and curdling away in my gut.

Come the hour, cometh nearly the entire school. Word had gone round faster than a forest-fire: fight! Danny De Vito was taking on Arnold Schwarzenegger. I'd never hit anyone in my life, and Chilton was known as the best fighter in the school.

When the bell rang for the end of the last lesson, it sounded to me like a death-knell. I walked up to the top end of the playground, a no-man's land where teachers never went, feeling a bit like Gary Cooper in *High Noon*. Only I was a lot smaller and much more frightened. My legs were shaking, and my face had gone pale – I knew this from the cloakroom mirrors. I should have gone home, and tried to forget about it. But I couldn't. I was more afraid of being called a coward than I was of getting hurt.

There was Chilton, waiting for me at the top of the playground, rubbing his hands and playing to the crowd that had gathered around him in a huge circle. They were buzzing with anticipation. I could see his fat face smirking at me above the heads of the gawping children as I walked up.

I pushed my way in through the wall. There was I, in the middle of the circle, and there was Chilton, not a dozen feet away, facing me. He looked enormous close up at this moment of truth, a big-boned brute, his thick features split by a crooked smirk of contempt. The shame of facing the school the next day if I bottled out now drove my quivering legs slowly forward.

Chilton kept the broad evil grin on his face. He knew it was going to be a piece of cake. As I came up within reach of him, he drew back one bullock-bone fist and hit me once, hard, in the mouth. For a moment I had no idea what had happened. I took off, backwards. Then my head hit the tarmac of the playground, and a new view of the constellations opened up to me. I felt the small gravel stones sharp in my cheek. My head was ringing, and my mouth was wooden, thick and heavy with the pain. From somewhere very far away, I heard the sound of someone laughing, then cheering. I tried to draw breath, but there was a big empty feeling where my lungs had been. I stayed down.

When at last I managed to sit up, feeling sick and very sorry for myself, I saw everyone walking cheerfully away, frisky with the excitement of what they'd seen. Tears of agony and shame burst from my eyes. I'd been beaten, without putting up a resistance. I wasn't born for this violence. I was a lover not a fighter. Then I felt a little hand on my shoulder, a comforting touch. I looked up to see the little boy with the thick glasses, the put-upon shrimp whose honour I'd been foolishly defending.

Was it foolish? Perhaps not. I hadn't exactly done a Rocky Marciano, but better to die going over the top than lie there cowering face-down in the mud all your life.

ChapterFive

WHEN I LEFT SCHOOL AT FIFTEEN, I COULDN'T AFFORD TO TAKE a full-time job. Most permanent jobs for juniors paid around one pound ten shillings – a week; but I was already earning twice that, and more, from all the part-time work I was doing. So while my mates were taking their first steps to what seemed to me a lifetime of boredom, against Nell's better nature, I was allowed to keep my part-time jobs going.

I'd started early in business, not just because of the cash it provided, but because I wanted to. I'm one of those nutcases who can't stop working. Which is strange, since my greatest pleasure in life is to lie in bed all day watching black-and-white movies while having cups of lemon tea served to me. I must be the laziest workaholic that's ever walked the earth.

When I was thirteen, I had three regular part-time jobs. A local morning paper-round; then, straight out of school, belt up to North Acton Underground, with my best mate Hurgy (Roger Van Engel), to sell the evening papers. Hurgy and I worked the stand on the west entrance to the station. We became dab hands at remembering our punters' choice of paper. Before they had a chance to ask, we'd have their *News*, *Star* or *Standard* at the ready. They were so pleased to be remembered, especially if they had a mate with them. It was a nice little boost to their egos, it made them feel important. I understand that. I still get a kick out of being recognized in a restaurant.

Christmas was bonus time for me and Hurgy. Our regulars would come staggering down the path full of the excesses of the works' party, waving their Christmas contribution. We took a small fortune in tips. It paid to look after your regulars, during the year.

My third job? Well every night, when the rush-hour was over and the last *News*, *Star* and *Standard* sold, I'd shoot off on my Raleigh eight-gear to the Park Royal industrial estate. My mum had a contract to clean a factory owned by a big medical services company. Inside this huge cathedral of a place were lines and lines of work-benches, looking like coffins in the gloom. Cold concrete covered the floor, and hanging high above from the rafters were rows and rows of fluorescent lights, all with tin-and-glass shades – thick with dust. It was just like a spooky scene from a Vincent Price Hammer Horror movie.

To save money I was only allowed to put on a couple of working lights: an excellent management decision seeing as how that meant I couldn't see what I was doing half the time. My job was to keep these shades spotlessly clean, and I had to clamber up to the top of the tallest ladder you've ever seen. I must have been desperate for the dosh, because clinging to the top of that ladder tested my bottle to the limit. There I'd be, like a monkey on a stick, perched precariously with my little bucket and cloth. I wiped and wrung out, wiped and wrung out again and by the time I'd come to the end of the last row, it was time to start all over again.

It was a back-breaking job, one of the worst I ever had, but it was good money – one pound ten shillings a week – so I stuck at it. But my recurring nightmare was that the ladder would go over, and I'd be clinging on for dear life to my half-cleaned light, praying that the workers would come to rescue me before my arms gave way, and I crashed to the concrete below. Most of my waking hours were spent living in fear of that evening job.

At last Nell took pity on me and put me to work cleaning the offices. Then it was sweep, dust, polish. Sweep, dust, polish. Not the coolest job for a Jimmy Dean clone to be engaged in. But it sure beat climbing the south face of the Eiger every night.

By the age of fourteen, I owed over one hundred pounds on the 'never-never' – guaranteed for me by my mother because I was still a minor. I'd bought a push-bike, some snappy clothes and a record-player. All this credit meant working flat out to pay the tick-man who came to the door every Friday evening for his instalments. With my expenditure starting to exceed my income, I had to take on a fourth job.

I became a baker's boy for Napier's Bakery, starting at five thirty Saturday mornings. That meant hiring one of my mates to cover for me on my Saturday morning newspaper round. He charged me ten bob, way over the going daily rate. But that still left me with twenty shillings' profit for the morning's work.

After a couple of weeks of being a baker's boy, I was in love with the job. I would have paid them to let me do it. It started getting good long before you could even see the bakery. Fresh baked bread. Has there ever been a better smell? It hooked onto my senses. First the nose, then the taste-buds, and then the legs. Sending them tearing up the road drooling for a chunk of steaming hot dough.

Then there was Lofty, my driver. He was a bit of a lad was old Lofty. He loved telling jokes! I laughed at every one of them just because he was telling them to me. There wasn't a pencil skirt, beehive haircut or a pair of white high-heels that passed our van that didn't get a blast from Lofty's two-fingered whistle. He was as tough as old boots. But he was kind to me; he liked to look after his apprentice roundsman. He tried for months, with no success, to teach me that whistle. I tried everything to get the hang of that girl-puller. But it was no use. Nothing! A shrill little feeble whimper was all I could manage.

In fact it was another forty years before I perfected it, courtesy of Zoë Wanamaker while we were filming *Love Hurts* in Israel. I was gob-smacked when she whistled for a taxi in Jerusalem. Needless to say, I pestered her mercilessly until she taught me how to do it.

I might have gone on with this piecemeal employment for a very long time, if my mum hadn't intervened. She came home one day and buttonholed me in my bedroom, singing my lungs out to a Slim Whitman record of 'Rose-Marie'.

'Bill, get your suit out, you're going into the film business.' Her firm had won the contract to clean the offices of the film company, J. Arthur Rank, in Mayfair. It had taken her less than two weeks to get her feet under the table and she'd got me an appointment with the personnel manager. I didn't need to be told twice. It was on with the Burton's blue-serge and off to Hill Street, W1.

All the way to Green Park underground station I was lost in my own fantasy world. The Rank Organisation! I was already preparing my Oscar acceptance speech. Pausing briefly on the way to the winners' rostrum, to shake the hands of David Lean, Ingrid Bergman, Cary Grant, maybe even James Dean himself. Smiling, benignly, down upon all these lesser film-making talents sprawled in admiration at my feet.

This was my big break. The personnel manager and I got on well enough for him to offer me a job. It was only as a messenger boy, but I didn't care. At last I had my foot in the door.

Most of the time I carried cans of film around London, making sure that everyone could see the Rank name. It felt good to let people see that I was in the film business. Sometimes, there were memos to be delivered to head office around the corner in South Street – a task every messenger boy dreaded. John Davis was the Chairman and we were all petrified of him. One look from him could make a strong man go weak at the knees. But there was one redeeming factor which made the visits almost pleasurable: the receptionist. Miss Jeffries was every young lad's dream woman. She dressed in that very formal Norman Hartnell look. Cool, sophisticated, untouchable. At least to my inexperienced young heart. She had those sort of legs that looked wicked in black. Long and slim, she didn't so much walk as glide.

I'd find any excuse to walk through reception. Just the smallest smile would set me up for the week. I'd lean as near to her as I could when I put her tea on her desk, getting my face as close to her as I dared, without making it obvious that I was panting for her. The slightest whiff of her Christian Dior perfume was enough. Of course, nothing ever came of my lust. Miss Jeffries was a woman, I was a boy: she hardly noticed me. That is unless I forgot to put sugar in her tea, which sometimes I did, deliberately, just to have another chance to drool.

There were six messenger boys, and the one who had been there the longest was invariably promoted to top dog. When a job

– any job – came up at Rank's Pinewood Studios, the head boy was expected to take it. The only trouble was that the studio jobs came up at random. There was never any knowing what you might end up doing. Whatever gap there was that needed filling, that's what you got. But that didn't fit in with my plans.

I was given an eighteen-carat piece of advice by an old editor: 'You want to direct Terry?' said the old boy. 'Then learn to edit. If you understand the business of editing you'll understand how to make a film.' Certainly, if David Lean could come up with films like *Great Expectations* and *Hobson's Choice* learning his trade in the cutting rooms, that was good enough for me.

Our particular building only dealt with the commercials Rank put on before the movie began. So it wasn't exactly the cutting edge of film making. But there was an editing suite in the basement, and as the editors were the only real film makers available to me I spent all my spare time hanging out in their cutting rooms.

After about a year in the job, I was finally promoted to head messenger boy. Shortly after that, a job came up at Pinewood: clapper-boy. But I didn't want to be a clapper-boy. I was going into the cutting-rooms. That was my route and as far as I was concerned, nothing else would do. I turned the job down. This was unheard of: it defied the natural order of things at the Rank Organisation. There wasn't a messenger boy that wouldn't have killed to get to work in the studios. That was the real film business. But no; not for me. Even my darling Miss Jeffries was concerned.

'Another opportunity might be a long time coming.' She was worried for me. It was worth not taking the job for the attention she paid me. But I knew what I wanted and nothing else would do. She was right, though! Jobs came and went. Grateful messenger boys thanked me, as they jumped the queue to Pinewood. Months went by, and no right offer. I was stuck.

Once again Mum came to the rescue. She'd picked up another contract. This time it was to clean the offices and studios of a brand new company that had just started up in Soho, making television commercials. So I left Rank and went to work for Television Advertising (TVA) instead. Within a few months the move paid off, they offered me a job as assistant editor. I'd taken my first big step to being a film director.

ChapterSix

IN THE MID FIFTIES, WHEN I WAS AROUND SIXTEEN, SOMETHING WAS going on. What it was, I didn't yet know, but there was no mistaking; something definitely was going on. Everyone under the age of about twenty was fed up with the idea that the grown-ups knew more, or were any better, than we were.

Our questioning of the society built from the ashes of two world wars hung in the air like petrol fumes. Volatile, dangerous, frightening to anyone born before the war. All it needed was a spark to blow their uptight little world to smithereens. One of the sparks came in the form of music. In particular, for me anyway, it was skiffle.

Skiffle was a word Chris Barber and Lonnie Donegan plucked off a 1929 Paramount recording of a 'rent-party' blues session. Donegan and Barber invented their own version of this down-home black music, and gave it this strange name. The whole point of skiffle was that it cost almost nothing to produce. Played on instruments knocked up out of any old thing that came to hand, skiffle music could be made by just about anyone.

I'd developed a taste for traditional jazz. After work finished at TVA, I'd be off to the Humphrey Lyttleton 100 club, 100 Oxford Street. My favourite group was Chris Barber and his Trad Band. One evening, during the interval, on came this bloke called Lonnie Donegan. Clutching an acoustic guitar, he started singing this strange new stuff, in a raucous, angry voice. By the end of the second song, that was it; I was hooked. Lonnie singing live had a fire and an anger in him that came right at you. Maybe he was angry about the fact that he got paid a one-off session fee of seven pounds ten for 'Rock Island Line', which then became a number one hit in America and sold millions.

Skiffle gave us something we'd never had before. Our own music. The more our parents hated it, the more we revelled in it. *'We don't care what Momma don't allow, play that skiffle any old how . . .'* All you needed were a couple of cheap guitars, a washboard and ten thimbles for the rhythm, a broom-handle, an old wooden tea-chest and a piece of string for the bass. Bingo: you had loud energetic music with a thumping beat. The laugh you had doing it and the feeling of freedom it gave more than made up for the horrible sound it produced. You might listen to that early rock 'n' roll blaring out on the flip-top two-tone Dansette, but you played skiffle.

All of a sudden everyone I knew was either in, or on the point of starting up, a skiffle band. It was like some weird mass popular uprising through music. One of the messenger boys at Rank, Pete, saw himself as a bit of a musician. His dad played banjo with the Sally Army and had taught him a few chords on the guitar. That qualified Pete as a musician in our eyes. So Hurgy, who volunteered to play washboard, and I press-ganged him into helping us start our own group. It was an uphill job, because what we knew about making music wouldn't have filled a postage stamp. Not that that worried anybody except Pete. You didn't want to spoil skiffle with any musical know-how.

So armed with our cheap guitars and bits and pieces we turned up at Pete's house in Putney for our first lesson. After getting to grips with a couple of chords we were really pleased with ourselves. But we were still missing a singer. Suddenly I found myself being nominated chief warbler by Hurgy, my so-called best mate.

'Don't be daft, I can't sing,' I said, getting a bout of the dry-mouth that's so familiar to nervous performers.

'Course you can!' Hurgy could be mischievous at times. 'What about when we're out after girls, sitting on the wall in the park. You sing Lonnie Donegan songs to them.' He was right. That'd teach me not to show off.

So, because the rest of them were too frightened to sing, it was left to me. And that's how I became a pop singer. The first gig we did, when we mistakenly thought we'd got the band together enough to perform, was a free concert for the staff at Rank. They'd let us practise in the screening-room at 11 Hill Street, off Berkeley Square, in our lunchtimes and after work. This was our way of saying thank you.

Miss Jeffries turned up. I peered at her through a gap in the curtains. All black stockings and perfume. I was so excited I shook like a leaf. That evening I sang like I'd never sung to a girl before. I harboured the fantasy that she would be so impressed she wouldn't be able to resist taking me back to her place, for a night-cap. As it was, all I got from her was a sympathetic pat on the shoulder and a warning not to give up my day job.

The din we made that day was horrendous. But we persevered, and took it seriously, because it was so exciting. The idea that a bunch of council boys could be musicians was almost beyond belief. The first paid gig we ever did (I can't call it professional) was at Wandsworth Boys' Club. We got £5 for the night, and every song had to be played in the same key, because I only knew three chords on the Framus steel-stringed acoustic guitar I'd bought for twelve pounds and ten shillings. It had a terrible action, which made the ends of my fingers bleed. But I didn't know any better. And anyway, I couldn't afford a decent one.

Like the Rank gig, the performance was a shambles. Being of unsound memory, I had all the chords and lyrics of the songs we were doing written out on sheets of paper which I balanced carefully on a rickety second-hand music stand. But as we were introduced, the curtains swished back, taking my stand with it. It was chaos. Bits of paper flying all over the place with everyone running around, trying to catch them. The curtains were quickly closed on this disastrous scene.

We got a new introduction, the curtain went back and sure enough away went my music stand for the second time. It was nearly twenty minutes before we finally got to play. With half my music sheets missing or torn underfoot, my professional singing début was not a resounding success.

In fact, it was an unmitigated disaster. I couldn't remember half the words, and kept getting the chords wrong. If I'd been in the audience I would have demanded my money back. Thank goodness the kids listening to this racket knew as little about the new music as we did. We just about got away with it, and it had given us a taste of showbiz, so we stuck at it. We got better because we could only get better.

TVA was based at Film House in Wardour Street, in the heart of Soho. It was an amazing place to be in the Fifties: so full of colour and life. Street-girls covered every corner. Tramps pushed their prams around full of God-knows-what. Seedy drinking clubs that catered for all sorts. Maybe ignorance is bliss but I never felt frightened or threatened in Soho in the Fifties. The film world brushed shoulders with the gangsters – and they left each other alone.

Being a local, of sorts, I got to know all the girls that worked the streets. 'How's your mum, Angela?' 'Business OK, Annie?' 'Like the dress, Sandra!' They looked on me as a brother and ragged me mercilessly, especially if I happened to be with a girl-friend. They'd shout out across the street, 'Give you a session for half-price Terry. It'll be better than last night.' Then they'd scream with laughter, when whichever girl was with me blushed her way down Wardour Street, me running after her.

They all ragged me except Doris (I've changed her name in case she's married to a vicar with nine grandchildren). Doris took a particular shine to me, and was very protective. She'd scold the other girls when they teased me. Maybe I reminded her of a teenage lover. Whatever it was, Doris had it in her head that I needed educating. It became her mission to pass on all her professional knowledge to me. And, to paraphrase Paul Simon, I must admit, there were times, I took some comfort there.

Soho was where all the clubs and espresso bars were, and this was where the skiffle craze was finding its voice. Because the other lads were still over at Rank, in Mayfair, I was the one who had to go round trying to get us a professional gig. As soon as I finished work every evening, I'd slog round all the coffee bars, begging for an audition.

Coffee bars fell into two distinct categories: Beatnik – all black polonecks and existentialism; and teeny-bop – beehive haircuts and bobby-socks. We played our music to the beehives and chatted up the girls dreaming of Jean-Paul Sartre. I spent most of my lunch hours hanging out in the Beatnik joints, a king-sized Stuyvesant drooping languidly from my fingers, and clasping a cup of frothy coffee. There was only one drawback: I hated coffee. Not just the frothy muck, any coffee. It tasted like lukewarm battery acid, but it had to be done in the cause of lust.

I spent many a happy hour sizing up these brainy girls with their spidery English good looks, trying to look clever, and wondering how to get inside their duffel-coats.

Joe Brown recently described these Fifties coffee bars as 'pubs for kids', and they were. They were pretty much all alike – there'd be a small ground-floor café, with linoleum floors and Formica tables. That was where the punters got the poisoned muck they called coffee before they trooped downstairs to the basement, where the live music was played.

It was downstairs, at night, under the street, that the real action took place. At night kids came out who'd never heard of existentialism, but understood perfectly about 'living for the moment' and did so on a regular basis in these basement cafés. They were the basements from hell: claustrophobic and cramped, with very low ceilings. There was usually zero ventilation, and they were always packed solid. I'd say most of these cellars could accommodate about sixty people, maximum, in safety. On an average night, with a good skiffle band on the bill, there'd be as many as four times that.

We finally got a gig in one of these sweaty little cisterns and, because the scene was still so small, word got round quite quickly that there was a new band in town. By now I could play about eight chords, which meant I could sing in more than one key, and although we still made a horrible noise, it was no more horrible than the noise anyone else was getting paid to make. The in-crowd started coming, and we did OK: which is to say they didn't pelt us with eggs and fruit, at least not all the time.

The Holy Grail of skiffle was the famous 2i's coffee bar. Daft name, great place. We all wanted desperately to play there, because that was how you got to be famous. Tommy Steele, Wally Whyton and The Vipers, Cliff Richard, Terry Dene, and anyone else you'd ever heard of, got started there. So, why shouldn't we?

The 2i's was run by Paul Lincoln and Ray Hunter, a pair of former wrestlers. It took me a long time to convince them that

Terry Denver and The Worried Men deserved a gig. We'd borrowed the 'Worried Men' bit of the name from the famous Arlo Guthrie song, and my opening line when we worked was 'We're called the Worried Men and when you hear me sing you'll know why.'

After a few weeks of badgering, Paul and Ray gave in, and some months later they even made us the resident group. This meant we played to audiences of two or three hundred a night, from 7 to 11 p.m., six nights a week, for a total of six pounds – or one pound ten shillings a week each. And they didn't feed us. That didn't matter though, as I was particularly friendly with one of the girls working the Gaggia machine and she made sure we were fed and watered. The privilege of playing at the 2i's, the thrill and the cool heat of being the resident band there, the trip of wearing the gear – and of getting the girls – was better than anything money could buy.

Evenings were for my James Dean mode. I used to strut around Soho in my Levi's and white T-shirt, wearing a red *Rebel Without A Cause* windcheater (I hunted for this garment all over England – it took me months and months to find one) and black-and-white baseball boots. I was the King of Cool with my tragically terrible Framus guitar slung round my neck for all to see.

I still thought James Dean was the business, even more so since my all-time hero had done the decent thing and died young, thereby guaranteeing himself immortality. But he was already getting to be old hat. So although he was always my hero I was compelled by fashion (if I wanted to keep abreast of the girls' taste) to move on to the Brando look. Marlon Brando had made *The Wild One* which was banned by the old fogies at the British Film Censors office. The red windcheater took a back seat to a Brando black leather motor-bike jacket, its collar specially stiffened with cardboard by Hurgy's mum so that it stood up per-manently at the approved Brando biker-rebel angle.

If you worked at your image, all other things being equal, girls took more notice of you. The only trouble was, once a girl did take notice there was a limited amount you could do together back in 1957. Kissing and fondling was usually as far as it went. The great terrifying spectre of 'getting a girl in the club' – and having to marry her – hung over all of us. God forbid we indulged in a bit of 'savage amusement', we'd spend the next few weeks praying for the girl to call with good news. Most of the time it just wasn't worth the strain.

At the 2i's we played on a tiny stage, about eight feet by four, raised up by a whole foot above the madding throng. This may well have saved our lives – it meant we had our own little pocket of air. We looked down as we played on this mass below us struggling for breath, sending up great waves of body-heat and the meaty oxtail smell of compacted human flesh. It wasn't a smell that I was unfamiliar with. I recognized and, in a funny way, welcomed it as my own. The smell of my earliest childhood, from the deep bomb-shelter under Acton Park.

We were all just kids, be-bopping about down there. The girls wore flowery flared skirts, with little fluffy sweaters that buttoned up the back pulled tight over their armour-plated conical brassières, and cute little flat black pumps with bobby-socks; or they wore black-and-white dog-tooth check slacks with side zippers and short-sleeved cotton blouses. The boys wore jeans, if they could afford them, or slacks and shirts with tweed jackets; and every one of them used about half a pot of Brylcreem to get the quiff that came sprouting off the front of his head, like the prow of a ship.

The most important thing we had to learn, now that we were semi-professional, was how to work an audience. Being the singer, this job fell to me. I had to talk to the huddled masses, fire them up, get them on our side. And that was the bit I loved. Talking to an audience, relating to them, is something nobody can teach you – it's 90 per cent confidence, and 10 per cent practice. And although, all my working life, I've harboured severe doubts about my ability as a performer, I've never lacked confidence taking on an audience one-to-one.

As it happens these coffee-bar kids were as excited about hearing this new music as we were playing it. They didn't need a lot of encouragement to get totally caught up in these 'American-African' work-songs that we were thumping out: one push and the whole room would be jumping.

'Gonna jump down, turn around, pick a bale of cotton, jump down turn around pick a bale a day . . .'

People fainted all the time in the airless heat, but there was never any break in the show. Those who happened to be standing nearest to the person who'd passed out simply reached down, picked up the oxygen-starved body and, in one seamless move, shuffled it out of the cellar, backwards over their heads. I got used to watching a lad – or more frequently a lass – being manhandled over the heads of the crowd in the tiny gap below the ceiling. When it arrived at the back of the room, the prostrate carcass was shoved straight through the little skylight and out onto the pavement. Once the fresh air in the street had done its reviving work, the person who'd fainted would dive straight back down into the throng again for more.

The record industry, fuelled by the skiffle craze, began to explode. But everyone expected it to be a nine-day wonder. The old-timer agents would sit around in their old-timer agent restaurants, shaking their heads, muttering, 'It'll all be over in a week or two,' and we believed them; we felt we had to get going, get a record out, we were terrified of missing the wave before it broke and the whole thing fizzled out. We were terrified that we'd wake up and find life had gone back to its normal dull old routine.

Even I thought the skiffle craze would die out pretty soon; but like everyone else in the world, I was wrong. The energy that exploded in the 1950s never did go away – it just kept on growing bigger and bigger, until it became one of the biggest driving forces in the world.

Being resident band in the 2i's, we were convinced it was only a question of days or even hours before we made it big. Every day we'd be waiting for a producer to walk through the door, and discover us. It happened all the time to other acts, why not us? Harold Wilson said that a week was a long time in politics. He should have been in pop music. A week to me felt like a lifetime.

The nights went by, gig after gig, and nothing happened. We'd just about given up all hope when luck struck in the form of Jack Good. He was already a legend in his own right, the absolute king of TV rock 'n' roll, for having invented the first TV pop show: *Six-Five Special*. He wanted to set up the first live rock 'n' roll outside broadcast. Since it was the Mecca of pop music, Jack had chosen the 2i's as the venue. The night he brought his team to give the 2i's the once over, we played out of our skins. We had to impress him, we were desperate to get an appearance on that show. It was too good an opportunity to miss. We were the resident group after all, we felt we deserved to be on it.

After the set was over and the kids had gone home, we hung around trying to look casually busy, praying for a nod from Jack to tell us he liked our performance. At last Jack confirmed that as the resident group, he wanted us to open and close the show. None of us slept that night. We spent hours on the phone to each other planning the minutest details. Did we need to buy new instruments? What gear should we wear, which songs would show us off to our best? What a break! This was it. Terry Denver and The Worried Men live on nationwide TV. Live on the BBC! There was no end to the possibilities I predicted for myself and the other lads.

But first, there was the little matter of doing our first live TV show. There was no room for mistakes. I was so nervous when the moment came to sing that I could hardly open my mouth. I had no idea whether we were good, bad or indifferent, I was numb after it was all over. But Jack seemed happy enough for us to be encouraged to think that we'd done the job. We went home and dreamt about the fame and fortune that was coming to us.

But, nothing whatsoever happened. I don't know what I expected – a mountain of record contracts in the mail? A posse of agents ambushing us from a Soho doorway? Some hope. Nothing happened. Zilch. Life went on as usual. It was back to the day job at TVA, and the evening gig at the coffee bar.

This was very bad news. We could hardly help noticing that the crowds at the 2i's were dwindling. We all had the cold feeling in our guts that the days of the skiffle craze were well and truly numbered. Rock 'n' roll was taking over. None of us could do rock 'n' roll; that kind of music wasn't our thing and we weren't up to it. In our hearts we understood that our days of playing together in a skiffle band were coming rapidly to an end. And it wasn't long before they did. As quickly as it had started this weird form of music, that had done its job of breaking the teenage ice, went into a rapid decline. Nobody wanted it any more.

Just as I was resigning myself, once again, to a lifetime stuck in front of an editing desk, I got a call from Jack Good asking me to go round and see him. He had a proposal for me.

I got to his flat just after Sunday lunch and he came straight to the point. 'You are not going to make any headway in television with a name like Terry Denver.' I sat there open-mouthed while the implications of what he was saying to me gradually sunk in. Jack Good, the famous producer, thought I was good enough to go solo. I stayed to hear more.

Jack had seen something different in me: something mean, moody and magnificent. Which I wasn't about to argue with, since that was exactly how I'd seen myself since my first visit to *Rebel Without A Cause*. Jack's idea was that I should do a couple of *Six-Five Specials* and become an English singing version of James Dean. But there was nothing mean moody or magnificent in the name Terry Denver. It had to go.

We were sitting on the floor in his living-room, scratching our heads over a new name, when Jack's wife, who'd just had a baby, came in clutching the infant on her hip. Jack smiled up at her.

'Hello, *Liebling*,' he said, by way of introduction. 'We need a new name for "Terry Denver" here.' She moved across to the bookshelves in the corner of the room, picked a book out and threw it across to me. I caught it: it was a paperback book of names for girls and boys.

'There,' she said, 'have a look in that. I was just going through it to get a name for junior here.' She jiggled the baby, which was making rainforest noises.

The girls' names were first in the book, and the very first one that caught my eye was 'Faith'. This seemed to me to have a good ring to it. I'd come up with the notion that a combination of two names that were also everyday words would be particularly clever: when people used these words in everyday speech, it would make them think of me. 'Faith' was good, then, because it was used in lots of expressions, like 'In good faith', 'Faith, Hope and Charity', and so on. The first boy's name that took my fancy was 'Adam'. It also qualified: 'I don't know him from Adam', 'Would you Adam and Eve it?' And of course it had biblical connotations too.

When Jack's wife came back into the room, I piped up, ''Ere, *Liebling* – what d'you think of Adam Faith as a name then?' They both fell about laughing at the monumental ignorance of this little scruff from Acton. Jack called his wife *Liebling*, which is German for 'darling', for the very good reason that she was German, but I thought *Liebling* was her name.

'I think it's a terrible name,' said Mrs Good, chuckling. 'Truly terrible.'

'What do you think, Jack?' I asked.

'Bloody awful,' agreed Jack. 'But better than the one you've been using up till now, at any rate.'

* * *

40

When I got home, my mother answered the door.

'I've got a new name, Nell,' I told her, jumping up and down excitedly on the step.

'Oh yes?' she replied. 'And what's that then?'

'Adam Faith,' I told her, all bright-eyed and expecting at the very least a bouquet of flowers.

'You're not coming in here with a name like that!' she laughed. 'And for God's sake keep your voice down in case the neighbours hear you. We'll get laughed out of the flats.'

I couldn't see what everyone was on about. I loved the name. It sure beat Bill Nelhams. Which if the old lady had had her way, I would have been stuck with, for the rest of my life.

Back in the peace and quiet of my bedroom, empty for once, I lay on the bed and let the day's events wash over me. It hit me like delayed shock. In one easy sweep, I was a solo artist with a new name. Stunning, exciting, mind-blowing, but what about the other Worried Men? We hadn't quite got to the point of going our own ways and were still trying to put together something that could stand up in the rock 'n' roll scene.

I'd argued with Jack to let the boys back me. But, as far as he was concerned, it was solo or nothing. That was my first lesson in the ruthlessness of show business: I left the group – and Adam Faith was born. And although I could never have known what it was going to mean to my life, something very profound had happened, Terry Nelhams had acquired a 'Siamese twin'.

No sooner had Jack Good taken me in hand than my number came up for National Service. National Service was another reason there were no teenagers in the Fifties. All the aggression and energy of Britain's adolescent rogue males was defused on the parade-ground, or in the jungles of Malaya. And it would defuse my showbiz career all right if I didn't manage to get out of it.

I'd watched this very thing happening to another pop star, Terry Dene, who'd had four top-thirty hits between 1957 and 1958. Then the army got hold of him. He managed to get out, on medical grounds, after six months, but during that time the business had moved on, he'd lost his place in it, and he never recovered. It finished him. I knew my number was about to come up. And as the date got nearer and nearer, I grew more and more desperate. I had to find some way of stopping the army from wanting me.

The first thing I thought of was swallowing soap to make myself sick just before the medical. They told me everybody tried that. Then I thought of pretending to be deaf. 'The oldest trick in the book,' scoffed my mates. The date crept ever nearer. In desperation, I went to see a private doctor, in Harley Street.

'Yes,' said this distinguished man, peering at me over his gold-rimmed half-moon spectacles, 'what can I do for you?'

'I'd like you to cut one of my toes off,' I told him.

'What's wrong with your toes?' he asked.

'Nothing,' I replied. 'I just don't want to go into the army.'

Politely but firmly, he showed me the way out.

'I'll pay you!' I shouted desperately as he shut the door in my face.

All that afternoon, I trudged up and down Harley Street, trying to convince one of these expensive private doctors to cut off my toe. Every single one of them refused. It was only a toe, I thought bitterly – I'd still have nine left to walk with – bunch of spoilsports. If I'd had the stomach for it, I would've cut the bloody thing off myself.

As it happened their lack of compliance was just as well; National Service was scrapped just before it was my turn to be called up. It was as if I'd been on Death Row and somebody suddenly came along one bright sunny morning and said, 'It's OK, you can go home now: they've abolished hanging.'

ChapterSeven

GETTING A BREAK ON TV AGAIN, ESPECIALLY WITH JACK GOOD, was a chance of a lifetime. I intended to give it all I'd got. I had myself a new name, now for the image.

I was still very stuck on my James Dean look. Fortunately for me, so was Jack. So there was no changing that. Although I did stand myself a new pair of 501s. By now jeans were a familiar sight in London but you didn't want your jeans to look like any old jeans. You had to make them as cool as possible. There was a whole ritual, which we'd learnt from articles about Yankee kids, to go through before you could call your 501 blue-jeans your own.

Denim was notorious for shrinking, so that meant buying a pair that were at least two sizes too big for you and, the minute you got home, putting them on and jumping into a hot bath. To get the amount of shrinkage required, you had to spend at least an hour lying prostrate in the bath, submerged up to the waist. I normally passed the time trying to keep my latest Mickey Spillane paperback above the water-line. If you think that sounds uncomfortable, try this: to make the jeans tight enough for it to look like you'd grown a second skin, they had to dry on you. And to prevent them bulging on the knees or, worse, the bum, you had to stand up till they were dry.

So, all in all, it was a three- or four-hour self-inflicted torture session. It wasn't easy in a small flat, finding somewhere to get yourself dry. Mum had very strong views on wandering about the flat in sopping jeans. One time, when I was just finishing my hour's soaking, she called me for supper. Not wanting to interrupt the process, I padded out to the sitting-room leaving a tributary of water in my wake. Nell went potty. She slung me out onto the balcony and sent my steak-and-kidney pie out on a tray. So there I was in the pitch dark eating my dinner standing up, in midwinter, catching my death of cold. I wasn't allowed back in the flat until me and the 501s were bone dry.

Another major drawback was that as your jeans slowly dried on you they got tighter and tighter and your legs went numb from corpuscle shortage. It usually took around four or five hours' continual usage for the waistband to ease off enough for the blood to start flowing again. It was like having a couple of hours of severe pins and needles, but it was worth all the pain and agony. What you were left with after the masochism was the coolest pair of jeans in the world.

As Jack wanted me to keep my Jimmy Dean uniform going and I'd got my new name sorted, there wasn't much left for me to work on for my 'make-over'.

I wore out the mirror trying to figure which bit of me would produce a change to impress Jack Good. I needed something that didn't frighten the girls off but could look different enough to get me noticed. Then it struck me, my hair. I'd change my hair. I was in the mood for a change anyway. I was getting bored with all the work it took to maintain the eight-inch quiff. Every day you needed to cake on half a jar of Brylcreem to make it stand up as it should. After a couple of hours this sticky white grease set solid like a motor-bike helmet, even a stick of dynamite couldn't ruffle it. The trouble was, in the Britain of 1958, nobody had heard of styling hair for men. I wanted a haircut that no-one had seen before. I wanted an Adam Faith cut.

By chance I got to hear of a bloke in Chiswick called Eddie Jones who was getting a reputation for doing to men's hair what women took for granted: styling. This news was manna from heaven for me. Trying to achieve the perfect Dean look, I'd already had a go at curling the golden locks. I'd heat my mum's tongs up on the gas stove and stick in a quick curl. I had reason, on many occasions, to be grateful to my cowboy hat, especially in bad weather – wind and rain can play havoc with a burnt scalp. When the burns got too bad, I tried some of my sister's rollers. But I lived in fear of a girlfriend turning up unannounced and catching me in my hairnet.

I discussed my dilemma with Eddie at great length. He pushed the thatch back and forth thoughtfully and then without wasting another moment he took up his scissors and went to work. Off came the quiff. Out in the wash came the Brylcreem. And out I slithered from Eddie's chair a new man. Without knowing it Eddie had created *the* Adam Faith trademark. That funny little crop, tight to the head, with a short fringe probably became my most recognizable feature.

As usual when I got back home, everybody fell about laughing like drains at my 'new look'. I didn't care, I loved my new haircut. It was different, as different as it could be from how I'd looked before. And I was just following a pattern in my life that I'd established long before. I wanted to be different.

To the Nelhams family show business was uncharted territory – an unknown, frightening world. So, half the ribbing I got for my efforts to break into the big-time was a lot to do with Mum and Dad being embarrassed and worried that their middle son would end up with a gigantic six-egg omelette all over his ambitious face.

Mum and Dad weren't the only ones who were nervous about where all this showbiz stuff would lead me. Terry Nelhams was nervous; in fact, scared to death. Nothing's worse than volunteering to be at the front over the top, only to be taken out with the first bullet.

Another thing that disturbed me was that I could lose track of Terry Nelhams. My Siamese twin, Adam Faith, was getting bigger and stronger every day. It was fun having an alter ego, but I didn't want him taking me over – I needed to hang on to my own identity. I already had a life, I didn't want someone else pinching it from me.

Until the hurricane of change started hitting Britain about 1957, almost all families replicated themselves through the generations:

45

if your dad was a brain surgeon, you'd automatically go to university and become a doctor. If you grew up on a council estate, you got a lowly paid menial job – unless you were born lucky. This still happens today, to a certain extent, but at that time it was an almost infallible rule.

Boy, was I lucky – I was born at the right time. The old Britain had been like a huge flat piece of glass, with no bumps or cracks in it and it was about to get hit by a mighty sledge-hammer. This strange new creature called the teenager was whacking at this lovely smooth uniform surface – shattering it and breaking it up into thousands of little pieces. And one of the little splinters, that flew up and didn't come back down to its former place, was yours truly.

I went back to Jack Good with my new identity. I did two *Six-Five Special*s with him for the BBC, singing cover-versions of current US hits. The *Six-Five Special* format turned out so successful that some bright spark of a promoter decided to turn it into a live concert called *Road-Show*.

They asked me to go and I accepted. It looked like a sure thing. Spurred on by Jack Good's confidence in me, I handed in my notice at TVA, and off I went, still singing covers of American hits like 'Hello, Mary Lou'.

The tour was a success, and I had the time of my life. I was in the spotlight, and I absolutely loved it. But, like a lot of jobs in show business, it was short-lived.

Suddenly, I found myself unemployed and next to broke. I'd blown my wages from the tour on wine, women and Wimpys. A wave of panic – which I've become familiar with over the years – came over me. I'd been used to a regular wage, which allowed me to plan some sort of budget for living. I wasn't used to getting great dollops of money and making it last through the lean periods. I was still naïve enough to think that every gig I had would last for ever, giving me enough money to enjoy the luxurious lifestyle that I'd enjoyed on tour.

'Never worry,' said the ever-helpful Jack. 'Something will turn up – have a word with my agent.' I had a word, and having signed me up, Jack's agent got me a record deal with EMI, working for a producer with a big reputation, Norman Newell.

Norman and I made two records, a cover version of Jerry Lee Lewis' 'High School Confidential' and 'Country Music Holiday'. The trouble was he had made his reputation with acts like Shirley

46

Bassey and he had about as much knowledge and, I suspect, interest in rock 'n' roll as my mum. Both records were diabolical and neither did a thing.

I'd had my chance, but it had all been a flash in the pan. I'd blown it. Well, Adam Faith had blown it. It was time for Terry Nelhams to take over. There was nothing for it, I had to go back to work.

Life could sure as hell go on without Adam Faith. In fact, in some ways it was a bit of a relief. The prospect of going back into the film business was no punishment for me. Adam Faith had thrown away our chance to have fame and fortune. Terry Nelhams couldn't do any worse.

Luckily I'd hung on to my Association of Cinema & Television Technicians union card. What kept the ulcer juices flowing was the thought that the movie business had moved on and left me out in the cold. But I got a job almost at once as an assistant editor for Danziger Studios at Borehamwood.

Danzigers were notorious in the film business for being careful with money. All their films and TV series were done as cheaply as the Danziger boys were allowed to get away with.

On one of their regular sweeps over studios costs, some bright spark had come up with the idea of reusing the spacing set between the sound effects on a roll of sound film. I was put in a hut in the middle of a car park, where they stored all the used sound-effects tape from the studios. My job was to take the spacing out and splice them together for use again. I wasn't exactly directing *Ben-Hur*, but at least I was back in the film business where I belonged.

On the very first day on this interesting new assignment, I opened the door to the hut, and stepped back smartly as a large can of tape rolled out and landed on my foot. It was a jungle in there: miles and miles of film crawling across the floor like snakes. What I needed was a machete not a tape-splicer. I could hardly get in. Naturally, being Danzigers, there was no heating in the hut. In that freezing winter of 1958/59, fingers dropping off with the cold, I started on the mountain before me.

There was one compensation. One of the girls that worked at the studio took pity on me and would come and spend her lunchtimes in my little hut. Somehow the fact that there was no heating didn't seem to matter when my pretty blonde friend was around. She could warm up an igloo. We spent many a happy hour laying around that hut, talking of each other's dreams and ambitions in the movie industry.

I spent weeks and weeks slogging through the forest of tapes, and Terry Nelhams was a contented man. Peace – just me and my rolls of film. No more putting myself on the rack of showbiz. As the months went by and winter turned into spring, the space in the hut got bigger and the pile of cans got smaller.

Finally, someone must have decided I'd served my punishment, because they put me on the *Mark Saber* TV series. It was one of those typical early black-and-white, private detective shows but it did have one fantastic gimmick. The lead actor only had one arm and that became the show's trademark. He would steer the car with his arm through the bottom part of the steering-wheel and change gears with his hand. It fascinated me. I thought it was so cool. I tried it a couple of times in Hurgy's brother's car, when he was giving me driving practice. But all I did was attract the attention of the local militia.

I was happy at Danzigers, but it was time to move on. Just up the road was a film people pub. I met a bloke in there one lunchtime who tipped me off that there was an assistant editor's job coming up at National Studios. This was a leg up because National was turning out slightly more upmarket stuff than Danzigers.

So I moved and spent the next six or nine months at Elstree, working on two television series: *William Tell* and *The Invisible Man*. My job was to dub on the sound effects – all the thuds and thunks, the arrows quivering in the trees and all that kind of thing. And I loved it.

I was in one of the cutting-rooms one morning, fiddling with a chase sequence, when suddenly a voice rang out along the corridor: 'Anybody know an Adam Faith?' There was a short silence. I stopped winding film. The spool clacked round and round in front of me, while I sat there, completely paralysed.

'Anybody know an Adam Faith?' barked the unknown voice again impatiently. 'There's a call for him!'

'Er, I know him . . .' I shouted. 'I'll take it and give him the message.' None of the people in the cutting-rooms knew about my brush with show business, I'd kept it quiet out of embarrassment. I'd no choice but to pretend that Adam Faith was somebody else, Judas that I was. But I didn't owe Adam Faith anything. He'd lost the plot and couldn't expect to come back into my life whenever the fancy took him.

I picked the receiver up as though it were wired to the mains, and put it to my ear.

'Ullo, Adam,' said a northern voice, 'it's John here, John Barry.'

My heart was already going nineteen to the dozen, but now it started hammering at warp speed. I'd met John when he was the musical director of the *Six-Five Special Road-Show*. A call from John could only mean one thing.

'Hello, John,' I said, as quietly as I could. 'What is it?'

'We're starting a new show with the BBC,' said John. 'A pop music show called *Drum Beat*. It'll be a rival to *Oh Boy!* [This was Jack Good's new TV show, only by now he'd defected to ITV.] I've told the producer you ought to come along for an audition.'

I lowered my voice to a whisper. 'I can't, John,' I hissed, 'I'm working here, in the cutting-room.'

'Oh,' he grunted, 'all right, then – as you like. I just thought you'd be interested, that's all . . .'

My brain started to turn somersaults. I was torn right down the middle. On the one hand, compared with most of my mates back in Acton, I was in fragrant green clover with juicy pink flowers, earning about £25 a week, or just over twice the national average. With a bit of 'double-bubble' for overtime on a Saturday and Sunday, I'd sometimes been taking home five times what my dad brought back in his own weekly pay-packet. It was regular money and I wasn't in a rush to throw it away.

On the other hand, Adam Faith was yelling out to me. He was sitting next to me – my twin – in front of the editing machine making my head spin. 'You still want to be a star. Don't try to fool me. You want to be so famous that you can taste it. Go on, don't miss this chance. Go, don't hesitate!'

I decided to throw caution to the wind and we made a date for the following week.

I still had nine days in which to change my mind, assuming of course that my editor didn't change it for me first. I needed his help on this one, so I decided it was time to tell him the truth about Adam Faith. He listened while I stumbled through my unlikely tale, and then said simply, 'OK, don't worry about it. Go to the audition. Just take the day off, I'll cover for you.'

49

The audition was in a rehearsal room on the Goldhawk Road, Shepherds Bush. I rang the BBC number John had given me, and said I was coming along. It didn't take long standing in that rehearsal room to realize that the BBC were very serious about this show. They'd had enough of ITV, with the help of Jack Good, stealing the hearts and minds of the new breed of TV viewers. They were determined that *Drum Beat* would compete with the best ITV could throw at them.

Drum Beat was going to be an all-new, fast-moving show, based around live artists singing the latest hits. Not terribly original – Jack Good had done that with *Six-Five Special* years earlier. But during the year or so I'd been back at work all these TV pop shows had really taken off. Every kid in the country tuned in to them. If you became a teen favourite now on a show like *Drum Beat*, your chances of stardom were extremely good.

Just when Terry Nelhams thought he'd got his life together again, here was Adam Faith breaking down the door.

I went through the songs they'd asked me to audition on the day, and when he'd heard me out, Stewart Morris, the producer, thanked me and pronounced that time-honoured phrase, 'Don't ring us, we'll let you know.' I went immediately to John Barry in the studio.

'Look,' I said, 'I'm not trying to be funny or anything, but I need to know right now whether or not Stewart's going to offer me a contract. If I don't know, I can't do this. I can't risk losing my job.'

John Barry looked down at me with a twinkle in his eye. 'Don't worry,' he said gruffly. 'They're going to give you three shows, with options – on their side – for another twenty-three.'

I thought about this. Three shows was great. Three shows was wonderful. But three shows wasn't enough. I needed the whole series, or nothing. It meant risking everything, my whole future; I needed to minimize the risk. I tried again. 'Look, John, it's all or nothing for me here. If I'm going to give up work, I've got to have the lot, a contract for the whole series.'

I think John did his best to help me, but what I was demanding was out of the question. The offer was three shows, at a flat rate of £60 a week, with the possibility, if I cut it, for the rest of the series.

Well, I thought! There's no way I'm going to get more than

three shows – Adam Faith didn't exactly have a track record of success. I might get enough out of the first three to put down a deposit on a car. More than anything else in life at that time, I wanted a Ford Consul. Going out to Elstree and back on public transport every day from Acton was getting to be a nightmare. I had to take three different buses, followed by a train, then meet my editor for a lift. I was getting up at dawn every day to be at work for nine. It was harder than flying to Spain, and probably took longer.

The car I wanted cost £200, and I needed an £80 deposit. That ought to be well within saving distance.

I told my supervising editor they wanted me for the three shows, and that to do them I needed to rehearse Thursday afternoons, all day Friday, and all day Saturday.

'Can I have Thursday afternoon and Friday off?' I asked. 'And I'll come in after the show on Saturday and work all night Saturday and all day Sunday at the weekday rate of pay to make up for lost time. That way we would be ready for dubbing as usual on Monday.'

He thought about this for what felt like an hour.

'All right,' he said at last, 'I'll cover for you; but only for these three shows, OK?'

For the next few weeks, I got virtually no sleep at the weekends. I'd finish the show at Riverside Studios in Hammersmith on a Saturday night, grab a quick Scotch and ginger in the bar, jump in the car (which I'd secured with the first week's *Drum Beat* money) then tear out to Elstree and start cutting.

Finally, the last of my allotted three shows came round. Now, at last, for a bit of rest and relaxation, I thought. Sunday mornings in bed, Mum bringing me a nice cup of tea at about eleven o'clock – luxury. I couldn't wait. I was so tired I was on the point of having a nervous breakdown – except they didn't exist in those days. I put my coat on, said a fond goodbye to the cast and crew of *Drum Beat*, and made a beeline for the exit. I was just about to shoot through it and burn the tarmac getting over to the pub, when the producer appeared out of nowhere.

'Ah, Adam,' he said, 'I wonder how you'd feel about doing another three shows?' I didn't know whether to groan or cheer. I nodded glassily at him and croaked, 'Thank you.'

'Jolly good. That's settled then. See you next Thursday.'

Next day, hollow-eyed with fatigue, I staggered in to see my understanding editor again, certain that his understanding was about to give out. 'I've got to do another three,' I said. He looked at me gravely for a little while. Then he said quietly, 'You can't go on like this, you know, Terry. Look at you – you're killing yourself. You've got to make your mind up what you want to do.'

'I know,' I said. 'But honestly, this is it, I promise. They're never going to take up the option for the rest of the shows.' I was amazed that Stewart Morris had kept me on for so long anyway.

'All right, Terry,' he said wearily, 'but this is positively the last time.'

And it was the last time. Because a week or two later the roof fell in on me. I went in to Elstree on the Monday after the fifth show. There was a message telling me to go and see the studio manager, a woman called Aida Young. Nobody had to tell me what it was all about. I'd been living in dread of getting a summons from her. As I walked towards her office I had that horrible feeling you get when the big boss crooks the finger and you know you're going to get the bullet.

I sat in front of Aida Young quaking in my size seven and halfs. She gave me the hanging-judge look.

'Hello, Terry,' she said, coolly. 'Do sit down.' After a short pause to inspect this underling in front of her she went on, 'You know, it's a funny thing, but I don't seem to have seen you round the studios very much recently, do I? Particularly on Thursdays and Fridays?'

I swallowed the can of baked beans that had suddenly lodged in my throat.

'Haven't you?' I mumbled.

'No,' said Aida thoughtfully, as though the whole thing had only just occurred to her, 'I haven't.' She raised her voice a notch and hit me with the killer punch: 'But I do see a lot of you on a Saturday afternoon, at six o'clock. Because my children watch a certain television show called *Drum Beat*.'

'Oh,' was all I could say. The game was up. My tongue clung to the roof of my mouth like it had been stuck there with superglue.

'Listen,' Aida said, as kindly as she could, 'either you're going to be in show business, or you're going to work for me as a film editor. Which is it going to be?'

'Can you give me a day?' I asked. She stared at me stonily. I was sure she was going to say, 'No.' But she nodded: 'All right,

I'll give you one day – but that's all.'

Under the circumstances, I thought this was pretty fair.

I called Stewart Morris.

'Stewart, I got hauled in by my boss at work today, and I've got to know: are you going to keep me on the show until it's finished?'

Stewart hedged. 'It's not time to take up the option,' he said. 'I'd need time to think about it . . .'

'Don't think about it,' I said, 'because I haven't got time. I've got to see her again first thing tomorrow. If you want me for the rest of the run, please tell me and if you don't, no hard feelings, I'm going back to work.'

'Oh, all right,' Stewart replied. 'Go on then: you're on for the six months. Don't say I never give you anything.'

Back I trotted to see Aida Young the next morning. 'I'm leaving,' I told her.

'Are you sure you're doing the right thing?' she asked. Well, no, actually. I didn't know! My editor was due to start work on a new movie – *The Guns of Navarone* – in a few weeks' time and he'd already promised me the job as his first assistant. It was a big chance for me. At the very moment when they were about to promote me to first assistant on a big new picture, here was Adam Faith butting in and making me resign from my fantastic film job.

Very seldom in life have I regretted the things I've done. It's the things you don't do that haunt you for ever. At that particular moment I wasn't at all sure that the decision I'd taken wouldn't turn out to be one I'd regret. Of course, I could never have predicted what an extraordinary life that decision was going to lead me to.

ChapterEight

AFTER A FEW MONTHS OF APPEARING ON *DRUM BEAT* I FOUND MY life changing. People were beginning to recognize me in the street. I loved that. It puffed me up no end when people asked for my autograph. I still find it immensely flattering.

The first time it really came home to me was one evening, after one of the later *Drum Beat* shows. I'd arranged to meet my new manager, Eve Taylor, at the pub opposite the studios.

Eve was John Barry's manager, and he'd persuaded her to take me on. At the time I was very pleased she'd agreed to represent me. Nobody else had taken a particular interest, and Eve Taylor had a fearsome reputation for fighting for her artists. As I was still shell-shocked from the disasters of my earlier attempts to take showbiz by storm, this suited me down to the ground. What I lacked in confidence she made up for in aggression.

She was a fearsome sight when she was in full flight. God help anyone who disagreed with her. There's many a promoter, agent or even her artists who could have used a month in rehabilitation after a five-minute going over from Eve. This woman made Cruella de Ville look like Snow White.

She'd use every trick in the book to get what she wanted. Emotional blackmail, tantrums, threats and, if all else failed, she wasn't backwards in coming forwards with the old water-works. Screaming blue murder, she'd threaten all sorts of dire consequences if anyone dared cross her. She was the commandant from hell. A dreadful woman.

I very soon came to rue the day I'd signed that five-year contract giving Eve Taylor a franchise on my life. But for now, I was a young, inexperienced kid, dying to be famous, so I let her get on with it.

When I got to the pub, Eve Taylor and her husband, Maurice Press, were already sitting at a table with their drinks. I went to the bar and ordered my usual, Scotch and ginger. I paid for the drink and was about to join Eve and Maurice when I was stopped in my tracks. A pretty young girl, who I'd already noticed earlier in the audience, stepped in front of me and blocked my way.

'Adam, can I have a kiss?' she begged.

Blimey, have a kiss? Was she joking? I would have happily emptied my pockets into any charity box for a taste of that incredibly pretty mouth. She looked so young, and beautiful, her long black hair falling across her shoulders. Her eyes smiling silently, but saying everything. She didn't have to 'plead' for a kiss, or anything else for that matter. I put my arms around her, and we made a very fair attempt at devouring each other, right there in the middle of the pub.

This was the first time anything like this had happened to me. I liked it and, whatever else show business could offer, this was enough to keep me in it until they nailed down my box.

When my head stopped spinning, and the heart slowed to a pace that allowed me to move, I went over to Eve and Maurice. Eve glared at me. 'You do not, ever, ever make love in public view with any girl that comes up and asks you for a kiss,' she hissed. 'That is not the way a star behaves.'

Of course she was right, but that was one of the main reasons I'd signed up to share life with Adam Faith. And if there was one thing that banished all thoughts that I'd made the wrong decision, it was that kiss. I made a point of never bonding with fans in front of Eve again. I didn't want her spoiling my enjoyment.

That was probably the first and last time I was able to ignore anything Eve Taylor said to me. I was not at all certain that I had the talent to succeed on the road I'd chosen. I was insecure, so I allowed, and even encouraged, Eve Taylor to take over my showbiz life completely. Adam Faith was there to do what he was told.

It was around about this time that I met the first girl I was to fall really in love with. Hurgy, who stayed on in the film business after I went fully pro, decided that we should take up ice-skating. Not for the exercise you understand. He'd heard from another pal of his, Dave, that Richmond ice-rink was packed with girls. That was enough for us. Hurgy with Dave in tow picked me up from rehearsals one evening and off we trotted to Richmond to check out Dave's information.

None of us could skate so we spent most of the time sitting with our Cokes, leaning over the barrier, checking out the talent. Dave spotted a couple of budding Jane Torvills and pulled Hurgy onto the ice. They did a few circuits, looking like out of control windmills, desperately trying to keep up with the two girls. Each time the girls went by, I tried hard to look like a chilled-out pop-star. But my heart was already banging against my back bone. One of the girls never took her eyes off me. Which was just as well, because mine were burning a hole right through her. She was stunning. Long blond hair, beautiful lean features, slim body and a golden tan. She had a cool confident look about her that was incredibly attractive. Finally, the girls decided that we were worth their attention and glided over to where I was sitting, drooling over the barrier. Hurgy and Dave came crashing to a stop beside them a couple of seconds later.

Then my heart gave way. The one I would gladly have married there and then spoke, 'Hi, I'm Verna and this is my sister.' She had the softest and most beautiful accent I'd ever heard. 'We're American. It's nice to meet you.' I'd only ever heard that sort of voice on the movies, and I was totally, utterly and completely captivated.

They sat down with us and we talked. Verna and I became lost in conversation. The rest of the world ceased to exist for the next couple of hours. If Verna had told me to jump off Beachy Head to prove my love for her, I would have. We'd arranged to meet them a couple of days later at the rink. But as we drove home, Dave dropped his bombshell. He'd spotted her first, so she was his.

That was the unwritten law of pulling, you didn't poach your mates' girls. I had to concede, but I was devastated.

What neither of us had taken into account was Verna's thoughts on this agreement. It was typically stupid of us to think that we were going to have a say in where a woman chooses to lay her heart. No man ever pulls a woman: she decides whether she wants him and then condescends to let him think that he's the big Don Juan.

So it was with Verna. She had already made up her mind and Dave and I had no say in the matter. Next time we all met up at the ice-rink, Verna and I became an 'item'.

Verna's father worked for an American company with interests in Europe. They'd rented a fantastic house in Weybridge which became like a second home for me and Hurgy. I loved it out there. It reminded me of Ruislip: fields, open spaces and houses at the end of long drives.

Verna and I had an idyllic summer. We'd bowl around the Surrey countryside in my old Consul, teenagers in love, doing all the things that teenagers do when they are in love. She was the first girl I'd ever talked to properly. She was very bright and introduced me to all sorts of different music, books and the art of discussion.

One time she wanted me to meet an old boy who was a friend of the family. Verna idealized this professorial man. We were invited for dinner at his house and I knew she wanted me to make a good impression. I rehearsed all sorts of what I thought to be intellectual subjects to make Verna proud of me. Fortunately, fate took a hand. I had one thing in common with the old man, the works of Edgar Allan Poe. We sat through the whole dinner discussing Edgar's books. The evening ended with the Professor reading *The Black Cat* to us, one of my favourite Poe stories. It was a wonderful night. Verna was proud of me and I basked in the glory. I'd made her happy.

A few months later I picked Verna up as usual on the corner of her road. I'd been banned from the house after her father had come home to find us both semi-naked and unspeakably drunk on his finest claret. When she got in the car she was in floods of tears. Her father had just told her the terrible news that he was to be transferred to Switzerland which meant, of course, that she would have to go with him. I was going to lose my love.

We tried to keep the relationship going but it was no use. With

57

her in Geneva and me on the road we reluctantly grew apart. We met several times in Paris, and occasionally in Geneva and London. But finally her dad was moved back to the States and we lost touch. My first broken heart.

During the early days of my love affair with Verna I was still working on *Drum Beat*. As it neared the end of its six-month run, I began to get that old familiar feeling, worrying about where I was going. There was nothing in the pipeline. You don't get to be a star covering other people's hits; you have to have a hit of your own.

Whilst I was on *Drum Beat*, Eve had convinced a record company that I was a chance too good to miss. Actually, she could have sold cocaine to a Colombian drug dealer. With twenty-odd shows on mainstream TV behind me, she had persuaded them that I was a lad worth backing and they had agreed to let me do one record for them, to see how it went.

Isn't it amazing how the circle goes round. My new record company was Top Rank Records. Rank wanted to get a piece of this new action called teenage music and, although it was a bit late, had started a record company. I was the second artist to be signed, after Craig Douglas.

This time I couldn't miss. New manager, new haircut, six months on a major rock 'n' roll TV show. I was set to fly. Do I need to tell you what happened?

We went into the studios, made the record 'Ah, Poor Little Baby'/'Runk Bunk', released it, and just like the two I'd made for EMI, it was greeted by the teenage record-buying public with overwhelming indifference.

Once again it was Terry Nelhams, the Acton Vale flats and unemployment looming on the horizon.

In the meantime there were still a few *Drum Beat*s to be done. We did the show live from the BBC Riverside Studios in Hammersmith, and I always looked forward to show day. The studio was full of girls: secretaries, canteen girls, researchers. It was a great place to spend your Saturdays. During a break in rehearsals, I was hanging out in the office corridor, posing as a successful pop singer in case one of the girls walked by, when I heard my name being shouted.

'I thought I'd find you here.' John Barry came striding up to me. 'I've got a song for you,' he said. 'Come and have a listen to it.'

I followed John Barry to the piano, slightly upset that he'd dragged me away from my pulling site, and for what? I'd sort of resigned myself to the fact that I would never find that one magic life-transforming song.

John Barry's pianist, Les Reed, was sitting at the piano, with a songwriter, Johnny Worth, standing beside him.

'Johnny's written a song,' said John Barry. 'Have a listen now and see what you think.'

Les struck up, and Johnny started singing.

John Barry and I looked at one another when it was finished. There was no need to say anything. It was brilliant. John Barry was right: 'What Do You Want?' had my name all over it. My heart started pumping. Maybe, at last, this was it. The Song.

'Yes!' I said, 'Yes, yes, *yes*! I want to do it.'

No-one has ever found the fail-safe formula for making hit records. If they had, they would bottle it and make a double-dyed Jimmy Goldsmith-type fortune. But, even with my limited experience of hits I couldn't miss this one. '*What do you want, if you dont want money?*' had success written all over it.

Eve Taylor convinced Norman Newell and EMI to bite the bullet and take another chance with me. So everything was in place. Thanks to the two Johns – Barry and Worth – I was back on the pitch, just dying to prove that I could score the winning goal. For days I practised the song. In the bath, in bed, in the car. Every opportunity I warbled out that simple but clever little ditty.

Although I didn't have an inkling at the time, I was about to get the break that would transform my life. My best mate on *Drum Beat* was Roy Young, a great rock 'n' roller. He covered all the Little Richard songs, which were easily the hardest to carry off, if you didn't happen to be Little Richard. One afternoon, Roy collared me in the studio canteen. 'Hello, Tel. I've got to go to Oxford to take my driving test,' he said. 'Will you drive me there?'

'What do you mean, you've got to take your driving test?' I asked. 'You can already drive!' Of course he could drive. We'd been out in his car on enough double-dates for me to know that.

'Yes, I know I can drive,' he said patiently, 'but I haven't actually got a licence. I drive illegally, see? So I was wondering if you could take me up for the test, 'cos I can't drive to the test-centre myself, can I?'

The boy had a point. So I drove Roy Young up to Oxford. In his car.

As we bowled up the A40, Roy sang me a new song he was about to record. What a song! It was fantastic. 'Bound to be a big hit, Roy,' I told him. 'Congratulations! You'll be visiting the estate agents when that's released.' As it turned out, Roy's record was about as successful as my first three.

'What's yours like?' he asked. I sang him 'What Do You Want?' I gave it my best shot. He turned in his seat and glared at me, shaking his head, like people do when the new puppy shits on the carpet once too often.

'You can't sing it like that!' he exclaimed, 'It's a great, great song, but you're killing it. It'll die of boredom if you sing it like that. So will the audience.'

'Like what?' It wasn't that I was hurt, just scared. The old warning lights were beginning to flash.

'You're singing it way too straight. You've got to bend it a bit – put your mark on it.'

I sat there, staring at the road. A black cloud filling the car. I turned to him, desperate. 'How would you do it?' Roy was a compassionate lad. He took pity on me.

'Sing it through again for me,' Roy said. He listened, thought about it for a minute, and then started to sing. When he'd finished, he made me have a go. Line by line, word for word, he took me through it. We sang 'What Do You Want?' all the way up to Oxford, and all the way back again. By the time we got back to London, I felt I'd got the message.

My act of kindness, driving Roy to Oxford, was about to pay off in spades.

There were seven days; just one hundred and sixty-eight hours; or ten thousand and eighty minutes; which is God knows how many seconds, before I had to walk into that recording studio, and I used every single waking one of them. Determined to stick with Roy's advice, I twisted my voice this way and that. My vocal cords went to places no vocal cords had ever been before. God knows what the neighbours in the Vale flats thought. But by the time invasion day arrived I felt ready. I was high on the excitement of doing something original. I was finally putting myself into a song. Thanks to Johnny Worth, John Barry and Roy Young, I'd got what I needed, something that was different, something that was mine and mine alone. I was ready for the fray.

And that is how I became an 'original' sound.

And how Roy Young finally got his driving licence.

Cliff was already on Columbia, one of EMI's labels. So to make sure there was no conflict they shoved me on Parlophone. I was a bit disappointed, because Parlophone wasn't exactly the coolest label to be on. In those days it was a comedy record label. The only hit record I'd ever heard of on it was 'Any Old Iron' by Peter Sellers, which had got into the Top Ten in 1957. But for pop music? It was a graveyard, and I didn't fancy it one bit. You can't market a pop singer like a comedy artist. I was worried if there was anyone at Parlophone who knew anything about my kind of music. Still with my past record I was lucky to get any deal. So Parlophone it was.

We recorded in Abbey Road's No. 2 Studio, soon to become a legend in its own lifetime for the amount of hits that came out of it. First Cliff, then me and later the Beatles.

Norman Newell, my producer, head-shy from his previous experience with me, got his assistant John Burgess to sit in on the session. Being into what he called grown-up music – Frank Sinatra, Shirley Bassey, all the big Columbia label stars – Norman probably thought that it would help if he had someone in the control box who was a bit more *au fait* with pop music.

It was just as well, because the minute old Norm heard my twisted, strangulated, bastardization of Roy Young's interpretation of 'What Do You Want?', he freaked.

'You can't sing it like that!' he said. 'That's a great song, and you're making it sound horrible. Why don't you sing it a bit straighter?'

Christ! Now what was I supposed to do? Norman sounded like the flip side of Roy's coin. They both hated what I was doing, but for completely opposite reasons. If I'd already had a couple of hits under my belt, I would have been prepared to go fifteen rounds with Norman to get my own way. But, as it was, all I had to boast about were three disastrous failures. All those hours of practice, gone for a Burton. I was completely stumped. I was in trouble with a capital S.

Once again John Barry came up trumps. 'No, no,' he said, 'We'll do it Adam's way. Trust me Norman, it'll work. It's unusual.'

'Unusual!' said Norman. 'It sounds ridiculous! We can't have it going out like that!'

They argued back and forth, with John Burgess as referee, while I stood between them like a tailor's dummy. In the end, and to my amazement, John won the battle. John was a proper musician, he could read music, so I suppose Norman felt relatively safe with him. It turned out to be one of Norman's best decisions.

John's pizzicato string introduction, his whole arrangement of 'What Do You Want?' was brilliant. I had no idea just *how* good John was at the time – but like Norman I was happy to put myself in his hands.

Joining up with John Barry was one of the luckiest things that happened to me. Between him, Johnny Worth and me we had numerous hits. It was such a joint effort that when I got my first silver disc (250,000 sales) for 'What Do You Want?' I was quite prepared to have it cut in three, so we could all have a piece. Of course the two Johns wouldn't hear of it.

The recording took three hours and was released by EMI in November 1959. Any anxiety I should have felt about how the record would be received had been temporarily replaced by a new-found career. I'd been offered an opportunity to act in a TV cop show called *No Hiding Place*. The part was right up my street. A surly, rebellious tearaway runs over a policeman and leaves him dead in the road. Great! Very James Deanish. Hollywood was beckoning and I was hooked.

But one review of my new single did cut to the quick. A panellist on *Juke Box Jury, the* television record review programme, smirked, 'This record should do well in China, they'll be the only people who will understand it.' That review gave me a lot of pleasure when 'What Do You Want?' got to number one.

People ask me all the time 'What has been the most exciting moment in my career?' and given that so many things over the past thirty-five years have been extraordinary, it's hard to know what to choose. But if I was put in front of a firing squad and made to pick out something, it would have to be the very first time I heard that 'What Do You Want?' had gone into the charts.

It had been out for about three weeks, and we'd been getting the odd vibe that it was selling. Every now and again, EMI sales would ring up Eve Taylor and report, 'It's going well: it's sold 1,400 in one day . . .' or whatever. This was good but not good enough to penetrate the charts. The record was just 'bubbling under' as they say in the trade. We were just a handful of sales away from the Hit Parade.

When I'd finished doing me thespian bit on *No Hiding Place* I had nothing to do, so my attention swung back round to 'What Do You Want?'

Everyone in the record business lived in a state of suspended animation on the day the charts were announced. The biggest weekly telephone call was the one that came over from *New Musical Express*: if you got that, you'd made it.

On chart day I'd sit around Eve Taylor's office in Hay Hill near Berkeley Square, chatting up Jan, Eve's Miss Moneypenny. Between lustful thoughts I'd pray for that elusive phone call telling me I was in the charts.

We waited and waited, but there was no call. Six o'clock came and still no call. Eve and I left the office and started home, deep in depression. We'd just reached the bottom of the hill, and were about to wind our weary ways to our respective homes, when there was a God-almighty scream from behind us. It was Jan.

'Eve! Eve! Adam! Adam!' she yelled, like an evangelist at a prayer-meeting. She came belting down the hill at us, gasping for breath.

'What?' we asked her in unison. 'What, Jan? What's happened?' I wanted to ask if she'd changed her mind about coming home with me for the night.

Jan straightened up, with the biggest smile you ever saw on her face.

'You're in. They've just rung! NME's just rung! It's in the Hit Parade!'

A record in the Hit Parade. Terry Nelhams – excuse me – Adam Faith had a record in the Hit Parade. I couldn't take it in. It couldn't be true. It couldn't possibly be true, could it?

But it was true. 'What Do You Want?' was in the charts at number eighteen. Unbelievable!

ChapterNine

WHEN 'WHAT DO YOU WANT?' STARTED SHOOTING UP THE charts, it was *mind-boggling*. No other word for it. And there was nothing, absolutely nothing, I could have done to prepare myself for what was about to come. Some of the first astronauts that went to the moon had their whole outlook and values on life scrambled like a ball of wool after the cat's been at it. Well, that's what it felt like to me when 'What Do You Want?' hit the heights.

Countdown had started at eighteen. Next week it stood at eight. Then after just three weeks in the charts it hit number one, and it was lift-off. Terry Nelhams was left standing, shaking his head, looking up in wonder, whilst Adam Faith sat astride the rocket, arms stretched wide, screaming 'Come and give it to me.'

The rocket had hardly left the launch pad before mission control – with Eve Taylor in charge – went into action. There were photo sessions, interviews, radio and TV appearances. It was madness, and it was all happening in the blink of a gnat's eye.

With no time wasted, a forty-odd venue, one-night-stand

concert tour was put together. Rehearsals, new show clothes, money in my pocket – advanced from Eve – life was great. It was a complete fantasy and I lapped it up. And all the time, there was Eve Taylor pushing the buttons. By Christmas, a few weeks later, I was on the road. A new town every night.

Touring was a bit of a shock to the system. I was nineteen and, like most teenagers in 1959, I'd hardly moved outside my own town. I had certainly never, by choice, been north of Watford before. It was a different world 'up North'. Greyer and poorer than I'd been used to in the cushy south. People were different, more reserved and well mannered. Shy almost. It was like visiting another country to me.

The first night of our tour was in York. I stood in the wings, shaking with excitement and nerves. A stage-hand touched my shoulder and nodded to a gap in the curtains. 'They're bloody mad,' he said shaking his head, as bemused by it all as I was. I stood and watched from behind the curtain, for a minute, waiting for a very young Jimmy Tarbuck, our compere, to announce me. It was the most fantastic sight I'd ever seen. There were all these females screaming, their bodies twisting and jerking, some waving their knickers, frenzied in a kind of mass hysteria. All these young girls out there, howling for me!

When I ran out in front of them, a gale of sound crashed up and over me, like a physical force – two thousand voices screaming at full pitch, on and on screaming. I just stood there, deafened, unable to think or move. I'd suddenly discovered what it meant to be a star. It meant standing in front of hundreds of hot, supercharged girls, screaming at the top of their voices. It meant heat, noise, manic energy, and sex. I looked at it, and I loved it.

The more they screamed, the more I loved it. It was obvious what you were supposed to do – smash all that sexual energy straight back at them. So that's what I did. I wanted every girl in the audience to feel that I was there just to make love to her. It was as basic as that, and as simple as that, and it was no act: I meant it – I was living every young man's dream.

I couldn't wait to go on stage every night, to get that massive charge from all those women out front. It was mass seduction, with me as the only man up there for a couple of thousand girls. Heaven, I thought, I'm in heaven.

After every show there they'd be baying for blood. Every exit covered by patrols of girls ready to bring the rest of the pack if they spotted us trying to get out. They were wise to all our attempts to escape unnoticed.

Bert Harris, my roadie and partner in crime, spent half his time perfecting escape routes. We tried everything: laundry baskets, dressing up as a very short policeman, trying to wait them out. When all else failed we used battering-ram tactics. A flying wedge of burly policemen would hustle me into the back of a black Maria and slam the doors on me as if I were a criminal. Apparently Paul Anka would come straight off stage, climb into a disguise, go out through the pass-door and calmly walk out with the audience. Bert and I never plucked up enough courage to try that one.

We never took our own car to the gig. Any vehicle a pop singer left a show in would be plastered in lipstick, kicked and scratched to perdition, and would need a respray between gigs. More than one was nearly overturned by hundreds of kids rocking it. It was no joke. The mob knows no conscience. But sometimes it was my own fault because I'd encourage it. It was a measure of your success. The harder it was to get out of the theatre, the more wanted you felt. The more cars that needed a respray the more successful you felt. It was the same collective mania the Beatles faced two or three years later, and David Cassidy after them.

Damage to property, and sometimes people, was pretty routine. Later, when I did a show at the Theatre Royal in Dublin – the biggest in Europe then – we had fantastic stage-door action. A dozen or so cars outside the theatre were wrecked. Not because the kids were hooligans, but because in their excitement they forgot themselves. They were everywhere. Scrambling up onto cars to catch a glimpse of the action. And they were, I'm sure, very surprised and sorry when the bonnets and roofs they were standing on gave way beneath them as the vehicles collapsed.

As I was struggling to get to the car after the first night in Dublin, one girl got hold of the end of my scarf and started pulling. Her friend thought this was a great game and joined in. Not realizing what was happening, my brother Dennis started pulling from the other side, shouting at me to get into the car. The girls held on tight. It was like a tug-of-war. With me as the knot in the middle. Everywhere was noise and confusion. The scarf tightened and tightened, until it was biting into my neck. I started to choke. It was like a Tom & Jerry cartoon, with my neck getting thinner and thinner, only it wasn't funny – the world around me was gradually turning black as my airway cut off. I finally broke free and collapsed onto the back seat, sucking in great mouthfuls of air through my scalding throat. When I looked in the mirror, back at the hotel, the skin around my neck was a mass of great red weals and friction burns. One look from the doctor and I was off to emergency, for a layer of transparent skin. My neck looked like a parquet floor with a cover of polyurethane.

But there was another side to the coin: the loneliness of touring. You'd imagine that with a thousand girls screaming to get your trousers off every night it would be a piece of cake to indulge in what the naturalists call copulation. Well, contrary to popular opinion, it was the devil's own job to get to meet girls on tour. There was very little opportunity. You were in the town for only one night and were either locked up in a hotel room, praying for something good to come on TV, or you were at the gig. If you did go out for a quick breath of fresh air, you took your life in your own hands. If more than one girl saw you on the street, they were more likely to tear a piece off you for a souvenir than jump in between the sheets.

More often than not, when the show was over I went back to a dreary, depressingly faded, impersonal hotel room. The comedown off the drug of playing in front of several hundred yelling people was extremely hard to handle. That's why bands like The Who or Led Zeppelin smashed up their hotel rooms. It beat sitting there on your own thinking, 'Why, after that fantastic gig, with all those people screaming for me, aren't the walls lighting up at my magnificent presence? Why am I sitting here, like an ordinary person, twiddling my thumbs, eating a dead ham sandwich?' Most of the time it was a lonely life, and I hated to be alone.

I could have asked Bert to sit up with me all night chatting, but somehow it wouldn't have been quite the same. Most of the time I just craved the company of a woman. What always surprised me was that, in spite of all their enthusiasm in front of the stage, getting women to come backstage was nigh on impossible. That's not to say I didn't try. It was first on the agenda the minute the curtain went up.

I developed a system. At each new venue when I went on stage, I'd get Bert to stand in the wings. While I was singing the opening number I'd scan the first dozen or so rows of the audience. With minute attention I'd search for a girl. There were no criteria for selection, she didn't have to be the prettiest, the sexiest, or the most likely. It might be her hair that caught my attention. Maybe her legs, her smile, how her breasts filled her sweater, even her shoes. There are very few women in the world that haven't got something alluring about them.

When I'd spotted that special little feature that attracted me, I'd count the number of rows back to where she was sitting. Say, six rows back, centre aisle, twelve in from the left. Then, I'd startle the lead guitarist by awarding him an unexpected guitar solo. While the boys were trying to figure out where the heck they were, I'd belt off-stage. 'Right, Bert! Blonde, pink jumper. Six from the front, left of stage, twelve in.' Just before the end of the show, he'd go and stand by the appropriate row, waiting for the girl to leave her seat.

'Excuse me, my dear.' Bert had a fatherly charm. 'Adam would like to say hello to you backstage.'

This sounds incredibly calculating, and it was I suppose; but what other way is there of meeting girls if you're in a different town every night? As a pop star, even then, I had a lifestyle that was entirely out of sync with normal living. I never went to pubs, never saw the real world, I only talked to 'ordinary' people when I was giving them an autograph. I lived in a cocoon, like the emperor of China.

Most of the time and to her infinite credit, the girl would tell Bert where to get off. 'Adam Faith! Who the hell does he think he is? Tell him to get lost,' or, 'How dare you speak to me like that?' Occasionally, one would pluck up the courage and come round backstage.

One girl, I'll always remember her, in Doncaster, came into the dressing-room, and I started showing off in front of the boys, clowning about, being stupid. 'Whoa, boys, look at those legs!' I shouted as she came in. 'Aren't they fantastic!'

'Yes,' said the girl in her flat Yorkshire accent, 'they are, and they go all the way up to the top, then they start getting cheeky, like you – so watch it!'

That put me firmly in my place, and taught me not to show off at the expense of someone else.

Some, just a few, I would end up making love to. People used to say to me, 'You're all right, you can have any woman you want . . .' But you can't. People and feelings don't work like that. Those women screamed at me while the show was going on, but

I came to realize it was for their own agenda. They didn't necessarily want to jump into the Slumberland with me – they wanted to release something in themselves. They might all like to fantasize about it, but doing it for real was a totally different matter. Only very occasionally would the two things come together – the fantasy wish and the reality – and there'd be a one-night marriage, made in hysteria.

One time I was on my way to Brighton to do a gig at the Essoldo cinema and I'd invited two friends along to see the show. One was a redhead, one was a blonde. To my undying shame I can't remember now who they were, their names, what they were wearing, not even their faces. What I do remember is that they were a lot of fun.

That afternoon on our way down to the coast, me driving, we were all over each other like cheap suits. How the hell we didn't end up ploughing through a fence and sliding end-upwards in a field was more down to luck than driving skill. Come to think of it, I don't think I would have cared where we would have ended up, as long as it was locked together in some carnal combination.

It wasn't that the girls and me were particularly close friends. It's just that we were, well, you know, close. Close enough for me to be already planning that after the show I was going to break the world land-speed record, from Brighton to London.

So, knowing what delights would be awaiting me on the journey back to the Smoke, the act couldn't go fast enough. The trouble was, that while I was warbling away on the boards of the Essoldo cinema, drinking up the unadulterated worshipping, Bert had sent a message on stage informing me that the girls had decided to start without me.

Before the curtain even had a chance to fall, I took off at a pace that wouldn't have shamed a cheetah on heat. I hit that dressing-room at a hundred miles a second. What greeted me wiped out all thought of a quick getaway. The girls had got bored with waiting and had decided to practise the tango, stark naked, on a table in the middle of the room. Before I had a chance to consult my Victor Sylvester handbook on ballroom dancing, someone was banging on the door.

I prised open the door just enough to squint out. It was the theatre manager. Panic flooded my head, 'Oh my God, they've found out!' The police cell and the 'Monster of Depravity' newspaper headlines flashed in front of me. I squeezed myself through the crack in the door. I was no bigger than an emaciated sparrow in those days, so I managed to do it with the minimum exposure of what was going on behind me. What a relief, the manager was smiling.

With him was a woman of about forty, who looked exactly like Vivien Leigh. Behind her was a sulky young man, who looked like the sort who 'helped them out when they were busy'.

I stared at this tableau for a second. Oh no! Not Vivien Leigh! Not here. Not now. Not while . . .

The manager stepped forward with a broad grin. 'Adam,' he said expectantly, 'this is Miss Leigh, who wanted especially to meet you.' Miss Leigh stepped forward with her hand out-stretched. I shook it automatically.

Vivien Leigh, one of the world's all-time most celebrated actresses, star of *Gone With The Wind* and *A Streetcar Named Desire*, semi-detached wife of Laurence Olivier, and one of the all-time 'good lookers', here, at my dressing-room door. I was supposed to invite her in. There was no way. What the hell was I going to do?

'Ah,' I stuttered. 'Right! Er . . . Hello!' My brain ground into gear: they'd given me two, interconnecting, dressing-rooms. 'Could you . . . would you mind coming to the other door?' I said. A frown appeared on the manager's face, but they turned, and began walking along the corridor. I whipped round. The nymphettes were still at it, unfazed by the idea of a larger audience. If anything, they were getting even friendlier, and by now they had my backing group to cheer them on.

I shot through into the other room and wrenched the door open. Vivien Leigh came in and sat down. She was beautiful, with a dainty sexuality that smouldered with powerful intensity. Deep, mesmerizing eyes, like smoke.

It would be nice to say that Vivien Leigh was the world's most charming and fascinating woman. That we had a wonderful and entertaining chat, but I was oblivious to anything except what was going on next door. Not for the first time, my basic instincts were taking over.

At last, Vivien Leigh stood up and held her hand out again. She was leaving.

The moment the door closed behind her, I was straight into the next room, which now looked like a cross between an advanced ballroom dancing masterclass, and a *Playboy* centre-fold.

Just when I was beginning to feel like Wall-Flower of the Year, boom, boom, boom went the door again. This time I ignored it. There looked like an 'Excuse Me' coming up and this was one dance I didn't want to miss. Somebody else could answer it – one of the band.

The sods! They ignored it too. A second knock, more insistent this time. What was it with this place? A bloke does a hard show and can't get five minutes' peace to relax after work.

'What, what, *what?*' I swore, out loud. The door did well to stay on its hinges as I flung it open, all caution lost to the wind. '*What?*' I screamed. Outside, pouting slightly because I'd kept him waiting, was the sulky young man.

'Vivien's compliments.' He smiled. 'Would you like to go back to her house, and have dinner with her this evening?' I stared at him blankly.

'It would be a private dinner,' he added encouragingly, 'just you and Miss Leigh.'

'Er . . . I'd love to go,' I stuttered, 'but two of my cousins came to see tonight's show and I've got to take them back to London. Sorry about that. Maybe some other time. 'Bye!' Having delivered my puerile excuse, I closed the door on the lad and returned to the mayhem.

There are very few things I truly regret in my life. Saying no to an evening with Vivien Leigh is one of them.

ChapterTen

I
T TOOK ME A TIME TO GET USED TO THE IDEA THAT I WAS ABOUT TO
make a lot of money, and that it was there for the spending.
When I played that first tour, my brother Dennis came with
me to keep me company. We were very sensible and booked ourselves into digs in York. It was the middle of winter and the city
was gripped in a fearsome cold spell.

We shared a room in a freezing boarding-house. And when I
say freezing, I mean exactly that. I woke up the first morning,
shivering with the cold. I couldn't believe it, there I was lying
under a pile of blankets and a quilt, and yet my teeth were playing a tune that a xylophone player would be proud of. 'Christ,
I'm going to die of the cold,' I thought, '*in bed*!' I clamped my jaws
together to stop my teeth clacking. The single electric bar had
gone out. The meter needed another shilling and I was too rigid
with cold to feed it. I lay there for a while, going slowly numb,
fantasizing about the headlines. 'Pop star found frozen to death
in York boarding-house.'

There was a strange, translucent light in the room that hadn't been there the day before. It took me a while to work out where this light was coming from. Then I looked at the windows: frost flowers had spread their beautiful icy petals right across the panes – *on the inside.*

Dennis, in the next bed, slowly came to. We shivered at one another.

'Christ,' he said, 'it's like Eskimo Nell's in here. I'm freezing! Aren't you?' It was a stupid question that didn't deserve an answer. 'Come on, we're getting out of here.'

We cursed and shuddered into our icy clothes, hopping about on the arctic linoleum, paid the landlady for the week, ran out of the front door and dived into the car. That was even colder, if possible. We sat there and revved it up, then drove around the quiet streets at top speed until we saw the biggest hotel in town. Dennis strode up to the desk.

'Have you got central heating?' he demanded.

'Yes, sir,' replied the startled night clerk.

'Does it work?'

Imperiously: 'Yes.'

'Good. Book us a suite, then, the warmest you've got. We're moving in.'

Luxury is warmth, warmth luxury. It was like changing planets, that hotel – about as different as you could get from the icicle-infested hovel we'd just quit. Yes, the staff wanted to park the car, carry the luggage, make the beds and do our every bidding – but above all it was warm.

Not all boarding-houses were as bad as that one in York. There was one that was superb, much better than going to a hotel. It was called Mrs Bradley's and it always smelled to me of perfumed panties. It was at 12 Street Lane, in the posh area of Leeds – quite a big house, with loads of bedrooms, some of which Mrs Bradley let out to 'theatricals'.

Mrs Bradley – imagine Shelley Winters as she was in *Alfie* and you have a pretty good idea of how she looked – was a warm, lovely woman who enjoyed having people from show business in her house. The all-pervasive brothel smell was explained by the fact that she managed part of the house as an 'escort' service. Anytime I stayed at the house I was never aware of Mrs Bradley being hassled by the police. In fact I seem to remember that the Law and Mrs Bradley lived in happy harmony.

73

Strangely, in spite of its nocturnal activities, Mrs Bradley's wasn't in the least bit sleazy; for twelve shillings and sixpence per night, you had clean, comfortable, warm accommodation, with a great breakfast, and no stupid rules. If you staggered in at 3 a.m. after a gig, there was no problem about raiding the fridge, making a cuppa, or taking a girl to bed. It was great, great fun, and all the top stars stayed there.

The Milverton Lodge, in Manchester, was similar to Mrs Bradley's, only even more like a full-scale re-enactment of Sodom and Gomorrah, especially in the Annexe at the back where we always stayed.

Places like Mrs Bradley's and the Milverton Lodge were famous in the business because it was so difficult to find anywhere in the early Sixties where you were allowed to have female company with you. Whenever anyone found a good place word went round the tours like wildfire.

Most places, especially hotels, wouldn't allow a girl within a mile of the bedrooms, under any circumstances. One time at the Midland Hotel, Manchester, I had another one of my 'cousins' visiting me and I went to take her up to my room. It was three o'clock in the afternoon. No matter how much I pleaded with the hall-porter, he wouldn't let me and the girl upstairs on our own. In the end he allowed us to go up to the room escorted by one of his assistants, on the condition that while we had afternoon tea, his man stood at the open door to keep an eye on us. If one of us did manage to smuggle a girl into one of these morality zones, it was considered a great coup.

One thing that John Barry helped me to understand was the power of money. Early on in that first tour, he came back to the Midland Hotel in Manchester, where we were staying, and calmly announced that he had just bought a new car. He was a cool dude, John.

'What?'

'Yeah, I was wandering around, saw this American car dealership, saw a Chevvy in there, went in, and bought it.'

'You're joking,' I said.

'I'm not joking, it's outside. See for yourself.'

I moved to the window. There, in the street, was this spaceship. It was a huge great mass of fins and chrome and aerials. I *loved* it. 'Got to have one, got to have one.'

'They've got a Ford Galaxie down there,' John told me. 'A real beaut – yellow and white. Go and have a look.'

I was in that car showroom before you could say 'flash bugger'.

Twenty minutes later, I'd traded in the two-tone Ford Zephyr which had replaced my old Consul and had whitewall tyres and twin aerials on the tail-fins, had written out a cheque for the difference, and there I was sitting outside the hotel in my new £2,800 American Ford Galaxie, bibbing my horn for John to come and see. A Galaxie. Amazing. I wanted a Ford Galaxie, and I just bought it. I hadn't even bothered to give it a test drive.

It suddenly hit me. I was rich. There wasn't a shop in the world I couldn't go into and buy whatever I wanted. Incredible!

It was another breakthrough. I was finally understanding how my life was changing.

If I needed the odd spot of encouragement to believe that I was now bizarrely rich, I needed even more to believe that I really was this famous pop singer, Adam Faith. The breakthrough on that front came when I was on my own.

There are moments that touch you and stay with you all your life. I was staying at the Turk's Head, in Newcastle – since pulled down. On the first morning there, I came out of my bedroom and started walking along the corridor. Just before I reached the T-junction at the end, I slowed down, I could hear someone singing. I stopped and peeped round the corner. While he was redecorating the ceiling, a painter was singing my song, 'What Do You Want?' A strange eerie chill of pleasure came over me.

I'd been running on hyperbole, buoyed up by the thrill of it all, and yet never quite believing in it. This voice had the grab of reality. People were singing my record – it was real. I really did have a hit. Kids were singing it on the school bus, char ladies humming it while they scrubbed steps. I didn't have to keep on telling myself that it was real. This wasn't happening to anyone else, it was happening to me. I wasn't Terry Nelhams living on borrowed time, I was Adam Faith, the famous pop star. It was time to start getting used to it.

ChapterEleven

MY MANAGER, EVE TAYLOR, WAS A CRUEL AND DESTRUCTIVE woman, who liked to control people through intimidation and the abuse of power. She looked and sounded like Thora Hird, and behaved like Attila the Hun. People in the business either feared her or hated her – usually both. If she didn't get her own way, she'd scream and rant at you until she did. Once her jaws were clamped on your tender parts, they didn't open until she'd got what she wanted.

I was easy meat for her: she simply played on my insecurity. She encouraged my belief that I was out there in the limelight under false pretences; she perpetuated my fear of failure by always insinuating that without her, Adam Faith would cease to exist. In this way, she kept an absolute hold over me. Eve seemed to know where I should be going, so I was happy to let her lead the way.

In fact, though, she had no vision. Her management philosophy was deeply entrenched in the dark ages of 'Variety'. She didn't understand this new music, only smelled the barrels of money that smothered it.

The best example of this was a song called 'Lonely Pup In A Christmas Shop'. It was definitely a huge hit in the making. It was also patently obvious that this was a song that no self-respecting rock 'n' roller would go within a mile of. John Barry argued against it, but by now Eve had such a tight grip on things, even he gave me up as a hopeless case. So, sure enough, Eve was able to play on my desperation to keep the hits coming, and got me to take a look at it. Here I was, supposedly 'the bad boy of pop' – as opposed to Cliff Richard, who was the good boy – thinking seriously of recording this kiddie's ditty.

I didn't want to be the good guy. Cliff was much more at ease with that image. I wanted to be the one the parents were frightened of. I liked people to think that if Cliff Richard and I were walking towards them with cut-throat razors in our hands, they'd expect Cliff to use his for a shave, and for me to use mine to slit their throats. It was a pretty daft idea in itself, but I still saw myself, underneath all that gloss, as James Dean with a shiv in his belt. Bad boys do not sing songs called 'Lonely Pup in a Christmas Shop'. It can ruin their reputation. But having had five hits in a row, it was vital to keep the successful run going and good songs were getting harder to find.

Despite knowing the song could be disastrous for me, I let myself be bullied and browbeaten by Eve into recording it.

The song was a big hit, all right. But for me, it was the beginning of the end and it nearly buried my record career. It attracted universal derision from the critics and the fans alike. It was a ridiculous, stupid thing to do, and it served me right. It was against all my instincts, and was one example of how little control I had over my singing career.

But even the wormiest of worms can turn. And it was not long after this that I won one of my only victories against Eve Taylor.

The winning formula that John Barry, Johnny Worth and myself had built up was already coming apart at the seams. John Barry was so busy with his own career it was becoming difficult for him to find time to work on my stuff. Johnny Worth was now writing hit songs for other artistes and I took it as a personal betrayal if somebody else went into the charts with one of Johnny's songs.

Of course the two Johns had a perfect right to their own careers. But when you are the lead man in a success of that sort, it gets so that you begin to believe that you are the monarch, and everyone else that works with you are your obedient subjects. You expect to be the centre of everybody's world, and for them to jump at your every whim. The two Johns were now jumping to their own whims, and I didn't like the feeling of being hostage to someone else's career. It angered me that John Barry had the cheek actually to be interested in his own career. He wasn't totally and utterly dedicated to me, so I wanted a set of musicians who answered to me and me alone. I got out of my pram, stamped my foot, and demanded to have my own backing group.

You'll excuse me if I take a few lines here to explain that it wasn't just me being megalomaniac. It got so that John's busy life was holding up my recording career. One album – I can't remember which one – was so late being completed the release date had to keep being put back. The effect of that was that I lost some of the momentum that had been built up by the single's success. So I wanted my own musicians who could record with me.

Eve resisted my move to form my own group with every argument she could muster. She was very wary of anyone coming into my life who might undermine her influence over me. But I was determined to have my own way, and eventually Eve backed down. The Roulettes came into existence.

The first set of lads I got in to form The Roulettes were a disaster, so I sacked them all except one, Peter Thorpe, who'd become a great friend. Then one of The Shadows gave me the name of a great bass player, John Rogers, who brought his own drummer and lead guitarist with him. Pretty soon, though, John came to me and said that Peter Thorpe wasn't cutting it – he just wasn't good enough to keep up. So I hired in a temporary replacement, and paid Pete to take six months off. I told him to go away and lock his bedroom door, and practise playing his guitar all day, every day, until he came up to speed. After six months he was up to speed, and we took him back on, and that was The Roulettes sorted out.

My lack of passion for singing gave Eve Taylor licence to take over my career completely and that started to spill over to my private life. By now I'd got used to the lavish lifestyle of the successful pop singer and that gave her the leverage she needed to pull the strings. Eve had absolute power over me, and she knew how to use it. I loved the roughneck look – torn jeans and scuffed-up leather jacket – that's what I wore on that first glorious tour. But for the second, Eve made me wear a suit; she transformed me into a prissy twit who did the job not for the fun and for the thrill of it all, but exclusively for the money. All the time preying on my insecurity.

Eve didn't just force me down paths I had no wish to take, she made sure all kinds of other avenues were closed to me. She stopped me taking opportunities simply by not telling me about them. Years after I'd finally got rid of Eve, the film director Lindsay Anderson came up to me at a party.

'So you're an actor now,' he said. 'You say it's what you always wanted to do. So why didn't you do that play for me at the Royal Court back in 1960?'

'What play?' I asked.

'I wanted you to work for me in a play I was doing at the Court. I told your manager, Eve Taylor.'

'I never knew about it,' I told him. 'Eve never told me.'

Of course she never told me! She knew damned well that I would have killed for the opportunity to work with Lindsay. She also guessed that if I'd gone into the Royal Court at that age, I probably never would have come out again. That would have killed the Golden Goose all right. If I'd taken that part I'd have been on £20 or £30 a week, max. Eve would have been missing out on a ton of money every week. You could see why she might want to keep me in the dark. And to make sure I kept right on singing, she buried one of the greatest opportunities I ever had to act.

Why didn't the Royal Court just phone *me* up and offer me the job? Because it didn't work that way. God help anyone who approached an artist direct. There would be writs or threats flying all over the place. Managers protected their pot of gold, like a starving man protected his last crumb.

Eve was part-promoter of the Faith tours, and she was taking a huge cut of my income on the sly over and above the 30 per cent she already took legitimately as my manager. Sometimes, she was promoting the whole tour herself – she'd pay me £1,000 for the week, take £300 off the top as her manager's fee. Another 10 per cent went to Maurice as the agent, which left me with £600. That seemed fair enough. What I didn't know at the time was that she was raking off three or four times what I was getting, in her hidden role as the promoter. Later I was to find out that this was normal practice with managers in those days; and given some of the arrangements other artists had with their management teams I was probably less exploited financially than most.

But what upsets me more than the money I might or might not have missed out on was the squandering of my singing career. There was so much more that could have been done to develop it. But with Eve there was no career, just money.

Eve didn't just block my chances of acting: she even sat on brilliant PR opportunities. I only knew about the invitation to go on the BBC's flagship talk-show, *Face to Face*, because Eve had never heard of the programme.

'There's some kind of talk-show that wants you on,' she told me one day. 'It's called *Face to Face* or some such rubbish – but they've only offered fifty quid for you, so I'm telling them to get lost.'

'No, no. For God's sake. Tell them that I'll pay them to let me do it. It's the most prestigious programme on television.' All of a sudden she was interested.

Face to Face was the show to watch on British television in 1960. It was compulsive viewing. The idea behind it was to get the top person in a given walk of life to talk as intimately as possible about themselves and what they did. The first of its kind, its list of interviewees was second to none: Martin Luther King, Evelyn Waugh, Bertrand Russell, all the great and the good went on it. One week they would have King Hussein of Jordan, the next Augustus John, the painter, followed by Carl Jung, Henry Moore, and so on. An invitation to appear on it as 'a young singer representing pop music', as the invitation sweetly put it, was quite exceptional. It was a sign that the changes sweeping through Britain were coming to be recognized as fundamental.

The show's host, John Freeman, was extremely clever at getting people to open up; his questioning was deft and incisive, without seeming aggressive. And, for its day, the style of the show was entirely original. The camera stayed locked on the face of the person under scrutiny, it never cut away to John Freeman. It was as if the viewer, and not the host, were asking the questions.

My invitation to appear on *Face to Face* came about quite by chance. The show's producer had a teenage daughter called Liz. He went home one day and said, 'Guess what? We're having a popular singer on our show!'

A rare early sighting:
Pamela and me watching over
the twins, Roger and Christine.

Acton Vale flats, still lurking.
Ours was the top one.

Mean, moody and magnificent, James Dean, *East of Eden*.

Me as James Dean – East of Acton.

The place that launched a thousand hips – the 2i's coffee bar.

Six-Five Special, BBC TV, November 1957 with my best mate Hurgy on the washboard, far right.

Eat your heart out, Elvis – *Drum Beat*, BBC TV, 3 April 1959.

Recording 'Someone Else's Baby'
in Abbey Road No. 2 studio
with John Barry, October 1959.

Adam and Eve – Eve Taylor,
the Agent from Hell.

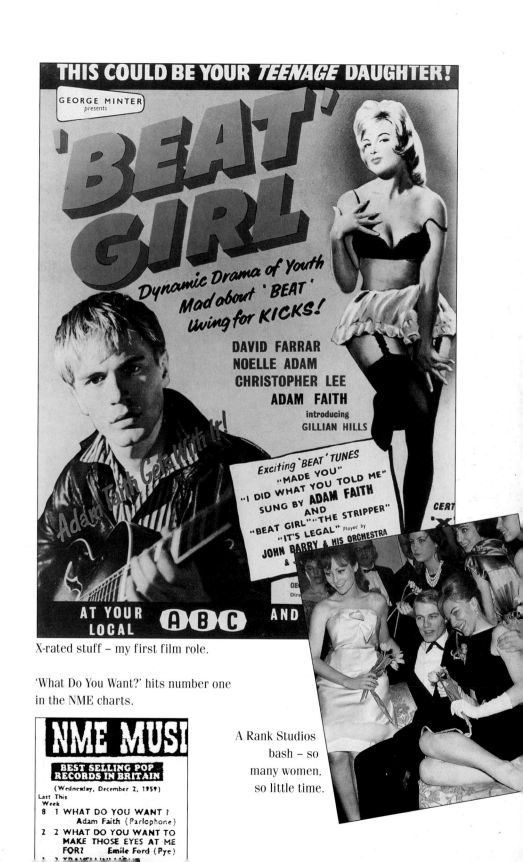

THIS COULD BE YOUR *TEENAGE* DAUGHTER!

GEORGE MINTER presents

'BEAT' GIRL

Dynamic Drama of Youth Mad about 'BEAT' living for KICKS!

DAVID FARRAR
NOELLE ADAM
CHRISTOPHER LEE
ADAM FAITH
introducing
GILLIAN HILLS

Adam Faith Gets With It!

Exciting 'BEAT' TUNES
"MADE YOU"
"I DID WHAT YOU TOLD ME"
SUNG BY **ADAM FAITH**
AND
"BEAT GIRL" "THE STRIPPER"
"IT'S LEGAL" *Played by*
JOHN BARRY & HIS ORCHESTRA

CERT 'X'

AT YOUR LOCAL **ABC** AND

X-rated stuff – my first film role.

'What Do You Want?' hits number one in the NME charts.

NME MUSI

BEST SELLING POP
RECORDS IN BRITAIN

(Wednesday, December 2, 1959)

Last This
Week

8 1 WHAT DO YOU WANT ?
       Adam Faith (Parlophone)

2 2 WHAT DO YOU WANT TO
       MAKE THOSE EYES AT ME
       FOR?   Emile Ford (Pye)

A Rank Studios
bash – so
many women,
so little time.

Live at Wembley – the 1960 NME Poll Winners concert.

ALL THE EVES GO FOR ADAM

Girls mob him on the stage

BLOND beat singer Adam Faith was mobbed yesterday by about thirty screaming teenage girls who invaded the stage while he was singing at London's Albert Hall.

Adam was one of the stars of the Great Pop Prom, a two-hour barrage of rock and beat entertainment, organised by the romantic weeklies Roxy, Marilyn and Valentine.

Five thousand cuddle-some-most of them girl-made it a "house full" turn-out.

Adam Faith was in the middle of "Singin' In the Rain"—when it started to rain fans.

Girls rushed from the centre and the sides and climbed on to the dais. They pulled and tugged at him, planted kisses on his lips and cheeks, tore at his red jacket, still he kept on singing.

Commissionaires forced them back.

The show, it, aid of the Printers' Pension Corporation orphans' fund, was an immense success. There were cheers and longing for other stars.

On the bill were his-panders Emile Ford, the

By PATRICK DONCASTER

John Barry Seven and Cliff Richard's accompanying group The Shadows, who currently top Pop Prom with their "Apache" record.

There were also Cliff's singing discovery Dave Sampson, singing sensation Johnny River Peter Elliott, the band of Bob Miller and his Millermen, the music of the Billy Wood Five.

Ace disc girl on the act was pertly-pigtailed Cherry Wainer who also beat out a drum duet with her partner Don Storer.

Appearing as a compere was ITV's Jackie Rae.

● Producer Tito Burns struggles to rescue Adam Faith ("mike" in hand) from over-enthusiastic fans. Adam just went on singing.

This is why I went into show business? September 1960.

Pan-Galactic line-up, 1960. From left to right: Billy Fury, Jess Conrad, Gene Vincent, Jo Brown, Eddie Cochran, me, Marty Wilde.

'Poor me ' – My second No.1.

Cliff Richard and me rehearsing for the
Royal Command Variety Performance,
May 1960 (Cliff is on the left!).

Who's that woman standing next to
Lonnie Donegan?

Getting sketched by Feliks Topolski, for the BBC's flagship chat show, *Face to Face*, December 1960.

Tudor Court, Esher – my own little home in the west.

My 21st, with Mum and Dad.

I get my first (BBC) TV series, September 1962. Backing by The Roulettes. From left to right: John Rogers, me, Peter Thorpe.

Smash kills Adam Faith's guitar

Worse than words can say – John Rogers is killed in a crash on the way to a gig in Sunderland.

Mandy Rice-Davies, leaves the smoke of scandal behind her at Heathrow, 1963.

ADAM FAITH AND THE ROULETTES

Jackie, my wife, before we met, heralding my appearance on TV.

...was killed ...avelling van in which ...of a stationary ran into the the A1 near Grantham. lorry on colnshire. Lin-

The van driver, manager Mr. Peter Cotter, 22, of Stratford-on-Avon, Warwickshire, was detained in hospital with multiple injuries.

Mr. Rogers's mother, Mr. Matilda Rogers said...

The gang's all here – the Faith team at work. Clockwise from me: Janice Sherbourne (secretary); The Roulettes – Bob Henrit (drums), Peter Thorpe (rhythm guitar), Mod Rogan (bass) and Russ Ballard (lead guitar); Doris Askham (fan club helper); Eve Taylor (manager); Alan Shalet (accountant); Maurice Press (agent); Dennis Nelhams (PA); Bert Harris (roadie); Angela Miall (fan club secretary); Vincente Catala (butler); Angelina Catala (cook) and Lesley Miall (fan club helper).

Following in the footsteps – Sandie Shaw on piano, Chris Andrews playing it.

The Beatles and The Rolling Stones head the December 1964 chart – just a little bit of competition.

Top Ten

Here is an up-to-date list of the ten best-selling records compiled by "Melody Maker."

This Week	Last Week	
1	(—)	I FEEL FINE—The Beatles (Parlophone)
2	(2)	LITTLE RED ROOSTER— The Rolling Stones (Decca)
3	(4)	I'M GONNA BE STRONG— Gene Pitney (Stateside)
4	(6)	DOWNTOWN—Petula Clark (Pye)
5	(13)	PRETTY PAPER—Roy Orbison (London)
6	(3)	ALL DAY AND ALL OF THE NIGHT— The Kinks (Pye)
7	(1)	BABY LOVE—The Supremes (Stateside)
8	(16)	WALK TALL—Val Doonican (Decca)
9	(5)	THERE'S A HEARTACHE FOLLOW- ING ME—Jim Reeves (RCA)
10	(—)	A MESSAGE TO MARTHA— Adam Faith (Parlophone)

Taking an early bath from the horrendous South Africa tour

Daily Mirror

4d.   Saturday, January 9, 1965   ➔   No. 18,989

ADAM FAITH ARRESTED AS HE FLIES HOME

£55,000 poorer, but I was so glad to be home.

MIRROR CORRESPONDENT: Johannesburg, Friday

BRITISH pop-singer Adam Faith was taken off an airliner and put under arrest tonight, as he was about to fly home after cutting short a stormy concert tour of South Africa.

The arrest was made on a warrant issued because of a civil court action launched against 24 - year - old Faith by the manager of a Cape Town theatre.

The British Overseas Airways VC10 jet was on the point of leaving Johannesburg's Jan Smuts Airport after a half-hour technical delay, when a woman deputy sheriff from nearby Kempton Park went on board.

Warrant

With the deputy sheriff — middle-aged Mrs. R. Malan—were two lawyers representing the Cape Town theatre manager, Ron Quibell.

Mrs. Malan walked to the seat where Faith was already strapped in for take-off. She asked: "Are you Adam Faith?"

Faith said: "Yes."

Deputy Sheriff Malan said: "I have a warrant for your arrest.

In the airport's VIP lounge, Faith was told he had been ordered to appear at the Cape Supreme Court, Cape Town.

And he would not be allowed

Deputy sheriff Mrs. E. Malan shows the warrant to Adam Faith.

Jackie: one look and I was in love.

'Take good care of your baby...'
I think we got engaged around this time.

We wanted a quiet
little wedding. Caxton
Hall, 19 August 1967.

Icons of our times – Dame Sybil Thorndike with Noel Coward – two of my life's greatest influences.

Jack looks great but what *was* I thinking of?

As Feste, in *Twelfth Night* at Northampton Rep, February 1970.

Hands up! Birth of our daughter and only child, Katya, in 1970.

Budgie hits the unsuspecting airwaves, April 1971.

On location with Charlie Endell, aka Ian Cuthbertson, 1972.

'Oh really, Dad?' replied Liz, her eyes lighting up at this un-paralleled piece of news. 'Which one?'

'We're thinking of doing a chap called Cliff Richard.'

'What?' she said. 'You can't do him. You've got to do Adam Faith.' Liz was one of my fans, and not one of Cliff's – and on such little things turn the great wheels of our lives.

When I got to Lime Grove, to tape *Face to Face*, on 11 December 1960, there must have been forty or fifty journalists gathered to watch the hanging. John Freeman had a fearsome reputation: some had called the experience 'torture by television'. The press were there to see the blood being spilled – my blood.

'He'll slaughter you,' they shouted as I went in. 'He'll tear you apart. You shouldn't have agreed to go on . . .'

In the event, I found Freeman's style very gentle, very subtle, and not at all intimidating. I think he was particularly kind to me, because of my youth. Then again, I was used to answering ques-tions – I'd done that interview so many times already, a thousand times over in fact, with local reporters writing for the local papers up and down the country. They were much more eager with the scalpel than John Freeman and because they didn't have his immense charm and intellect, and thorough decency, they tended to use their operating instruments like baseball bats.

In the process, without even realizing it, I'd become a talker. In fact, I'd become much better at talking than I was at singing. So when Freeman started prodding, I was in my element. John Barry's dad had come up with a useful piece of advice: 'If Freeman asks you an awkward question, just pretend you don't understand, and ask him to repeat it. That will give you time to think about your answer.' In fact the advice came in handy when John Freeman asked me about money. It was a taboo subject in polite circles, so I needed time to dwell on my answer, and I made use of my little trick.

It all seems so tame now. But in fact *Face to Face* was the next big landmark in my life after 'What Do You Want?' The coverage that interview got in the press, and the impact it had on my image, was enormous.

One of the biggest differences it made was that I crossed over to a new audience; suddenly I'd become acceptable to an older, middle-class audience. There was a strong opinion at the time that rock 'n' roll music was the work of the devil, and that any-one who sang it was the devil's own instrument. Elvis Presley got on the end of this in the States. Even skiffle, and this is really hard to believe, was looked on like some early form of punk. Lots of people in the country saw me as a kind of Sid Vicious. They said it was me, and others like me, who were undermining the moral fibre of the nation. Whole sections of the Establishment were getting up and sounding off against these rebellious kids who were using their devil's music to corrupt the nation's youth.

The Archbishop of York made a speech in which he said that young people were being corrupted by the lyrics of Adam Faith's songs. Some middle-class parents who'd never listened to a bar of pop music in their entire lives fell for this, hook, line and sinker. Of course it was all rubbish, but I revelled in it, it was good for the image. I liked to be thought of as the 'Rebel with a Cause', bringing down the establishment.

But to parents it was very real. They actually believed that lyrics like, 'Say what you want, and I'll give it to you, honey – wish you wanted my love, baby . . .' were eating the heart out of the nation's morality. In an attempt to defend their children from this terrible corruption, they'd ban them from having pop stars' posters on their bedroom walls or from playing the records.

But *Face to Face* showed people what the average pop singer was really like. Instead of the unwashed, sex-crazed oik they expected, they saw Mr Reasonable: a well-dressed, well-scrubbed and reasonably well-mannered boy called Adam Faith, who could actually speak joined-up sentences. John Freeman concentrated on the real human being, as opposed to the Frankenstein's monster created by 'What Do You Want?' That interview has probably turned out to be the single most important influence on people's opinion of Adam Faith.

It was great for me, because it allowed Terry Nelhams a voice. To me that interview wasn't given by Adam Faith (in any case what did he have to say? He was only two years old). Terry Nelhams spoke that night, and told Faith to keep his mouth well and truly buttoned.

Face to Face has reverberated all through my life. And so, too, has that peculiar split personality Freeman so cleverly uncovered that night, the real and the show-business versions of whoever it is that I am.

Eve Taylor had a business partner called Colin Berlin. Colin was the best negotiator I've ever met. It got to the point where I wouldn't move anywhere without him – he used to come with me on the road. I looked on him as a mate, as much as one of life's great fixers.

Like me, Colin thought Eve Taylor was basically a nutcase. We talked all the time about getting rid of her, and setting up a new management team together. We figured that if we could prise me away from the she-devil we could set up our own management company with me as its first client. Our idea was to bring on new acts on the back of my success.

I never knew what the financial arrangements were between Taylor and Colin Berlin, or indeed Maurice. But they were tied up financially. Colin, like Maurice, was probably in on the profits from the tour. That wouldn't have been unusual, but who the hell would ever get to know about it. Anyway I didn't much care. Colin was my friend and I trusted him with my life. Also Colin was one of the funniest people I'd ever met. And boy, oh boy, am I a sucker for anyone who can make me laugh.

Despite his business arrangements with her, Colin's dislike of Eve was certainly genuine; so by the time my contract came up for renewal, in 1963, I'd made up my mind: with Colin's help, I'd leave her and set up in partnership with him.

The terrible day came round for me to go in and give the awful Eve the short goodbye. Colin shared the same suite of offices with her in Great Russell Street, and sat at his desk, making encouraging faces at me, as I steeled myself on the threshold of her room. This was it. I was ready. Nothing was going to shake my resolve. I walked into the dragon's inner lair with my chin held high and my shoulders squared, ready to do battle.

Taylor was behind her desk. The minute I saw her I knew that I would have preferred being at the dentist having root-canal work without an anaesthetic.

My resolve was firm, 'Look Eve, about this new contract . . .'

That's all I needed to say. She reared up on her hind legs, like Beelzebub. Her nostrils flared, and she snorted down her nose at me. A terrible noise that might once have been speech came out of her iron throat. I tried to hold her gaze, but I could see the demon ready to jump out of her. I folded up like a pricked balloon before that terrible glare. I can't remember even what she said; it was enough that my eyes fell, cravenly, to the floor.

On the desk in front of Eve was the new contract, ready for

signing. Imperiously, she pointed at it. My hand, like a zombie's, stretched out and took up the pen.

A moment later, I was back outside, having signed on with Eve Taylor for another five years. I couldn't look Colin in the eye. But then I didn't have to: he knew. I'd let my friend down and I was ashamed.

To understand why I signed against my will I'd have to be regressed by means of deep hypnotherapy. I'd like to think my abject cowardice was located in some deep-seated childhood trauma. But to my dying shame, I think it was just that this woman dominated me, totally and utterly, by the mere force of her unspeakable personality.

Her whole power hinged on my insecurity as a singer. And I can't believe it now that I let her get away with it. Maybe it's to do with having a strong woman as a mum. Maybe Nell never did me any favours, fighting my battles for me when I was young.

ChapterTwelve

SO MUCH HAPPENED, SO QUICKLY, TO ME AFTER THOSE FIRST
records went into the charts that it's difficult now to
unscramble it all. And if there wasn't enough going on in my
working life (although, I've always considered show business
more of a blessed dream than work), there were the practicalities
of running a private life to contend with. Here I was earning
undreamed of sums of money, with number one records, and a
face that was more well known to most teenagers than the prime
minister's, and yet I was still living in my mum's council house.
To boot, my great spaceship of a car was taking up four parking
spaces in front of our block of flats. With all my pop-star trappings, I was beginning to feel like a cuckoo barging about in the
wrong nest.

It's one thing for people to stare in amazement as a neighbour
wins the football pools. It's quite another to have it rammed
down their throats. Big cars, visiting journalists, other show-
business people coming to visit. I'd turn up with another pop
singer one day, a new girlfriend the next. At times, it must have

seemed like the circus had arrived in the neighbour's front room.

In 1960 I signed to do the movie *Beat Girl*. It was my first chance, on the big screen, to make my James Dean dream come true. I played a 'Teenage Rebel' just like Jimmy. I didn't get to rebel in the flaming sunshine glamour of California like him. I had to make do with the Chislehurst caves in Kent. But I was in my element. A dream had come true, and the big bonus for me was working with Shirley Anne Field. From the very first time I walked on to the filmset and caught sight of her, there was never any doubt in my mind that I wanted her. She was beautiful. Her shock of red hair framing a face with fine features, like china. She had a gentle, kind manner that wrapped round you like a warm blanket. Being a little older, and a woman, she knew so much more about relationships than me, a gauche cocky teenage boy. Shirley Anne was the first 'woman' I'd been out with and she taught me so much about love.

Mum adored Shirley Anne and would sit at the kitchen table with her, talking for hours about life. It was as if Shirley Anne had become one of the family, and Nell harboured dreams of Shirley and I becoming a permanent item. But both our careers were taking off and inevitably we went in different directions. Films for her. Endless tours for me. To hold on to a relationship for any length of time was not on the agenda. Everything mitigated against a normal relationship. Not least the pressure from the fans. If the fans found out that your heart belonged to another, that was it; instant death. They would desert in droves. You were theirs and if you wanted to keep their loyalty and devotion, you'd better not be overly unfaithful. Break that rule and you could kiss goodbye to your career.

You could have girlfriends, it just made sense to try to keep them under wraps.

It was about this time in the early Sixties that there were one or two little surprises which my overnight rocket-trip to stardom brought out of the family woodwork. Now that I was in showbiz, I needed a passport to go abroad. I asked my mother if she had my birth certificate.

'No,' she said tersely, 'and I've no idea where it is.'

Dennis said he'd go down to Somerset House, and have a dig around. But he came back after several hours of searching empty-handed, with a bewildered look on his face.

'You're not registered,' he told me.

'Don't be daft,' I replied, 'everyone's registered – it's the law.'

'I'm telling you,' insisted Dennis, 'you're not registered.'

We went back to Mum.

'Don't be silly,' she blustered, 'of course you're registered. It probably just got lost in the war, or something. Dennis must have missed it. Tell him to go back and look again.' Dennis went back, returning once more without the certificate.

'Look,' he said, 'I'm telling you, there's no record of Terry's birth.'

'Nell?' I prompted.

'Go back again,' she said at last, 'and look under "Nelhams-Wright".' We stared at her. Where the hell did 'Wright' come from? It wasn't Nell's maiden name.

Off Dennis went again. Third time lucky?

Bingo! Dennis came up trumps: I was filed under 'Terence Nelhams-Wright'; the only one in the whole of Somerset House. For nineteen years I'd lived as another person. I was waiting in the kitchen when Nell got home from work. 'What's all this Nell?' I asked, waving the certificate at her. Not an unreasonable question under the circumstances.

'Oh, well,' she told me grudgingly, 'when we went to the Register Office in 1940, it was the war, we were rushed. When we went in the man behind the desk said, "Name?" Your dad said, "Nelhams", and I said, "Wright". The registrar was such a bad-tempered, impatient bugger he couldn't wait for us to make up our minds. So he put down Nelhams-Wright.'

'OK,' I said, not really understanding. 'So why do you call me Bill, then?' Which she did often, but which, as it happens, didn't really faze me, because I never had been fond of the name Terry.

'Because I always wanted to call you William.'

'Well, why the bloody hell didn't you? What was stopping you?'

'Well, when we were going into the Register Office, we hadn't decided on a name for you. As we were walking in, me and your dad looked at one another, and I'd just seen a removal van going by with "Terence O'Donovan, Removals" marked on the side – so when we were asked for a first name I just blurted out Terence. I always meant to have it changed later, but I never got around to it.'

87

So because the registrar was a grumpy old misery, I got lumbered with a name I never liked. It took a bit of swallowing, this rigmarole. I never broached the subject with her again, but in my more reflective moods, I couldn't help wondering who was this person Wright? Was there a William wandering around the world, who knew more about me than I did.

Of all the children I am the only one with the name Wright attached to him. Whether my dad was really my father, though, or the mysterious William, is something I didn't care to find out at the time. I got my passport and, with the question of my origin left unanswered, went off to Majorca for a bit of light relief.

By great good luck, I met the perfect holiday companion: her name was Mandy Rice-Davis. She was wearing a mini-skirt and a suntan. She had a great figure, short blond hair and a face that had character as well as being pretty. On top of that, she was full of fun and laughed all the time. Which considering that already, at the age of about twenty-two, she was going through the nightmare of having every journalist in the world chasing her for the untold story was a remarkable tribute to her humour. I'd read all about her, along with Christine Keeler, being paid to whip Conservative Cabinet Ministers for a pound a stroke, or walk across them naked in her high heels. The *News of the World* had provided a breathless nation with all the gory details. That whiff of the devil gave her a grown-up glamour that made her all the more attractive.

The second he clapped eyes on her, Maurice told me to stay well clear of Mandy. Set against what Mandy had to offer, this advice slid off me like so much butter in a hot pan. The trouble was she was running from the press. We both caught the gossipy attention of the Brits who were holidaying at the same hotel and it was difficult to get away from the prying eyes.

To get around this, we made a date for the evening. I planned to drive way out into the countryside, right up into the mountains to the north-east of Palma. So with hair slicked back, shirt opened just enough to show a bit of tan, and smothered in a gallon of Brut, I hired a car and off we went. Hyperventilating in anticipation of what could turn out to be one of the most memorable nights of my life, I found a likely spot and parked the car. There was no way, we were sure, that anyone could spot us here. Outside, it was pitch-black. We kissed for a while, and then just when we'd got to that halfway stage between doing it and not, there was a sharp metallic knocking on the windscreen. We looked up. The car was surrounded by shadowy figures in the darkness.

'Oh God,' I thought, 'bandits! They're going to rob us and beat us and leave us for dead.' Then, uniforms came into focus. These bandits weren't bandits, they were soldiers. Their leader, in a peaked cap, was bashing on the glass with the muzzle of his rifle. The man standing next to him shouted something that I recognized as, 'Get out of the car, now!'

We buttoned and zipped ourselves frantically back together. Shaking with fear, we climbed out. I spoke to the officer-in-charge in Spanish. He told me he was arresting us on suspicion of spying. When I asked him why, he pointed behind him to a fence topped with thick rolls of barbed wire and with a very large sign on it that somehow, in our haste, we'd managed to miss. I picked out the word, PROHIBIDO, in large black letters on a white background. We'd parked right outside a top-secret Spanish army installation, at one o'clock in the morning.

At the time, the Gibraltar question was causing one of its periodic flare-ups between Britain and Spain. No wonder they thought we might be spies. The young officer in charge of this detachment interrogated us for what seemed like the rest of the night: why were we there? What were we doing in this area so late at night? Didn't we know it was a military zone? Had we been intending to take photographs at first light, perhaps?

In the end, I told him, man to man, that I'd just been trying to have sex without anyone watching, for a change. He let us go, laughing, on the grounds that if we weren't English and therefore spies, we were English and therefore mad. A judgement we were very happy to settle for.

Throughout all this, Mandy was a real sport. We didn't progress our relationship any further, it was all too fraught. But whenever I see her name mentioned anywhere, I wish her well. She was the kind of person you only wanted good for.

When I got back from my hols my mother had another surprise in store. Pam, Dennis and I were sitting round the kitchen table sharing a packet of custard creams and a pot of Typhoo, when the front door banged open. Mum was home from her morning job.

'Put the kettle on again, I've got something to tell you,' she said. She leaned back on the sink, looking down at me. After a moment's silence, she said, 'Me and Dad got married this morning.'

'You did what?' I mumbled.

'Married,' she said. 'We just got married.'

'But . . .?'

'Me and Dad went to the Register Office this morning on the way to work,' she explained patiently, 'and got married.'

Pam, Dennis and I stared at each other for a second, then broke into uncontrollable laughter.

'But – what the bloody hell did you want to go and get married now for, after all these years?'

'Because you've gone into show business and you're famous now,' replied my mother. 'We thought we'd better do it in case the press got hold of it.' It was simple to Nell, her lad needed protecting and that was that.

I think it was the sweetest thing my mother ever did for me. All her life, she'd despised convention, yet she'd cared enough to go and get married for me. In her own strange way, I think it was an act of love.

My relationship with Verna was still bubbling under, but with her in Switzerland we were finding it more difficult to make something of it. We neither of us wanted to let go of the love that we'd shared. Although deep down, we both knew that the clock was ticking, we tried to keep things going by meeting in Paris.

Eve Taylor got more and more twitchy about the press finding out about me travelling to France for my love trysts. In one of our discussions – which meant she screamed, and I listened – she persuaded me (which is a nice word for brainwashing) that Verna and I had to become an undercover operation.

To throw the press off the scent, I took to disguising myself on my excursions across the channel: a pair of clear-glass glasses, a black beret, and a big jacket with the collar turned right up around my ears. I thought it looked very French.

One time walking through customs, looking like a spy from a black-and-white 'B' movie, my cover was blown. Trying to mingle unnoticed with the rest of the travellers, I was shaken rigid by a voice shouting out across the customs hall. One of the customs men had spotted me. 'Wotcha Adam,' he yelled. 'How was Paris!'

Some disguise! I spent the next ten minutes signing autographs, making feeble excuses about how I came to be travelling, looking like a complete berk. I didn't try that one again. It was easier to get Verna to come to England.

By that time I'd moved my mum into a new house in Sunbury-on-Thames. It was built from scratch, to her own plans, in a cul-de-sac near the river. My dad had a modest dream fulfilled.

I lived there for a while, in much the same way as I did back in the council flat, only with more space. At least now I had my own bedroom, which was essential if I happened to bring a girl home to stay the night. Mum didn't mind, but there wasn't a girl who woke up in bed with me who wasn't freaked out by the sound of my mum's voice announcing the arrival of our morning cuppa. They'd dive under the sheets like scalded cats. Slowly emerging as they got used to Nell's completely unfazed behaviour, as she'd sit on the bed catching up on the news. Most of them, coming from a more conventional background, had never come across anyone quite like Mum before. But it got too crowded and it was time to get my own place.

Dennis, who by this time had thrown in his job, was working with me full time, and went looking for a house for me. Because I had particular attachments to the Weybridge area – where Verna had lived – I asked him to concentrate his search around there. He covered every estate agent within a few miles of Verna's old house. Thank God she hadn't lived on the Isle of Skye or on Mull; I would probably have ended up buying something there.

After a couple of days Dennis arrived at the recording studios, where we were trying to put the next hit together. Breathless with excitement he burst into the control room and shouted, 'I've found you the perfect house.'

Chapter Thirteen

TUDOR COURT WAS NOT THE PERFECT HOUSE OF MY CHILDHOOD dreams. I'd always imagined living in a big white mansion at the end of a long drive somewhere remote in the countryside. Tudor Court was right in the middle of the claustrophobic commuter belt, it had no drive and it was all beams and leaded windows. But, coming from a council flat in Acton, it seemed like a castle to me. I didn't know, or care, that it was 'mock'. It was a huge house, with grounds all round it, and I wanted it the moment the fancy wrought-iron gate to the front garden creaked open on its hinges.

I went into the new house with a carrier-bag full of clothes. There wasn't a stick of furniture in the place. But it was my first house and even though the electricity hadn't yet been transferred into my name, I couldn't wait to move in.

The first night, Dennis and I took a mattress from Mum's house and made up my bed on the floor of the master bedroom. We pottered about making cups of tea on a primus stove, until it was time for Dennis to go home.

That left me alone. I tried to sleep on my own in the huge

master-bedroom, but there was no way. I was not long out of a council flat with 48,000 people running about it at all hours of the day and night. Suddenly here I was, alone on my little mattress, in this gigantic room bigger than our entire flat. I was scared out of my wits.

The darker it got the more I cowered down under the blankets. At the slightest noise, I'd sit bolt upright until I couldn't stand it any more. In the pitch dark, I fumbled my way downstairs, dragging my bed behind me. I sat on the floor in front of the sitting-room fire, huddled up in my blanket, shivering with fright. I never slept a wink. It was the longest night I'd ever spent in my life. Next morning, I moved out of Tudor Court and went back to my mum's place in Sunbury-on-Thames.

Dennis and I spent hours wandering around this vast empty cavern of a place, trying to figure out what the hell to put in it. The only idea I had fixed in my mind was that I wanted my bed-room to be silver and mauve. I think I'd seen something similar in a Dean Martin film and his bedroom was always filled with women. I figured it was the colour-scheme that was working the magic for Deano, so that's how it was going to be for me.

Apart from that, I didn't have a clue. But then I was a council-flat man. I didn't know what taste was. I'd only eaten egg and chips up to then, so how should I know what caviar tasted like? Here I was, nouveau-riche, with absolutely no experience of having money or how to spend it. All I knew was that there was money coming in – a lot of money. Eve Taylor told me so. I'd shot straight from an average of £14 a week at Elstree to over £1,000 a week on the tour – equivalent to about £20,000 a week in today's terms. I was one of the first teenagers to have big money and since no-one had written the handbook on how to deal with it, I learnt as I went along. That meant some very expensive lessons.

The George Swank Hotel in Paris was the rendezvous place for me and Verna, and I'd taken a fancy to the Louis Quinze furniture that filled it. (If we'd gone to New York, I'd have finished up with a house full of art deco furniture. Impressionable? *Moi*? Not much!) But where to buy my Louis Quinze? I hadn't exactly been brought up with priceless antiques, so I had no idea where to start. Eve Taylor came to the rescue. She had a contact up in North London who was a furniture maker. So a house full of reproduction Louis Quinze stuff was ordered and expressly made. What I had yet to learn was that I could have bought the original antique furniture, for half the price.

Luckily for me, Dennis took a grip of the situation. No more reproductions. He had a natural appreciation of the finer things in life. Whatever it was we needed for the house he went out and bought the best money could buy. It was another lesson I've never forgotten: if you want something, especially antiques or art, buy the best. Even if the bottom falls out of the market, there will always be someone prepared to pay top price for the best.

Since I had to buy everything, new, from scratch, it cost a fortune to equip such a large house. Financing this new lifestyle took just about everything I earned.

Dennis's instincts were good, but not infallible. We made some horribly expensive mistakes. Art was one disastrous arena I played around in, and like the gladiators in the Colosseum, I got eaten alive. The house filled up with junk paintings that a first-year art student would have laughed at.

One of the things I've always loved about houses is the fact that frequently they come with very good stories attached to them. And despite its modernity and pretentiousness, Tudor Court had an interesting history. A famous society medium and spiritualist called Estelle Roberts had built the mansion some time in the 1930s at a guess. Estelle Roberts had achieved national fame when a young child went missing in the north of England. The police suspected a local man of her murder, but without the body they couldn't charge him.

When the spirit was in her, Ms Roberts conducted her seances at Tudor Court in the persona of a 'Red Indian' chief. There was even a stone plaque of this chief's head set into the façade, to prove to any doubting Thomas that he lived there, in body. One night, in the middle of a high-society seance, Ms Roberts suddenly fell into a profound trance. Red Cloud (or whatever his name was) had entered her. In the deep, booming voice of the Chief, she intoned, 'Go to a path in the north by a crooked fence, near a yellow barge, by three oak trees with one branch missing [or whatever] lies a body.'

Among the people present at this upper-crust gathering was someone of importance in the government. At the excited request of all the other guests, this man had the medium's directions circulated to police forces nationwide. A PC on the beat some-

94

where in the north recognized the description of this place – it was on his beat. He went to the spot and found the buried corpse of the dead child. Estelle Roberts, it appeared, had given its precise location. The poor child had been horribly murdered; the suspected man was subsequently convicted, and in this way, Estelle Roberts became big news.

Estelle was long gone from Tudor Court but the spirit lived on, at least in my imagination, and I was bloody terrified. It got so I wouldn't stay in the place on my own. Someone in the family had to come and spend the night to keep me from dying of fright.

One night, my mother, who'd come over to stay, was asleep in the 'green' room, at the end of the house, with my dad. She woke up in the early hours of the morning to find a little old woman in a grey cloak standing at the end of her bed, touching her foot. This apparition smiled at her, then walked through the wall and disappeared. That was the straw that broke the camel's back. I couldn't live in my new house on my own anymore – I was too petrified.

Dennis decided that it was time to get some staff to look after me. He duly advertised and interviewed dozens of applicants. Finally he came up with a young married Spanish couple: Angelina, who was a cook, and Vincente, a valet. They'd been working at Sunningdale for a French diplomat whose wife had taught Angelina how to cook. At last I had someone to keep me company in my spook-filled house.

My mum wasn't the only one to see and feel things in Tudor Court. Chris Andrews, who was to write so many hit songs for me, could only spend a few minutes in the drawing-room before he'd be afflicted with the most horrendous headaches. He swore there was an unseen 'presence' in the room.

One morning I was lying in bed, half asleep, with my back to the door, when I felt myself being tucked in. Paralysed with fear, I tried to turn over to get a glimpse of whatever it was. But no matter how hard I tried my muscles wouldn't respond to my brain's messages. It could only have been a few seconds that I lay there rigid, unable to move, but it seemed like it would never end. Then, as suddenly as it had appeared, the feeling left me. Slowly, with my eyes firmly shut, I managed to turn my head towards the door. Then summoning all my courage I prized my eyes open fully convinced that I was about to be confronted by some ghastly apparition. Nothing; absolutely zilch. Did I imagine it? Was it Angelina taking care of her 'Señor'? Or was it the little old grey lady come back to visit the new master of Tudor Court?

As a result of this and the other manifestations, I became interested in the spirit world. If I was going to have to share the house with a load of ghosts I wanted to know who they were. I started to invite mediums from all over the country down to the house for the weekend, and held seances with my friends. I employed a shorthand secretary to sit in the corner while the medium was supposedly in touch with the other side. The secretary's sole job was to write down what the medium (and any spirit) might say. Overnight, the proceedings would be typed out and in the morning my guests would find written reports of what the medium had said about them lying on their breakfast plates.

I never did get to meet any of my unwanted lodgers, but it was fun trying. I don't really believe there is such a thing as the supernatural, but I'd like to believe in it. Hence the experiments.

It never ceases to amaze me how easily I took to my new lifestyle. I slid from the council flat to 'the manor born' without the slightest seam. I discovered that I had a natural instinct for the good life.

Every morning my golden retriever, Shadow, painstakingly trained by Vincente, would bring my newspaper up to the bedroom, and sit there patiently with it in his mouth until I woke up. Then, while I leafed idly through the day's news, Vincente brought me a cup of tea, followed by my breakfast on a tray; the bread toasted to exactly the colour I liked, the marmalade with the rind carefully taken out by Angelina before it was put in front of me.

While I was eating, Vincente would run my bath, making sure that the water was always exactly the temperature I preferred. A thermometer dangled from the taps especially for that purpose. My bath was scented with oil that I'd been told, and fully believed, came from Cleopatra's tomb. I had it especially flown over from Cairo by the case, and while I luxuriated in its exotic perfumes, my valet would lay out my clothes for the day. And so it went on. Formal meals, even if I was eating alone, took place in the dining-room every day. Vincente serving the food in his crisp uniform of black trousers, white shirt and cream linen jacket.

It was an elegant, old-fashioned lifestyle and I revelled in it.

There I was, a twenty-one-year-old council kid, with no-one to answer to, behaving like an eighteenth-century nobleman.

Angelina and Vincente came from a poor Catalan hill-village. They didn't question where I was coming from. I was their 'Señor' and my responsibility was to look after them. Their part of the bargain was to cater for my every need. We never mixed. They had their side of the house and I mine. The only time I went to the domestic quarters was if I was hungry in the middle of the night, and the only time they came to my side was when they were pandering to my needs.

Angelina was a great cook, but when she first arrived at the house she couldn't cook the thing I loved best in the world: English puddings. Trifles, crumbles, pies, tarts and jam roly-poly – I adored them all, especially steamed golden syrup sponge pudding. I couldn't live without it. Knowing this, Dennis, who'd been a cook in the Army during his National Service days, took it upon himself to teach Angelina the finer points of English pudding making. The trouble was Dennis had been trained in the army to cook for five or six hundred people at a time. When it came to cooking for two or three, he was not only useless, but positively dangerous. For the next few weeks we had a series of disasters in the kitchen, as Angelina and Dennis wrestled with great mounds of pudding-mix, producing acres of roly-poly, Himalayas of trifle, and syrup sponges that the four of us and all our friends put together couldn't hope to climb over, let alone eat.

Suddenly, one great day, Angelina got the knack. She came out of the kitchen bearing a beautiful, steaming, golden syrup pudding. It was drowned in rivers of honey-coloured syrup. On top of that melted great mountains of soft vanilla ice-cream and round the edges was a sea of real custard. It looked like a very bad car crash, but my god, when the first mouthful went in, it was like I'd died and gone to the great pudding bowl in the sky.

I became obsessed with that steamed golden syrup sponge pudding of Angie's. And when I say 'obsessed', I really mean obsessed: for three years I had that pudding, twice a day, every day. If we had someone coming, we'd have two desserts, one of Angelina's devising in case the guests didn't share my passion for the English delicacy.

In all the years that Angie worked for me we never had a personal conversation of any sort. But she knew that whatever happened I would see she was all right. For my part, I knew she

would die for me if she thought it necessary. It was an arrangement that worked very well and probably accounts for the fact
that she stayed with me for over thirty years. She was part of my
family and I hers. I couldn't have loved her more if she had been
my own mum.

In no time at all, besides a cook, a valet and Dennis the 'personal
assistant to Mr Faith', there was a full-time gardener. In fact it
didn't end there. As well as domestic staff I acquired a veritable
army of helpers for my business life. It was frightening at times
to think of the people who in some way or other relied on me for
all, or part, of their livelihood: Bert, Eve Taylor, Maurice Press
and Colin Berlin, Angela Miall, my fantastic fan club secretary,
and my accountant Alan Shalet.

Alan had been with me from day one and wasn't much older
than me. We'd met through Eve Taylor. Alan worked for her
accountant as a junior. When I signed to Eve for management,
anticipating that I would be needing the services of an accountant,
she introduced me to the firm who looked after her accountancy
and tax affairs. As I was only earning tuppence ha'penny at the
time, the senior partners didn't consider it worth their while to
look after a little snot-bag like me. So I was consigned to the
junior, Alan Shalet.

A few months later when 'What Do You Want?' went into the
charts I was descended on by the whole firm. Eve and I sat down
with all the senior partners to discuss the handling of my financial
future. But no Alan. The partners had decreed that I was now far
too important a client to be left in the hands of a junior. But I'd
formed a liking for Mr Junior Shalet and anyway, if I wasn't good
enough for them when I was earning zilch, there was no way I
was going to let them horn in now. On my insistence, Alan Shalet
was brought from his office (little hovel in the basement) and put
in charge of my financial affairs.

That turned out to be one of the best day's work in my life,
because without Alan's friendship and support I could never have
survived some of the hairy financial years that were to come.

So there I was, a kid, responsible for this huge team of people
looking to me to earn the pennies.

Money can be fun. It can also ruin everything. When it comes
coupled with fame it can tear the average family apart. Within a

year of getting my first hit, I looked up to find my money and fame driving a wedge through the heart of my family. This came home to me one day when my mother rang me up to complain that she couldn't get to see me any more. I asked her what she meant – she could see me whenever she liked, what was stopping her?

'Well,' replied my mother, 'since you ask, it's Dennis. He won't let me near you.'

'Come on over, Mum,' I said. 'Come over right now.'

It turned out that Dennis was taking his duties as minder-in-chief a bit too seriously. When my mother had left, I sat down and thought about what I could do to deal with this. Dennis was due back from some task or other later in the day, but I wasn't brave enough to confront him face to face. Instead, I did a very cowardly thing – something that I still, to this very day, wish I hadn't done: I made a list of all the ways in which I wanted to cut Dennis down to size. I wrote how I wanted to stop him controlling who did or didn't see me; I mentioned taking him off the board of some of the companies I'd been setting up; and I threw in a few other anti-Dennis clauses for good measure.

I left this memo lying by my bed, as if I'd been jotting down a few random thoughts and forgotten to dispose of it. All the time, of course, I knew full well that Dennis was bound to come in and read it. It was a hole-in-the-corner way of getting at him, and he was predictably upset. No, he wasn't predictably upset: he was absolutely heartbroken. He cried, and begged to know what he'd done to deserve this cruel treatment. When I saw how much I'd upset him I was shocked. I hadn't understood until that moment just how much authority my money gave me over people, especially the members of my own family. Like some despotic medieval princeling, it seemed that I could snap my fingers and break their lives.

This whole episode strikes me as even worse now that I look back on it than it did at the time. After all, I'd probably encouraged Dennis to keep my family at arm's length, so that I could concentrate 100 per cent on my new career and my new life; I didn't like having to deal with any of their problems or demands. With the money and the fame, I'd been instantly promoted to head of the family, in place of my mother or my dad. It was a role I hadn't sought, didn't want, and did my best to wriggle out of. Dennis just got on the end of all that.

Life was zooming along for me and I hadn't even taken the

trouble to find out what impact it was having on the rest of my family. I just ploughed on, letting my success crash over them without giving it a second thought. They were innocent bystanders who'd got their braces caught on a runaway train and were being dragged along with no chance of having a say in where it was taking them.

I'd become so obsessed with myself, I never gave anyone else's feelings the time of day.

One of the big benefits of being in show business is that it allows you to see the world while getting paid for it. It takes you to places you would never usually get the opportunity of visiting. In Autumn 1962 I jumped at the chance of doing a tour of New Zealand with John Leyton who had just had a massive number one hit, 'Johnny, Remember Me'.

We were in Wellington the windy city, and Robert Stigwood, John Leyton's manager, had invited us to a restaurant after the show. It was run by a very ebullient Keith Floyd-type of bloke, in his own very small house. What distinguished this restaurant, apart from its excellent food, were the two waitresses who worked there. They were both stunning beauties. The darker one of the two, as well as being extremely beautiful, had a body to die for, and looked like a cross between Louise Lombard and Audrey Hepburn. We spent the entire meal flirting with each other, and ended up going back to her place.

She lived on the top floor of an old wooden house on the other side of town. There was no bedroom, just a mattress on the floor in the corner of the sitting-room. Come to that, there was hardly any furniture at all, only books. Piles and piles of books everywhere.

The last time I'd slept on a mattress was way back in my skiffle days. In those days, all the girls who wore black slept on the floor. Many's the night I nursed an aching back, lying on a beaten-up old Slumberland, with my book of poetry under my pillow, wishing that I, and my Françoise Hardy clone, could be sleeping soundly on a comfortable bed in my mum's flat at Acton Vale. But it was the cool and seductive thing that young people did and it was just the kind of thing I'd missed out on since 'What Do You Want?' went into the charts.

Some years later Ray Connolly (the screenwriter and author) did an interview with me for *Queen* magazine, and in it he wrote that Adam Faith had never known what it was like to be a teenager – he was right. When normal teenagers were cursing the stale bread and struggling to find a shilling, I was swanning around in five-star hotels, quaffing great mouthfuls of vintage wine, to wash down the cordon bleu food. I'd missed all that managed poverty part of life, which most people go through in late teenage-hood.

But in this girl's room I felt for a moment what it was like to be a student – poor, but free of all the madness I was caught up in.

We made love most of the night, and I woke up at six in the morning to the sun kissing the tops of the buildings over Wellington. I was in a strange room; chilled by the morning breeze coming in through the open window, with a woman I didn't know, and worst of all, trillions of miles away from home.

I lay there for a moment, feeling totally lost, extremely lonely, and overwhelmed by the knowledge that I was just a little kid from Acton called Terry Nelhams. I felt like a toddler who's just learned to run, windmilling down a steep hill at top speed, with my little legs going as fast as they possibly could, but not fast enough: at any moment, the slope was going to catch up with me, and I'd fall flat on my face. It was the fear of the unknown. I'd had it from time to time since leaving home – but now in this strange room at the other end of the world, it threatened to engulf me.

I'd been telling myself that I was taking it all in my stride, that I was dealing with the money, the success, the stardom well enough. But of course I wasn't. You don't deal with fame; it deals with you. You don't change show business to make it fit in with you; it squeezes *you*, until you fit the shape it has decided to give you.

Living your life out in public all the time, like a monkey in the zoo, is one of the oddest and hardest of things to get used to. All around you are people, endless crowds of people, throwing buns and nuts at you to make you move around. You can catch the buns, or you can ignore them – but you can't stop the people watching. And every animal needs its own little hole to crawl into at the end of the day, where it can be entirely itself and on its own.

What made the incredible sense of loneliness worse was that while I was feeling sorry for myself in this simple little room, at the other end of the world, Kennedy and Khrushchev were threatening to indulge in fisticuffs with 10 megaton H bombs. The Russians were sailing full pelt towards Cuba with boatloads of nuclear rockets, and Kennedy had decided to stop them. The Cuban Missile Crisis was in full flight. I'd already blown half my tour wages on phonecalls to my mum. The minute we got the news that the US was setting up a blockade of Cuba, I was making plans to get the family out of England.

New Zealand being as far away from Cuba as you could get, I reckoned that it would be as safe as anywhere in the world, if the worst happened.

It's hard to imagine now just how real the possibility of a nuclear war was. But for years we'd lived with the fear that some lunatic would press the button that could blow us all to smithereens. And we'd only have a four-minute warning to say our last goodbyes. Here in Wellington, all on my little lonesome, it was a very unsettling experience to be away from home, especially when there seemed a very real danger that it could all have disappeared before I could get back to it.

One byproduct of worrying about the ultimate stupidity of man was that it made me reflect on what I did have. On the whole, I wanted the buns to keep coming through the bars of the cage – especially if they were anything like this beautiful girl lying asleep with the sheets crumpled up around her pretty, smooth, young shoulders.

I scolded myself for being feeble, got a grip, kissed my sleeping beauty gently on her forehead, and let myself out quietly.

I can't remember her name. I shall never forget her.

On that tour, things came to a head between me and The Roulettes. They weren't really cutting it as a group. At times it seemed like they were all playing different songs. It was time for me to read the riot act to John Rogers. After agonizing over what was to be done, we agreed it was time for a reshuffle.

When we got home John went to work on remodelling The Roulettes. His first new appointment was Russ Ballard. When I first met Russ, I thought that John had lost his marbles. This so-called genius that he'd been raving about was only just sixteen, and looked like he belonged in short trousers. Then he took out his guitar and played. He made magic and we had ourselves a lead guitarist.

So with Pete Thorpe on rhythm guitar, Bob Henrit on drums, Russ on lead guitar and John Rogers, as leader, holding the whole thing together, we were set to conquer the world all over again.

ChapterFourteen

WHY THE HELL WASN'T I EDUCATED? I FEEL SO FRUSTRATED, not having a sufficient grasp of the English language to describe her.

I was in a restaurant in Blackpool after doing a Sunday concert at the Queen's Theatre. At a very large table in the middle of the room was a girl. She was the most stunning girl I'd ever clapped eyes on. Sitting next to her was Cliff Richard. There were some roadies with him who were mates of Bert's, and we went over to say hello. While Bert caught up with the gossip from his mates, I swopped a few pleasantries with Cliff. Whatever it was that was being said, I wasn't taking it in. All I could do was stare. I never took my eyes off the girl, willing her to look up and smile. She hardly seem to notice I was there. The more I stared, the more aloof and unattainable she seemed to become. Bert and I ran out of things to say and we went back to our table. I was smitten!

As soon as we sat down I gripped Bert's arm. 'Bert,' I hissed at him, 'don't look round, but who's that girl sitting next to Cliff?'

Bert immediately twisted round his chair and looked across. 'Oh, that's Jacqueline Irving,' he told me. 'She's Cliff's girl-friend.'

'Cliff's girlfriend, she can't be!' I didn't want her to be any-one's girlfriend, except mine. I was distraught. 'She's fantastic-looking.' She looked like Brigitte Bardot and Faye Dunaway rolled into one, and I couldn't keep my eyes off her. She was blonde, about my height, with eyes that you wanted to look into and not notice the colour. The more I looked at her, the more I thought her the most beautiful girl I'd ever seen. But if she was with Cliff, that was it, there was no way. I slumped back in my red plush velvet banquette, trying to get used to the idea of living in misery for the rest of my life.

When she got up to visit the loo, I did briefly allow the thought to pass through my mind of sending Bert in after her to get her phone number. But no. She was Cliff's girl and that was that. Up to then I'd only envied Cliff for making a record as great as 'Move It'. But tonight, as far as I was concerned, he had it all.

I thought about Jacqueline Irving, a lot. This was a totally new and very unsettling experience for me. I'd found the girl dreams are made of, and there wasn't a damned thing I could do about it.

Then, a few months later, at one of Alma Cogan's wonderful parties, in Kensington, I saw Jacqueline Irving again. More de-pression. This time, she was on the arm of George Harrison. She was standing in the middle of the room, holding George by the arm, with the other Beatles standing around her, clowning about.

I was with a girl who was no mean looker herself, but I hardly gave her a glance all evening. My eyes followed Jacqueline Irving like a missile locking on to a target. The more vivacious and animated she became, the more depressed I got. Why wasn't she laughing at my jokes, listening intently to the fascinating things I would tell her? But again what the hell could I do about it? Cliff had gone, and now here was George.

I did make a few pathetic attempts at attracting her attention. A couple of jokes here, a few silly anecdotes there. All told just a little louder than necessary. But they fell a long way short of getting my love goddess's attention. In the end, deflated, I dropped on to one of Alma's huge sofas feeling very sorry for myself.

* * *

Life slipped back to its normal round of work, girls, work and girls. There were endless girls, a night, a week, a month, but nothing special was happening for me or them. There was something missing. I was having a time most people would die for, but I was getting lonely. I was beginning to get to the point where it wasn't fun to wake up with a one-night stand anymore. I wanted a mate. I was getting bored with sex for its own sake. I wanted more. At twenty-two years old I was bored with sex. *Sad*. I needed a break. Maurice and Eve were going to the South of France, so I decided to join them.

We stayed at a hotel in Juan-les-Pins, between Nice and Cannes. It was my first time in the South of France and it was love at first sight. Sun, fantastic food, beautiful, chic, sun-bronzed women. It was like being in a Cary Grant/Grace Kelly movie. Magical. Elegant long-limbed women splashed around in the waves, occasionally swimming out to the platforms moored just off the beach. If they weren't doing that they were water-skiing, looking like beautiful graceful animals at home in their natural environment.

I spent my time sitting on the hotel sun-deck, my feet dangling in the warm clear water, gazing enviously at the beach-bums joining the girls in their play, cursing the times I'd skived school swimming lessons back in Acton. Here I was, twenty-two years old, and I couldn't swim a stroke. The frustration of watching every girl I took a fancy to dive in the briny and splash about with some foreign yob became too much for me to put up with. I had to have a bash at learning this swimming lark.

On condition that he taught me when there was no-one else around, I hired this Algerian swimming-instructor. We'd meet in the shallows at six o'clock in the morning, whilst the beaches were still being cleaned and raked. After floundering around like a beached whale for five or six lessons, I became brave enough to venture out up to my waist, all on my own.

One morning, with the gentle Mediterranean swell lapping up to my belly-button, I stood enjoying the feel of the warm sun on my back, day-dreaming of when I would be able to cut through the waves, like Johnny Weismuller, pulling myself up in one graceful movement onto the platform, and straight into the arms of a beautiful girl.

Suddenly, a vision broke surface right in front of me: jet-black hair plastered to her neatly shaped head, huge deep brown eyes, full sensuous lips, and the seawater running in sparkling rivulets

105

down her statuesque suntanned body. Startled by her sudden appearance, I tripped and floundered backwards into the sea. She burst into a peal of laughter, showing off white, even teeth and a little pink tongue. She laughed and laughed, watching me as I tried to empty my lungs of seawater. When I finally stopped spluttering, I tried to talk to her. But I don't think she'd ever heard English the way I spoke it, so she just blinked in bewilderment. As I didn't have a word of French, we were going to get nowhere.

Then I had a brainwave: Maurice. I signalled to her to wait for me, and did an impression of a demented duck as I fought my way up to the beach. There's no way you can look cool and sophisticated trying to run through water a couple of feet deep. I dragged Maurice into the sea to where my mermaid was still waiting, the sun burning the droplets of water off her shoulders.

We introduced ourselves. Her name was Andrea and while she was waiting to start her training to become an air-hostess for Air France, she was living with her mum and dad in Antibes. Somehow or other, between us, Maurice and I got her to agree to come out for dinner with me that evening.

I spent all afternoon getting ready. I wanted to look the business for this one. The little Citroën hire-car screamed in pain as I belted up streets and screeched round corners in my haste to see her again. My breath took a sharp intake as I caught sight of her waiting on the corner of the square in Antibes. Suntanned skin looks good in white and Andrea had that French knack of making the most of herself. In her simple white dress she looked a dream.

We drove up to St Paul de Vence and ate at the Colombe d'Or. Probably one of the best restaurants in the world. I was anxious to impress. The setting was magical. Beautiful food, beautiful decor, beautiful people, everything was beautiful. Twinkling lights sparkling like diamonds in the darkness.

Andrea ordered the wine, introducing me to what was to become another joy of my life. And as we sipped our vintage Château la Tour we gazed into each other's eyes like a couple of love-sick kids. Which, of course, was exactly what we were.

We communicated throughout this tender meal by means of sign language, laughing shyly if our hands happened to touch. It was unbelievably romantic. This was the stuff of movies. I'd watched things like this at the Gaumont cinema all those years ago when I was a kid in Acton, and here I was living it for real.

For the rest of my holiday we spent every possible moment together. We ate, drank fine wines, sunbathed and laughed endlessly at my attempts to teach her English. I liked making her laugh. It was a lesson I'd learnt when I was knee-high to a black suspender belt: make a girl laugh and you're halfway there with her. We spent hours poring over a French/English dictionary, telling each other about our lives. She'd never heard about Adam Faith and was fascinated by the recognition I got if we bumped into any Brits. It was fun to see her face when one of them asked for an autograph. (I was to see the same look of puzzlement on the face of my young daughter, years later.) I tried to pass it off with a bit of *savoir-faire*, but in truth, it gave me a kick to be recognized in front of her.

My enthusiasm for work was rekindled by her interest in Adam Faith. It was nice to have someone to share him with. I couldn't wait for her to come to England and see for herself what this Adam Faith stuff was all about.

She eventually got herself on the London run, and would come and stay with me for three or four days at a time. Occasionally I'd meet her in Paris, at the Georges Cinq. Sometimes the *déjà vu* was so strong I didn't remember who I was supposed to be meeting. Andrea or Verna.

On one trip at the end of 1962, Andrea came and stayed with me in Bournemouth where I was playing Aladdin in pantomime. Angelina and Vincente set up home for me in a rented house just outside the town. It was a most bitter winter; people froze to death in their homes; no central-heating system was man enough to resist it. There was also a freezing wind blowing through my recording future. The Beatles were about to hit the music scene and change everything in their path. It was time for me to get up to date. As luck would have it, at this moment when I most needed him, a songwriter called Chris Andrews came into my life. Gums bleeding with hunger, he'd walked into Eve Taylor's office with a fistful of wonderful songs that he'd written. Eve, never backward in taking advantage of a starving man, signed him up for thousands of years and I was the beneficiary.

For the first time The Roulettes, my live stage group, and I went into the recording studios together. My most recent record

'What Now?' only managed to creep up to a paltry number 31 in the charts in January 1963, and a lot was riding on the new direction I'd chosen. The resulting recording session was to produce my next hit: 'The First Time' entered the charts on 19 September 1963. Its highest position was number 5 and it signalled a revival in my recording career.

Andrea and I kept our love affair going despite the distance between us. In early 1963 I read in the papers that the completion of the Aswan Dam would mean the flooding of the Valley of the Kings, which has some of the finest tombs in Egypt; the report said that the summer was going to be the last chance to see the tombs in their original state. All excited, I rang Andrea and we agreed that Egypt was a must. She had a three-week holiday coming up and we arranged to meet in Cairo at the Hilton Hotel a month later. Dennis, in his usual extravagant way, made my holiday arrangements. Andrea and I were going in style. After a couple of days in Cairo we were to travel by private plane up country to see the tombs. First-class hotel suites, and our own private guide. Andrea and I talked endlessly on the phone about the coming trip. We were set for a great time.

Four days before the holiday was supposed to start I met an actress in London. I only went out with her once, but, perhaps because she refused to take me seriously, I convinced myself I was entirely in love with her. Totally and utterly infatuated, I bombarded this woman with all sorts of presents, and flowers, and phonecalls. All to no avail. But I kept trying right up to the time I had to leave for Egypt.

I missed the flight to Cairo. Dennis drove me to the airport, giving me ear damage about my cavalier treatment of Andrea. He thought that she was the bee's knees and was furious with me for missing the flight. 'You've got no excuse. You had plenty of time. You missed that plane because you didn't want to go.'

'Nonsense, I was busy, that's all.' I tried to defend myself.

'Rubbish.' Dennis knew me too well. 'You missed that plane because you didn't want to go. You've left poor Andrea right in the lurch, on her own in Cairo.'

He was right. I had missed the plane because I didn't really want to go. I wanted to stay and woo my unwilling actress.

I got on the next plane, feeling guilty as hell, a feeling that was made a thousand times worse when I arrived at the hotel. Andrea was sitting in the lobby surrounded by her suitcases. They hadn't let her go up to our suite, because it was booked in my name. She'd been there for six hours. Trembling and pale, she was beside herself with rage. The second she saw me she went ballistic. I got both barrels: one in French and the other broken English. She had an amazing grasp of the vernacular, considering she hardly spoke English.

On the way to Cairo I'd decided to tell Andrea it was all over between us. I had planned to put this off until the last day of our trip, I felt bad enough as it was without ruining her holiday, but it was straining my good intentions to the limit as she lambasted me in the middle of the busy lobby.

We followed the bellboy up to the suite in ghastly silence. When he'd gone, clutching the piastres I'd slipped him, I looked around. The room we were in had been decorated entirely in red – the walls, the carpet, the curtains, everywhere you looked was a shade of deep red. It looked like a cross between a slaughter-house and a bordello. It was unimaginably horrible, exactly the colour of the blood I was likely to be spilling when Andrea got her second breath.

The décor seemed to make Andrea angrier still. She dumped her bag, opened her mouth, and falling back on her natural language, she let me have it again. A long torrent of earthy Provençal epithets, whose meaning I didn't need to have trans-lated, hit me full-frontal.

Backed up against the wall, my good intentions of not ruining her holiday went out the window. Before I could stop myself the words came pouring out. 'Look, there's no point arguing about it, Andrea, because it's over between us, anyway.'

Andrea's mouth opened and shut a couple of times. She stood in the middle of this big blood-red room, and looked at me with her soft brown eyes, as if she couldn't begin to believe what she'd just heard. I'd have given up my next ten hit records if only I could have taken those words back. Her features took on that slightly surprised, expectant look people have when they're about to cry. And then, with a great whooping sob, she burst into tears. I felt awful and twice as sorry. I moved across the room and tried to put my arm around her. She threw it off, spluttering, and flung herself down on the bed. She cried all through our room-service dinner, finally crying herself off to sleep.

I watched her sleeping fitfully beside me, looking so sweet and innocent, the way women do when they are at rest. I felt wretched and guilt-ridden for hurting her. My God! Three weeks of this, how were we going to last it out?

At daylight, the second Andrea opened her eyes, great tears began rolling down her cheeks. All through breakfast she cried, and all through that day on our tour of the pyramids. We had the obligatory camel ride round the pyramids with Andrea supplying enough tears to keep her mount in water for a couple of months. Everybody stared at us. It was clear from the dagger looks they shot my way that they thought I'd broken this poor girl's heart. And they were right.

I'd broken her heart. What could I do? She wouldn't let me comfort her, and yet she wanted me near by. The slightest hint that we'd do better to call it a day gave rise to fresh floods of tears, even more misery. Fortunately, I'd booked a private tour, so at least some of the horror of Andrea's unhappiness was kept private.

The days unravelled, one after another, in this terrible slow agony of tears. All through the beauty of Luxor, in the breath-taking riches of Abu Simbel, monument after monument, Andrea cried. Then we began to recognize a tour-party that was running in parallel with us, and they could hardly fail to notice us. We'd be walking around inside a cavernous tomb, when suddenly the entire space would begin echoing and re-echoing with the most heart-rending sobbing, as though the ghosts of the ancient Egyptians were mourning their dead. The more magnificent and moving a thing was, the more it seemed to upset Andrea. She knew I was leaving her: it was no good my telling her I wasn't worth it.

Somehow, the beauty and magic of our surroundings made everything that much worse.

In Aswan, we stayed in a cottage in the grounds of a wonderful hotel. The weather was so warm that, even in the evenings, everyone took their meals in the open-air restaurant. Here, for the first time in seven days, Andrea stopped crying. I thought we might risk dinner. We went outside, as evening fell, to sit among all the other guests, on the wide romantic veranda. The tables were spread with snowy cloths and sparkling cutlery, lit by the warm glow of candles. It was a perfectly romantic setting. There was a memorable view over the valley to the opposite hills, bluing slowly to grey as the sun went down behind them.

Everyone was dressed in fabulous clothes, there was the low murmur of conversation, the occasional chink of a fork on a plate. Smiling waiters circulated in the semi-darkness, attentive, discreet. All was perfect, it was one of those moments when the world is in harmony.

Andrea put down her spoon. She looked down at her plate, and a mighty tear splashed onto it, then another, and another, wetting the cutlery and the tablecloth. I put my hand on her forearm. She lifted her head, gazed at me through brimming brown eyes, and let out a heart-rending wail of misery. The whole room fell silent; I could feel all the other people watching and waiting. They weren't disappointed: the tears burst from Andrea in shuddering waves, threatening to fill up not only the hotel, but the whole valley below us into the bargain.

Inside, I was going quietly insane. I'd have gladly died on the spot. My single thought was to get her out of there, at all costs. I led her out of the room and down the path towards the cottage. I was so wound up that everything seemed sharper to me: the crickets joining in with Andrea, the palm trees black against the darkening sky, the heady smell of the tropical flowers. At last, where the path wound to the left, I thought it might be safe to stop. As I went to put my arms around this poor girl, I glanced back up at the hotel. There, on the balcony, lit from behind by the warm golden lights, were the other guests, like passengers lining the rail of a cruise ship. They found our horrid little drama so fascinating they'd left their food, and were straining down to see what we were doing in the dying of the light.

Why not just cut and run? Why did I sweat it out? The answer was I felt so appallingly, horribly guilty about Andrea that I felt I had to do whatever she wanted; and she was determined to go through with the holiday. Suffering her pain was my hair-shirt, her tears were my penance. I'd died and gone to Purgatory, but if I was standing outside the gates of Hell, she was already on the inside. I felt compassion for her, but there was nothing I could do. She knew, and I knew, that I no longer felt love.

After two weeks of this walking nightmare, we left Egypt. I'd arranged for us to fly on to the Lebanon. I thought that Andrea might at last, with the change of country, stop crying.

We stayed in a villa on the beach in Beirut. It was, again, a wonderful place. You could sunbathe and swim in the morning, then go off and ski in the mountains in the afternoon. We spent a day sightseeing around Baalbeck. In the evenings we went into town.

Beirut had the biggest casino in the world and they'd asked me if I was interested in playing it. So Andrea and I gave the place the once over. It was incredible, sort of like Las Vegas with yashmaks; all girls and gambling chips. I would have liked to do a gig there, but the management probably wouldn't want a woman beater on their stage. Andrea wept through the whole spectacular cabaret show.

On our last day, I left her at the airport. Back then, the terminal at Beirut was a bit like the one in the last scene of *Casablanca* – you walked right out onto the apron to board the plane. Andrea's flight back to France was due out four hours after mine. On my way across the tarmac, I stopped and looked back at her. Standing behind the chain-link fence that stood between us, she looked a tragic figure. Her fingers hooked through the wire, clutching at it, tears still streaming in long torrents down her cheeks. Going back on the plane to London I had the mixed feeling of relief and sadness that you get when a funeral is over.

I thought that would be the last time I'd ever see Andrea. But about twelve years later, when I was managing Leo Sayer, he was playing the gala at the music festival in Cannes. I was standing at the back of the casino one afternoon, listening while Leo did a sound check, when I heard this soft voice in my ear: "Allo, Terry.'

I looked round – and there was Andrea. She looked exactly the same, except for one very important thing: she wasn't crying. In fact she was smiling broadly at me. We started to talk. And from that moment until six o'clock the next morning, we were never apart. We sat in my room, after dinner, with a bottle of wine, and we talked and talked and talked, about what had been, and what might have been, if only, and if . . .

She was happily married, living in Antibes with two children. And we didn't so much as touch the tips of our fingers together during the whole night.

When the sunlight came gleaming through the curtains, she looked at her watch, jumped up like Cinderella, and exclaimed, 'Oh, *mon Dieu*, Terry, I've got to go!' She hadn't told her husband where she was.

I walked her down to her car. It was one of those extraordinary mornings in the South of France. The light was so wonderfully clear, and yet slightly diffused, the kind of light that has made

Picasso and so many other painters want to live there. The Croisette was empty of traffic, and there was her little Renault car sitting waiting for her.

'What are you going to tell your husband?' I asked.

'Don't worry,' Andrea smiled, 'I've got between now and Antibes to think of an excuse.'

We kissed, standing by the car, and said our last '*Au revoir*.'

ChapterFifteen

NOT LONG AFTER I GOT BACK FROM EGYPT I WAS BOOKED TO DO a spot on the Mike and Bernie Winters TV show, also starring Lionel Blair and his dance troupe. On our first morning in the rehearsal studio, Bert Harris and I were sitting in the empty studio waiting for the off, when the dancers arrived. I glanced at them, then sat bolt upright in my chair.

'Jesus, Bert, look who it is.' I could hardly get my breath.

Jacqueline Irving took a seat about six rows behind and to the left of us. My heart banged against my chest plate. I watched her. It was the blue denim shirt that really got me. Some women can wear beaten up old clothes and make them look like high fashion. Jackie was like that, and the poised way she was smoking her cigarette convinced me that this was a goddess, dallying on earth for her own amusement, and not a mortal. A feeling of teenage embarrassment, anxiety and nervousness swept over me. I felt ridiculously shy, yet at the same time I couldn't keep my eyes off her. I kept craning my head round, looking up at her, like a kid in assembly at school, hoping and yet almost fearing to attract her attention. I didn't have need to worry. She ignored me completely.

I couldn't stand it any longer. I had to make my move. I ordered Bert to go over to her and invite her out to dinner; with me!

'Naow,' replied Bert. 'Oi can't do that. You go and ask her.'

'Bert,' I insisted, 'go over there now and tell her I'd like to take her to dinner tonight.'

Eventually, I bullied poor Bert into shuffling over. I watched them talking, hardly able to continue breathing. At last, Bert came lumbering back.

'Well?' I demanded. 'Is she coming?'

'Naow,' said Bert, 'she ain't.'

'What are you talking about?' I was sure Bert hadn't asked properly. 'What do you mean, no?'

Bert had that smug told-you-so look on his face. 'She's not very happy with you mate. She couldn't believe that you would be so cocky as to send someone else to ask for a date. If you want to take her out you've got to go and ask her yourself.' Bert didn't have to be enjoying this as much as he was.

Being put in my place by women was getting to be a habit, but at least she had given me hope. We had a full day of rehearsals ahead of us. I just needed to find the right opportunity. Throughout the course of that entire day, I trotted around after my goddess, hoping she wouldn't notice I was behaving like a little lap-dog. When it came to meal break I made sure I positioned myself in exactly the right place where I could see her and her me. Trying to pluck up the courage to ask her out, I sat at my table and grinned at her like a Cheshire cat all through the meal. But as desperate as I was, there was no way I was going to expose myself to the humiliation of getting the brush-off in front of all the other girls. Because they were usually beautiful, with wonderful bodies, they were the target for practically every red-blooded oik in showbiz. And I knew enough about dancers to know that when it came to male artistes coming on to them, they took no prisoners. Also it didn't help me that by now I'd built up a reputation that scared off most nicely brought up girls. There was no doubt in my mind that they had all warned her to stay away from me.

But no matter what it took, there was no way I was leaving that rehearsal room without her. I finally managed to get her on her own for a couple of minutes and blurted out an invitation for dinner after rehearsals.

Not exactly bubbling over with enthusiasm she agreed. 'Why not?' Just hearing her talk reduced me to a small heap of rubble. But at the same time I was exultant. I'd asked her and she'd said yes! It was as simple as that. For the rest of rehearsals I was delirious with anticipation. Jackie couldn't go anywhere, sit anywhere, talk to anyone, without me leering at her from a safe distance.

I followed her everywhere; if she went for a cup of tea I just happened to be passing through the canteen at exactly the same time. If she was using the phone, by an amazing coincidence I needed to make a call from the next phone-booth. She went to the make-up room, I went to the make-up room. I was utterly *sad*. It was a wonder she didn't have me restrained for pestering her. If it was today I'd be inside serving time for stalking. My ridiculous behaviour reached its height when we came to rehearse the end of the show. For some absurd reason, the finale was the whole cast riding bicycles round and round the studio set. I fought my way through the mob of artistes and dancers, and manoeuvred my bike next to Jacqueline's. How I never knocked her flying in my haste to get alongside her, I'll never know. What was I like? Here I was, twenty-three years old behaving like a silly five-year-old. Much later Jackie told me that her and the other dancers had spent many a happy hour laughing at my soppy antics.

When rehearsals came to an end, I walked her proudly to my E-type Jag. What a fabulous car. I loved it to bits. It was a bigger star than me. If I parked it outside a café on the way to a show, there would be five hundred people crowded around it when I came out. When the car didn't even warrant a mention I was more than a bit deflated. Jackie climbed into it without so much as raising her eyebrows, as though it were a London cab. What I didn't know then was that owning material things for their own sake just wasn't on Jackie's agenda. Suitably chastened I set off in the direction of Esher.

'Just a minute,' she said, 'I thought we were going to dinner in London? I live in London.'

'I know you do,' I replied. 'I just thought you'd like to come over to my house for dinner – then I'll drive you back home.' I

116

wanted her on my own patch.

It took some doing, but eventually I persuaded her to come back to Tudor Court with me. As we drove, I sneaked the occasional glance at her: with Verna and then Andrea I thought I'd found the girl of my dreams, but this was different. This wasn't a dream, it felt more real than any girl I'd ever been out with.

As we drove through Richmond and Kingston we talked. She'd been brought up in Manchester, in a terraced house with an outside toilet, in a working-class family much like my own. Aged fourteen, she'd faked her way into her very first audition at the opera house in Manchester by the simple expedient of saying, 'Yes,' to everything.

She hadn't had a formal ballet training, and when the choreographer asked everyone to do a *plié*, or some other complicated ballet move, Jacqueline simply watched the other classically trained girls go through their paces and copied them. This girl had guts and incredible strength of character. With neither training nor qualifications of any kind, she'd become one of the most sought-after dancers around. A fixture in Lionel Blair's troupe, she was more or less continually employed on the top television variety shows.

I should have been shaking with excitement, after all, I'd been dreaming of this girl one way or another for well over a year now. But it felt so natural, as if I'd always known her. I couldn't wait to show her how I lived, the style, the sophistication. I didn't just want to impress this girl, I wanted her approval – of me, of my lifestyle. I already knew from the way she'd dismissed my darling E-type that she wasn't impressed by possessions.

I swung the car up in front of Tudor Court, jumped out and rang the doorbell. Here was my chance to show off. Vincente answered the door, immaculate in his starched white jacket and black trousers, the sheen of his dark hair matching the gloss on his shoes. At once I began jabbering at him in rapid, colloquial Spanish. I stole another glance at Jacqueline expecting her to be impressed. She just smiled the cool tolerant smile women save for men when they are acting like schoolboys.

I'd already phoned ahead to instruct Vincente to get the best wine breathing; Angelina to cook the best meal she ever made. Meanwhile, I gabbled madly at my guest, terrified of leaving a

117

moment of silence between us in case she bolted.

After a fabulous dinner we went into the drawing-room and sat on the Wilton, luxuriating in the warmth of the log fire, and chatted the night away. Tudor Court became a home to me that evening. We talked about décor. As I showed her round the house she came up with wonderful suggestions on how to make this bachelor pad into a home. It was a totally different experience to any I'd had with a girl at Tudor Court. It seemed like we were sharing it.

As we drove back to London, I could see she was more at ease with me, beginning to enjoy herself, her smile was wider and more spontaneous. She really was beautiful.

'Ah,' I thought, cockily, 'the old magic's done its work. I'm just about home and dry.'

Outside her flat, I switched off the engine, and waited for her to invite me up for coffee. She got out of the car, shouted, 'Thanks,' and set off up the steps at top speed. I leapt out.

'Hey, hey, hey! Hang on a minute,' I shouted. 'Can I take you out again?'

'I don't think so, no,' she called back. 'Thanks and goodbye.'

And she meant it. She refused absolutely to come out with me or even see me again. In fact, she told me the only reason she'd agreed to have dinner with me that night was because her usual lift home from Teddington had fallen through.

To me, this was a declaration of war. If she was going to oppose me in love, I had to prevail, whatever the cost to my personal dignity. I started pestering her. I kept on and on and on asking her to go out with me again, but the answer was always, 'No.' At last, after weeks of this, out of sheer weariness, she agreed to go with me to a film première.

The great evening came round. Jacqueline arrived looking more beautiful than ever. It was clear she'd laid out a small fortune in clothes for the occasion – new dress, new shoes, new coat – money she could ill-afford to spend. When we got to the cinema, dressed up to the nines, we found that everyone else was wearing jeans and sneakers. I'd forgotten, in my love-struck condition, that it was an Elvis Presley film.

Jackie was furious with me, and after the film, stalked off swearing never to speak to me again.

Thank God for Interflora and white lilies. Nine months later Jacqueline moved into Tudor Court.

ChapterSixteen

WHILE I WAS QUIETLY GETTING OBSESSED OVER MISS Jacqueline Irving, a great dollop of obsession was about to land on my doorstep.

One day, I was sitting in the drawing-room of Tudor Court when the doorbell rang. Vincente, in his usual unobtrusive way, came to the drawing-room. There was a lady at the front door, who was very insistent on seeing me. It wasn't unusual for a fan to come to the house for an autograph so, Biro at the ready, I nonchalantly strolled through into the hall.

When I opened the front door there was a woman standing there. In her thirties, she was wearing an unbuttoned imitation leopard-skin coat, over an old-fashioned twin-set. A very dated hat was perched on the top of her head, and two cheap cardboard suitcases sat on the gravel either side of her.

'Hello, darling,' she said, opening her arms. 'I'm here!'

'Excuse me!' I replied. What the hell was this woman talking about?

She persisted, 'I've come to live with you, Adam,' she said.

'Like you wanted.'

Warning bells started to go off in my head. 'Er, right, I see. That's very kind of you, but I'm busy right now.' Mad. Possibly dangerous. I felt Vincente's presence behind me. I nodded to him to take over and get rid of her.

'But you told me to come!' she wailed, moving towards the door. 'You told me to come and live with you!'

Vincente and I stood there, staring at this complete stranger, not quite knowing what to do next. Her face crumpled slowly in bewilderment and hurt. I wanted her to disappear. But there was something about her that was beginning to worry me; and not just for my sake, hers as well. She seemed so fragile and pathetic. On the edge. This woman was not well.

I ushered her into the drawing-room whilst Vincente bought her suitcases in. Once inside the house she seemed to perk up, and the offer of a cup of tea brought the first smile to her face.

Settled in on the Louise Quinze sofa she poured out her story. 'You've been sending me messages in your songs,' she explained with a mixture of pride and accusation in her voice. 'I've left my husband and two children to be with you. Here I am!'

Even though I was freaked out by this show of self-delusion, my heart went out to her. 'But I don't understand.' I tried to be as gentle as I could, explaining that I was sorry but I didn't know her from Adam. I couldn't understand what messages she was going on about?

She was about to give the French repro a soaking when I was saved by the bell. Literally! Dennis and Jackie had arrived back from a shopping trip to Kingston.

It didn't go down too well with our strange visitor when I introduced Jackie as my girlfriend. To avoid trouble, I whispered to Dennis to take Jackie and put her somewhere safe. After leaving her in the custody of Angelina and Vincente, Dennis came back to help me.

We sat down and smiled at the newcomer nervously. I wondered about calling the police. Then, bit by bit, it all came pouring out.

One year before, I'd been doing a summer season in Yorkshire, and staying in a rented house out in the glorious countryside between Bridlington and Scarborough. Every day, on the way to the theatre, Bert and I would drive through the village near the house. In the middle of this village was one of those lovely old raised-up walkways, lined with railings, built to keep the people out of the mud in the days before hard-metalled roads. This walkway fronted a row of small terraced houses, outside which, in the fine sunny weather, would sit the local mothers with their children, watching the world at its work going by.

Pretty soon after I arrived, I'd say within about three minutes, word flew around the village, that this pop singer Adam Faith was staying just up the road. The village women would watch out for me and Bert driving through every day, and wave furiously as we swept by. Naturally, Bert and I would wave and smile back. But we never ever stopped; we never got out of the car; and I'd certainly never spoken to any of the people who'd waved.

This woman on my sofa had rented one of those terraced houses for the summer. She'd watched me going by every day, and been on the end of my waves and smiles. Gradually, she'd somehow got it into her head that there was something very special between us. She believed my waves and grins held a coded message which only she understood, a message that was reinforced by the words of my songs, telling her to leave her husband and kids and come to live with me.

Dennis and I sat with our mouths hanging open in the face of this incredible obsession. What do you say to someone who has elaborated this kind of fantasy about you? No use patting her on the head and telling her it was a lot of nonsense. It had become a reality to her.

There were more tears. Accusations of me leading her up the garden path. You couldn't get angry, because she was helpless, in the grip of this obsession. She was totally lost and bewildered. Dennis was wonderfully patient and gentle with her, eventually getting it into her head that she'd made a terrible mistake.

He gently coaxed her home phone number out of her and left me to keep her occupied, while he went off to phone her husband. The poor man was beside himself with relief that she'd been found. She'd gone missing the day before. She had been making her family's life a misery with her obsession. In between apologies, he pleaded with Dennis to put her on the train back to Yorkshire.

When this was put to her, she got close to hysterics all over again. But in the end, and with a large helping of kindness, Dennis eased her out of the front door.

It was heartbreaking to see this unhappy woman crying her way up the garden path, Dennis bringing up the rear with her two suitcases. I closed the door on her, and went to explain the whole miserable nightmare to Jackie.

If this kind of fantasizing wasn't too much of a problem, the violence I was sometimes on the end of certainly was. I'm not talking here about the over-enthusiastic fan pulling a scarf – I mean directed, premeditated violence.

The first time it happened to me was in Ireland. I was on stage in a packed-out ballroom somewhere way out in the sticks, singing 'Poor Me'. Right in the middle of the song, I suddenly found myself flat on my back staring at the ceiling, with no idea how I'd got there. There was a ringing noise in my head, a stunning pain in my mouth, and my eyes weren't working properly. It felt exactly like the time I'd been thumped by the playground bully at school, only even more confusing. I sat up, shook my head, and promptly fell back down again. Some stewards came running on and carried me off. When I'd come round a bit, they told me what had happened: some great country boy standing at the back of the hall had taken vast exception to all these fine Irish girls screaming their heads off at this little English fellow. So he'd taken a penny out of his pocket – an old copper, that is, big and heavy – drawn back his arm and skimmed the coin with the full force of his body across the heads of the audience. It had hit me just under the nose and I'd gone down like a skittle. A couple of inches higher, and they reckoned I'd have lost an eye. An inch or two lower and my attacker would have achieved his objective. The penny would have sliced my tonsils off, taking the vocal cords with them. That would have been goodbye singing career.

A half-dozen or so tough local boys had been hired as security for the evening. When they found out what had happened, they ran to the back of the hall, grabbed hold of this Goliath and took him into a small room at the back of the stage, and proceeded to kick seven bales of the old proverbial out of him. Then they dragged the poor bloke to my dressing-room where I was recovering. The coin-chucker looked a sorry sight. All I had was a big fat wooden lip. He had two big fat wooden lips, a black eye and a bloody nose. His ribs looked like they were in pretty bad shape, too, the way he was nursing them.

'Pat here is going to apologoize,' said one of the roughnecks holding him up. 'Aren't you now, Pat?'

Pat mumbled something.

'No, no, no,' I broke in, 'it doesn't matter – let him go.' I was just happy that he was immobilized, I didn't want him stirred up again.

'It fockin' duz fockin' matter,' said the man, and he elbowed Pat hard in the damaged ribs. 'Fockin' apologoize!' he shouted. Pat apologized. He was then formally escorted out of the dressing-room by my self-appointed bodyguards, straight to the bar to share a pint of the 'black stuff' with the same blokes that had just duffed him up.

I went back on stage to finish the show and was treated to constant encouragement from Pat, propped up at the bar. That's Ireland for you.

That tour of Ireland, including the North, was to produce yet another harrowing adventure. I'd only been there a few days when word got out that the IRA were going to assassinate me. It seems they'd got the idea I hated Catholics and had said so on a television show. I hadn't ever said that, or even been on the show; but some pop star or other had said something about the Catholic religion on TV in England, and I'd been elected as the guilty man: I was English, a pop singer, and I was in Ireland. This wasn't just upsetting, it was downright terrifying. From that time on, the tour was conducted under armed police escort. It's quite disconcerting to sing with an armed guard standing right behind you.

Then there was blackmail. As soon as I got back from the tour of Ireland, somebody tried to blackmail me. I was learning that when you're in the public eye, a lot of people think you're there to be shot at, in one way or another.

Eve Taylor took a phonecall one morning in her office. The stranger on the line told her that he had photographs of me in bed with a man, performing all sorts of unmentionables. He wanted £20,000, or else it was the newspapers.

Eve immediately got in a total panic and called me. I held the phone away from my ear for a moment or two, as she tried to establish if it was true.

I can't blame her doubting me; the shock of taking that sort of call would be enough to unravel anyone. It certainly did me. I knew it was impossible for anyone to have photos like that of me – if I was left on a desert island with the best-looking bloke in the world, for a hundred years, I'd become an expert in self-satisfaction rather than do it with him. But it still shook me up that there was someone walking around London with evil intent on my well-being. After we calmed down a bit, we agreed that it was obvious that he'd mocked up some kind of fake photographs.

Eve called the police. They interviewed me and Eve. She told them the caller had instructed her to have the money ready in two days' time, when he'd come into the office in person and pick it up. This gave me some hope: he didn't want it thrown onto the top of a moving train, or left in a prearranged spot – he was actually going to come in himself and get the dough. This didn't strike me as overly bright. What was to stop the police arresting him when he came in?

The same thing crossed the minds of London's finest. They devised a cunning plan. A policewoman was to be installed in the office, posing as Eve's secretary. When the blackmailer came in to collect his cash, she'd be there to nail him. They told me to keep out of the way, and coached Eve in how to make sure the guy demanded the money, out loud.

He came in on the day, and sure enough, about three seconds after he'd asked for the loot, the WPC stood up and arrested him.

The case came to court a short time afterward, but the trial was held in camera. I was referred to throughout as 'Mr X'. And there was never a word of it breathed in the press. Nowadays, someone would have been onto the tabloids within minutes of that first call coming through to Eve Taylor's office, and sold the whole grimy lie, without a qualm, for the price of a bottle of beer.

It was a great relief when the trial was over and the black-mailer was convicted. I don't remember how long he got, but it was a considerable sentence. Not only was it a thoroughly unpleasant experience, it could have also threatened my career. In those days homosexuality was against the law. Mud sticks, and if it had, then 'bye 'bye Adam Faith. But I was lucky: my black-mailer was an amateur.

If some of the men hated me, some of the women wanted to tear Jackie limb from limb. In Bridlington one of them very nearly did.

Bert, Jackie and Dave Cohen, who had now become my drummer, and I went to a nightclub in town. Clubs were not my natural habitat, but after ten o'clock it was the only place open for food.

Bert found us a table in the corner and we set about our over-cooked steak and veg. Tackling my lump of shoe leather that they laughingly called a steak, I noticed that one of the young girls from the dance floor had spotted me and was headed in my direction. It wasn't unusual to be asked for an autograph, I was just a little bit annoyed that she had chosen the middle of my dinner to ask for it. Trying to look completely absorbed by my steak, I kept my eyes firmly on my plate, hoping she'd get the hint and come back after the meal. I could feel her presence looming, she wasn't going to go away. Nothing for it, break off from my dinner, give her a signature, and she'd go away. But that was the furthest thing from this girl's mind. She'd got it into her head that I was going to be her next dance partner. As I would rather have my eyes poked out with a hot poker than dance in public, I refused as politely as possible. She stood, swaying unsteadily in front of me, the words not seeming to go in. I don't know what she'd been drinking but it certainly wasn't water. Suddenly she turned on her heels and let out a stream of abuse as she went off. And as far as we were concerned, that was that.

I went back to my steak and just as I was wishing there was a chain-saw handy, so I could get into it, a great shadow fell across the table. We instinctively looked up. There in front of us was the dancing girl and this Centurion tank on high heels. Mum had come back with her to help persuade me to trip the light fantastic with her little girl.

Mum's massive arms slammed down on the table, catching the edge of Bert's dinner plate, sending it soaring into the air like a UFO.

'Naw, naw, take it easy love.' Bert gave a weak smile as he tried to defuse the situation before it got out of hand.

'Shut your gob.' That dismissed Bert. 'And you,' she looked at me. 'Too good for my girl are you? Who the bloody hell d'you think you are?' And that was the relatively polite stuff that came out of that ugly cavern of a mouth.

I sat there, my mouth flapping in silence. This was my worst nightmare. A scene in public. There's no way of reasoning with someone when they're tanked up on booze. We were in trouble.

At the height of this drunken tirade, I felt Jacqueline bristle beside me. She'd had enough of this woman trying to force her

125

daughter on her man; she stood up and gave this drunken lump of lard a verbal volley. My heart sank as I tried to restrain Jackie. But she now had the bit between her teeth and was prepared to fight to the finish. Instead of dampening down the woman's enthusiasm for a battle, it just poured petrol on the fire. Before we could intervene the woman lurched across the table with murder in her eyes.

'You stay out of this, you stuck-up little bitch. It's him I want.' My legs went to jelly under the table as I tugged at Jackie's sleeve. From then on it seemed to happen in slow motion. Jackie, incensed at Fatso's ugly, foul mouth, prepared to take the gloves off and get down to bare knuckles. After exchanging a few more pleasantries, Fatso got bored with debating the issue and drew back her sledgehammer of a fist. It was aimed straight at Jackie's petite, pretty chin. It never reached its intended target. Bert, deciding that the time had come to take a hand, stood up at just the moment when Fatso's knuckle sandwich was halfway to putting Jackie in hospital for a month. He got it full on his right eye. Staggering under the onslaught and howling with pain, he reached out to steady himself, and got entangled in Fatso's flailing arms.

That was the signal for all hell to break loose. Fatso and her daughter had a bunch of male friends in the club with them, and seeing their ladies involved in a dispute was just the spark they needed to indulge their primeval instincts for violence. The club suddenly erupted into war. It was like a scene from a cowboy film. Tables went flying, chairs were used as weapons, plates crashing everywhere. It was utter chaos, with us in the firing line. Somehow the manager got us to a small office in the corner of the club. Dodging the missiles that were whizzing all round us, he managed to hustle us through the door.

Once we were cowering in the fragile safety of this pre-fabricated room with its cardboard walls, I laid into Jackie. 'Rule one in show business: whenever trouble threatens walk away from it. Not turn it into World War Three.' More out of fear of what could have happened than anger, I accused her of starting the trouble. While we screamed at each other, going at it hammer and tongs, the club was being wrecked around our ears. Just when the door to our little room looked like it was ready to give up the fight under the weight of drunken yobs baying for our blood, the boys in blue came to our rescue. They formed a wall around us and marched us out to the street, and safely back to our hotel. Bruised but not bowed Jackie resumed hostilities, indignant at being blamed, and vowed never to go to a club with me ever again.

That night we ended up sleeping in different beds.

ChapterSeventeen

ONE EXCITING ADVENTURE ON THE HORIZON WAS ANOTHER overseas tour. This time to Hong Kong, Singapore and Kuala Lumpur. But before that, The Roulettes and I had to take care of our domestic work.

Eve had put together a four-month tour, and this time we were to play a week in each town. Normally I'd be looking forward to being on the road again with all its laughs and capers, but touring didn't hold the same fascination for me as before. Now that I'd met Jacqueline Irving I didn't want to be running all over the country. All I wanted to do, was to be at home with my new partner.

There wasn't a moment I didn't think about her. We'd be on the phone to each other for hours on end. Jackie tried to come with me whenever her work with Lionel Blair allowed, but Lionel was in great demand for television. That meant that Jackie had to be on hand in London for rehearsals etc., so as the mountain couldn't come to Mohammed, I went to her. When I couldn't stand being parted from her anymore, I started commuting

128

nightly, from all over the country. It was ridiculous really, because by the time I'd got home, it was too late to do anything except crash out with exhaustion. Then in the morning it was a quick cuddle and back to Sheffield or wherever, for the evening show.

All the travel was wearing out the car tyres and me, but I didn't mind if I got to see Jackie even for only a few hours. It became a challenge to see how far I could drive to prove my love for my girl. Anyway I was enjoying – something that was entirely new to me – the feeling of being emotionally anchored. For the first time in my life I started to think about the future. Then the most horrible thing happened.

It was May 1963 and I'd spent the weekend at home with Jackie. We were woken early Monday morning by the phone jangling in our ears. Peter Thorpe – The Roulettes rhythm guitarist – was on the phone sounding very distressed. The boys were driving in their Dormobile to Sunderland, to get ready for our next gig, when they'd hit another vehicle. John Rogers didn't survive the crash. Miraculously the rest of the lads escaped with cuts and bruises. I laughed at Pete when he first told me, I just couldn't believe it. I suppose that's not an abnormal reaction when you hear news that you don't want to believe.

When I finally got to Sunderland the boys were in a terrible state. We sat around the backstage of the theatre, staring at each other in a state of shock; shrugging our shoulders, shaking our heads and raising our eyebrows in that resigned way people have when they can't comprehend what's happened to them. There was nothing to be said that could have made any of us feel any better, we just sat there in awful silence. Sadness enveloped our show that night. The Roulettes played one short, and we dedicated our music to John Rogers.

With the tour of the Far East starting in nine days' time, we had to try to fill John's place. With the help of the local paper we made it known that we were in the market for a bass player. After despairing at the motley crowd of would-be musicians who turned up, we were getting desperate. Then we got lucky: this skinny, curly black-haired Teddy boy turned up. After a quick rendition of 'Twist and Shout' he was in. It wasn't an easy situation for John Rogan our new bass player to come into, but he won everybody over in no time, with his infectious humour, and easy-going attitude. It was too weird a coincidence that he was also called John, so the boys immediately christened him Mod.

Probably because he looked exactly the opposite in his draped jacket and drainpipe trousers.

As well as travel, this business gives you a better education than anything you can get in school. In the space of eight days Mod went from never playing anywhere more illustrious than The Rink, Hartlepool, to travelling the world.

First he played the Sunderland Empire, his home theatre, in front of his whole considerable family. On the Sunday he found himself in London for a midnight charity show at the Palladium. Then the very next day, having never been on a plane before, he was on his way to Hong Kong.

What a place! In Hong Kong everything was instant. You wanted a suit? They would make you one up in a day. Anything to get your hard-earned cash out of you. The lads walked into a tailor's shop next to the hotel, while we were waiting for our cars to take us to the airport. Even though there were only a few hours left before we caught our plane, the guy promised the boys he would deliver four suits to the airport. Sure enough just before take-off, four made-to-measure, stage suits arrived, costing £30 for the whole lot.

After Hong Kong, our next stop was Singapore.

The five of us arrived at the Goodwood Park hotel in the early evening when the linen-clad ex-pats are making a bee-line for their sundowners. The Goodwood Park was a major colonial event, all hardwood floors and potted palms and slow-rotating ceiling fans with rattan chairs and tables. When we were checking in, there was an invitation to join the manager in the bar for a drink.

We walked into the lounge-bar, all sweaty and creased from the flight, to find a man in an immaculate white suit. Standing at the bar with the manager, he looked for all the world as though he'd just stepped out of the pages of a Somerset Maugham story. It was Noël Coward.

There are people – and they are very rare – who go beyond normal stardom, who seem to grow bigger than life itself, and become part of legend. In my lifetime, I can think of Marlene Dietrich, Winston Churchill, Marilyn Monroe and Gandhi. Noël Coward was in that company.

What a thrill. His air was everything that represented stardom and sophistication – a spokesman for an age that had already gone by. It was a huge privilege to meet him.

We were doing a concert in Singapore the next day, and I invited Noël Coward to come along to it. When he agreed so readily, he could have had no idea what he was in for. We sat him down right in the middle of the front row, where he gleamed like a beacon in the darkness. There he was in his white linen suit, sitting in the Happy Valley stadium, surrounded by four thousand screaming Malaysian girls, all five times younger than he was.

After a show it's normal for an artiste to entertain guests in their dressing-room. Only we didn't have one for long. We hadn't had time to kick off our shoes before Mod let out an almighty scream. His mouth opened and shut soundlessly as he struggled to get his words out. With his arm pointing to the ceiling he shot out of the room screeching like the heroine in a monster movie. It took a second for the rest of us to focus our eyes in the gloom of the underlit room. Then it hit us, the walls and ceiling, which we'd thought were painted in black, were shimmering with thousands and thousands of cockroaches. We entertained our new mate Noël in the corridor, where we'd set up a temporary dressing-room.

As soon as I saw him, I bounded up to him.

'What did you think, Noël? Did you like it?' An endorsement from the 'great man' was something to treasure. He gave me one of his inscrutable smiles, and replied, 'Unbelievable, dear boy; unbelievable.'

I was thrilled. I couldn't wait to get on the phone to Mum and tell her that Noël Coward thought I was unbelievable. Only years later, when I was doing a play with Dame Sybil Thorndike, did I realize how very dryly he'd meant it. Sybil told me, in between fits of hysterics, that every over-eager artiste who touted his opinion on their performance got the same answer from 'The Master'. What he omitted to say was whether he meant unbelievably good, or unbelievably bad.

After that first meeting in Singapore, Noël Coward sent me my first invitation to one of his famous parties at The Savoy. I felt a big rush of excitement. You knew that the party would be filled with the sort of people you wished you could meet, but never got the opportunity to. Naturally, Jackie came with me. Like me, she didn't overreact to the invitation in any way – all she did was rush out and buy herself a new Balmain dress, black and sheer and short, with a diamond shape cut into its back, with new little court shoes to match, and got her hair specially done for the occasion.

I was standing in the middle of the room talking to one of the party's lesser lights, it could quite easily have been the Queen Mum, when suddenly I looked up and caught sight of Jackie, across the room from me. She was sitting on one of the lemon-yellow sofas, waving her hands while she told a story. She looked so young and beautiful, so animated and sparkling while she held court. On one side of her was Marlene Dietrich, and on the other Coward himself. Both of them were hanging on Jackie's every word.

It was as though time had stopped for a second or two, fixing Jackie before my wondering eyes in this fairy-tale scene. There was the woman I loved and would marry. The very same Jackie who not so long ago had been scrambling over piles of rubble on a bombed-out Manchester estate. Sitting at this high-society party in her *haute couture* outfit, captivating these icons of our times. What had happened to us? We had come a long way from our beginnings.

What was remarkable about Jackie was her innate sense of taste. She'd had no previous experience of decorating and furnishing a big house. Yet after a couple of visits to Tudor Court she had its measure.

Later when we'd settled in together, she told me that she'd hated what I'd done with the house from the very first second she stepped inside the front door. She hadn't mentioned it at the time, because I'd been so proud of what I'd done with the décor and she hadn't wanted to hurt my feelings. With a few deft touches she turned a house I'd managed to make look like a dentist's waiting-room into a home.

Jacqueline decided quite early on that Tudor Court was in bad need of a make-over. With the help of my old friend Eddie Jones the hairdresser, we set about the job and did a lot of the manual work ourselves.

One night, after an evening's paper-stripping, Jackie, Ed and I retired to the kitchen for a resuscitating cuppa. It was close to 1 a.m. and as we'd been at it since late afternoon we were ready to call it a day. Eddie happened to make a casual remark about

132

the tiles that ran halfway up the walls. That was enough for Jackie, she hated them, she thought they made the kitchen look like a railway station lavatory. She'd vowed that one day they would go. Too tired to argue, I agreed to let them see how easily one of the tiles would come off. That's all Jackie needed. She became like The Demolition Man on speed. A hammer and chisel appeared out of nowhere, and she and Ed set about the top row of green lavatory tiles. It was six o'clock in the morning before the last tile hit the dust. When Angelina came down in the morning, she ran around on the spot in panic. Seeing these three people covered in dust, looking like something out of a Mother's Pride advert, and wondering where her beloved kitchen had gone. Our nocturnal building activities set in motion a six-week rebuilding programme.

Eddie came every weekend and the three of us rebuilt the whole kitchen ourselves. Cabinets, wallpapering, painting. When we came up against a problem, I'd go to one of the local building suppliers and get advice. Tongue-and-grooved pine was all the rage in the Sixties so we had pine everywhere. Halfway up the walls, kitchen cabinet doors, even the floor. We took a whole night putting that floor in, with Angie keeping us going with sandwiches and gallons of tea.

It was six-weeks' sweated labour and we loved every minute of it. Jackie and I had found a common passion: a love of 'doing-up' houses.

When Jacqueline moved into Tudor Court, things were a wee bit twitchy at first. It was one thing for 'Señor' to indulge his natural urges, quite another to move someone in full time. Angelina and Vincente, being simple well-brought-up folk, were quietly outraged by my behaviour. Vincente had a particularly annoying way of showing his disapproval. His normal routine, after I'd left the bedroom in the morning, was to collect my dirty laundry from the day before. He always knew where to find it because I slung it into the same corner of the room. When Jackie moved in, he would studiously pick up my discarded rags and totally ignore hers. They would still be there when we went to bed that night. Vincente's attitude towards Jackie drove me completely mad. It got so I was ready to tell him to take a hike. Nobody, but nobody, was going to make my woman feel uncomfortable. Fortunately, before I lost my cool and went ballistic Jackie took a

133

hand. Quietly, she took Angelina aside and got her to persuade Vincente to let Angie pick up the clothes. Vincente's civil disobedience didn't last too long once he realized that I was getting very serious about Jacqueline Irving, and Tudor Court had a new mistress.

ChapterEighteen

'LIFE THREATENED BY SOUTH AFRICAN EXTREMIST stop IN DANGER OF ASSASSINATION stop AM UNDER ARMED GUARD stop REMEMBER I LOVE YOU stop'.

I read my words back to myself as I waited for the hotel operator to get me international telegrams on the line. It seemed like only yesterday that I was so excited to be offered a tour of South Africa. And now here I was locked – for my own good – in a hotel room in Johannesburg.

Touring South Africa was one of those job offers that was manna from heaven. Opening up new markets was important. There were only so many times you could tour around Britain before people got sick of the sight of you; an overseas tour took pressure off the domestic market. The Roulettes and I were all set to go and waited with bated breath until the final details were agreed. Then all hell broke loose.

A huge row suddenly erupted in the British press about the political system in South Africa. The fuss had been kicked up by a young British singer, Dusty Springfield, who'd been doing a tour of South Africa and, apparently, at a party, had attacked racism, and the South African government for endorsing it. Claiming that she wouldn't sing in front of segregated audiences, the reports said she stormed out of the party; and South Africa.

When she got back to the UK, Dusty found herself at the hub of an enormous media furore about this thing called 'Apartheid'.

Apartheid wasn't the world issue that it was to become later, and I really knew very little about it. South African politics were the last thing on my mind in the early Sixties.

Nonetheless, now it had become an issue with the press, there was no ignoring it. Chaos reigned for a while with Ronnie Quibel, our South African promoter, saying I must come, and the British press saying I mustn't. In the face of all the publicity, the South African authorities ordered me into their consulate to sign a piece of paper stating that I would not play to mixed audiences. Of course there was no way I was going to be a party to a document like that. So I politely declined, and had the distinction of having my passport stamped 'undesirable alien'.

We telephoned Ronnie Quibel and asked him what the hell was going on. He assured us that he would sort it out with his government in Pretoria, and would also send us a telegram confirming that we would be playing to 90 per cent mixed audiences. Based on the evidence of that cable my union, Equity, gave me their blessing for the tour.

Unfortunately the Musicians Union took the opposite position and The Roulettes were refused permission to go.

Maurice Press and I left early to find a replacement backing group. When we landed we were greeted by thousands of girls, spilling over the airport balconies. It was great but the edge was taken off our excitement because of the constant harrying of the press. They didn't believe Ronnie Quibel's telegram was valid, and that I was having the wool pulled over my eyes. I suppose if I'm honest, I'd been dubious about the tour from the time I was in the South African Consulate in London. But it was too late to worry about that. There was a tour to do and a group to find. We found a Rhodesian group, rehearsed for a couple of weeks and started the tour in Jo'burg. The shows went OK but the press were still sceptical.

The next thing was the *Daily Mirror* got one of their journalists to book tickets for one of the shows. When he turned up to collect them, the box-office girl took one look at him and refused to sell him the tickets. He was an Asian. The paper came straight to me with this story. A journalist asked me why I believed in apartheid; I told them that no normal human being could possibly believe in apartheid, and I was a normal human being.

When that remark hit the papers, something ever so slightly nasty happened. I got a call at the hotel. The man's tone was all the more menacing for being polite and measured: 'Don't criticize our politics,' said this anonymous voice, 'and don't interfere in our politics. Get out of our country and stay out – or we'll kill you.' Then he put the phone down.

My legs began to feel like a used tube of toothpaste as the courage squeezed out of them. What had I got myself into? When I told Maurice, I'm not sure whether he started sweating because of the assassination threat, or because of what Eve Taylor would do to him if he lost her golden goose. Maurice called the police, and we were put under twenty-four-hour armed guard.

Jacqueline was touring the Far East with Lionel Blair. And because in those days it was necessary to pre-book an international phonecall hours before you wanted it I was standing in my hotel bedroom, waiting to send her my telegram.

What a life! All I'd wanted to do was to come to South Africa, make a few pennies and go home with a suntan. And here I was, in grave danger of being sent home in a box.

This was another fine mess Adam Faith had gotten me into.

Maurice and I had a round-table discussion about the trip so far, and decided that in spite of all the problems, we would wait until we got to Cape Town before we made a decision on whether to go home. Being British-influenced, Cape Town was reputed to be a lot more liberal about segregation than the Afrikaners of the north.

We were handed over to six armed plain-clothes policemen when we got to Cape Town. From then on, Maurice and I were isolated from anything even approaching a normal way of life. There were always two heavies stationed outside the door of the hotel suite, and another four downstairs in the lobby. If we wanted to go out, we had to clear the arrangements with the chief heavy.

I needed to go souvenir shopping – I had a list a mile long for witch-doctor masks. Our guards escorted us through the hotel, clearing the lifts of passengers before we got in. Opening up a path in front of us, we swept through the lobby.

When we arrived outside the store, Maurice and I peered out through the wire mesh reassuringly welded over the riot-proof Land Rover's windows, while the two lads in the front got out and ordered everyone to vacate the store. Once they'd cleared the whole place of customers, Maurice and I did our shopping, and went home twenty minutes later laden down with spears and antelope skins.

On New Year's Eve, we were going stir-crazy with only each other as company, so Maurice persuaded our guards, who we'd become quite friendly with by now, to take us out for a break. They knew of a seamen's dive down by the docks, and off we all went.

After a couple of hours of peering vainly into the gloom for something prettier to look at than six bored gorillas, we got homesick for our luxury hotel cells. Surrounded by our centurions, Maurice and I said our goodbyes to the lady who owned the joint, and traipsed out.

Halfway down the dark passageway to the street a sailor came lurching towards us. He recognized me, and in a thick Scottish accent welcomed me like a long-lost brother. Arms wide apart, he staggered towards me, as if to embrace me in a bear-hug. He didn't reach me! Before you could say 'Glenfiddich, haggis and kilts', he found himself being bundled up the alleyway and spread-eagled across the bonnet of the Land Rover. With two six-guns pushed up his nostrils, he was frisked, then, reassured that he wasn't the 'Jackal', our lads treated him to a touch of GBH and sent him on his happy way. God knows what he must have thought about my security arrangements when he sobered up the next day. We hadn't had time to explain to our guards that probably all he'd wanted was an autograph for his mum.

That same week I was doing an evening show in the suburbs of Cape Town. Ronnie Quibel had again reassured us that the people in the Cape were much more relaxed in their attitude to apartheid. So I was looking forward to some trouble-free time.

Chance would be a fine thing! Halfway through an afternoon show the lights suddenly went up in the auditorium. The doors at the back of the hall were flung open. Down the aisle lumbered two big bull-necked South African policemen, armed and in uniform, preceded by a diminutive usherette. She led them down

138

to the front stalls and pointed to the middle of a row. There were two little girls sitting there, who can't have been more than ten or eleven years old. They shrank down in their seats, frightened out of their wits. The policemen signalled furiously at them to come out. They sat still. At this, one of these human Rottweilers waded into the row, grabbed these children by the scruff of the neck, and dragged them out. I'd long since stopped singing.

I watched, dumbfounded, as the police dragged these girls, by now almost hysterical with fear, up the aisle and out of the theatre. Just as they went through the exit, the whole audience burst into a round of spontaneous applause.

That was it, I'd had enough. The press, Quibel, assassination threats. Now this. Two defenceless young girls being man-handled out of the theatre in the middle of the act. The money, South Africa, they weren't worth it. I turned away from the mike and walked offstage.

Maurice was waiting for me. 'Those girls are Cape Coloureds. This theatre's for whites only. Somebody in the audience must have recognized them and complained to the management.'

Ronnie Quibel came bursting into the dressing-room. 'What do you think you're doing?' he screamed, the veins sticking out on his neck like knotted rope. I wasn't listening to his ranting and raving. No more singing until something was sorted out. I was in no mood for any more of Ronnie Quibel's managed truth.

Maurice and I had met a left-leaning lawyer called Arthur East at a party a few days earlier, and it seemed sensible to get some advice on our position.

Arthur wasn't very comforting. Ronnie Quibel could sue the socks off me if I tried to leave the tour early. And there was a strong chance that I would have to stay in South Africa until the court case, which could take six months to come to trial. Arthur advised us to play it cool with Quibel until we had a plan ready.

As it happened the Secretary to the Minister of State was pass-ing by Cape Town on his personal yacht. Early the next morning Ronnie Quibel, who'd been on the blower to Pretoria, was all excited by the fact that he'd managed to get this Very Important Person to grant us a meeting so that we could argue our case for playing in front of mixed audiences.

We all went along, and got nowhere. Waving Ronnie Quibel's telegram around, I naïvely went into a great diatribe about the evils of segregation. Despite Arthur's reservations, I was convinced that it would be a piece of cake persuading them to allow me to sing in front of mixed audiences. The goon in front of me was in no mood for a philosophical discussion on South African politics with a snotty-nosed pop singer from Britain. Without ceremony, he showed us the door, advising me to keep my trap shut and fulfil my contractual obligations with Ronnie. As a parting shot he also told me that if I knew what was good for me, I would keep out of South African politics.

On Arthur's advice we let him make arrangements to get us flown to London. There was a seven o'clock BOAC flight out to London that evening. He booked me under the name of Terry Nelhams, to avoid detection. Arthur's friend, who managed Cape Town airport, had arranged to drive us to a little work-man's hut out by the perimeter track. The plan was for us to hide in there, then slip onto the plane to Jo'burg unnoticed.

The first part of this cloak-and-dagger operation worked like a dream. The aeroplane taxied up to the little hut we were hiding in, the steps came down, we got in with our luggage and took off, waving goodbye to our new-found friend.

By the time we landed at Jo'burg the news had broken that we were trying to skip the country. The press were waiting for us in force.

The airport authorities, getting wind of all this, refused Maurice and me permission to use the first-class or VIP lounges – even though we had bought first-class tickets – and made us sit out in the public concourse. To amuse us, some of our fellow travellers spat insults at us. They made it quite clear that they would prefer us to be anywhere except their airport terminal. They didn't have to tell me twice; as soon as the flipping plane was ready for take-off, they wouldn't see my 'what's-it' for dust.

Over the next two or three hours, at regular intervals, the Tannoy informed us that our BOAC flight to London was to be delayed.

Maurice went off to send another telegram to Jackie for me.

'ABANDONED TOUR stop GOING HOME stop LOVE YOU stop.'

Eventually, one of the press boys strolled up and told us they were delaying the flight because Ronnie Quibel had taken out a summons for my arrest and a sheriff was on his way to arrest me.

Suddenly the captain of the delayed BOAC flight burst

through the air-side doors and ran up to us. He'd heard the same rumour and was determined to save us. Against the protests of the airport staff, who only just stopped short of physically assaulting us, our *Boy's Own* hero hustled us through immigration and onto the waiting VC10.

Eventually, the captain, after threatening to cause a major international stink, got his take-off permission and taxied to the end of the runway. Maurice and I heaved a huge sigh of relief. We took our shoes off and loosened our ties. Then we settled back to enjoy the trip home.

The engines were revved up, the wheel-brakes released and the VC10 started its take-off run. Almost at once it jerked to an emergency stop. We were thrown forward against our straps, with the airframe shuddering around us. The door flew open and the next thing I knew, I was staring down the barrel of a rifle. A woman in a buff-coloured C&A dress was telling me, like a prissy school-marm, to leave the plane. Her sidekick with the rifle nodded to the door and Maurice and I hurried off.

She'd just finished telling me that I'd broken my contract and unless I happened to have 40,000 South African Rand handy, I was going to prison, when we heard the plane start up and take off.

Forty thousand Rand was a lot of money (£20,000), and it was a Friday evening. The banks were closed. It was looking unpleasantly likely that I was destined to spend the next few days in a cell.

My legs were so unsteady as all this went through my head, I could hardly keep going. They marched me across the grass, towards the airport buildings. Maurice was huffing and puffing behind us, with our raincoats and hand luggage.

We turned and went through the doors of the terminal spur. A desolate corridor, wide and white, ran in a long straight line ahead of us back to the public waiting areas. As we walked forward, our footsteps echoed forlornly.

The second the press saw us a great snarling roar came up out of their throats. Over and over they were shouting, 'Adam! Adam! What's happened? Where are they taking you?'

'To prison, they're taking me to prison.' If the trembling fear in my voice could have been measured on the Richter scale, it would have pushed the needle right off the top.

They charged up the corridor, a great tidal wave threatening to engulf us. The Sheriff panicked and pushed me into an empty office to our left. Maurice and the deputy shot in after us.

We'd hardly got through the door when smack! the wave of reporters and photographers crashed in after us. Bearing us physically up before them, like so many corks, until the four of us found ourselves squashed right up into the furthest corner of this little room. There was fear in the faces of the Sheriff and her deputy. It was obvious they'd never had to deal with anything like this before. They stood between me and the press; the Sheriff clutching her warrant for my arrest, the deputy brandishing his rifle.

A silence fell over the room as the press and the law faced up to each other. The poor Sheriff cracked first and called for re-inforcements: the High Sheriff of Johannesburg himself.

While we were waiting for the great man to arrive, Maurice slipped out to send Jackie another telegram.

'ARRESTED stop GOING TO PRISON stop MORE LATER stop LOVE YOU stop.'

About an hour later the High Sheriff arrived. He looked like King Kong, only white and a lot less friendly. He'd been pulled off the golf course and was not best pleased. As a matter of fact he was rock-faced with fury. A huge man, built in the Afrikaner style, he had great fists trailing at the end of arms that were thicker than my thighs. He filled the room, ploughing his way through the pack of journalists like the blade of a snowplough, scattering them on every side.

Thrusting his great red beefy face right up close to mine, he shouted for me to get up. Being a well-mannered young lad – added to the fact that I didn't want my face smashed in – I obeyed. Trying desperately to get on his good side, I mumbled an apology for ruining his golf game. He didn't even blink. 'You're going to prison. Now! Deputy, take him out!' He turned on his heel and glared at the press.

Not one person moved. The press just stood in a solid diagonal line across the room, refusing to budge an inch. At last, one of the reporters said, in a thick Afrikaner accent, 'You are not taking him. You cannot put this man in prison. You simply cannot do it! If you take him, you're going to have to take me as well.'

A voice just behind him, on his left, firmly grunted, 'And me.'

Then a woman's voice, 'And me.'

142

'And me,' 'And me,' 'And me.' They all joined in.

The High Sheriff went mad. He stormed at them, snorting with rage. Nobody wavered. He raved and he ranted. None of it had the least effect.

The Afrikaner journalist moved forward a few steps. The High Sheriff glared at him, purple in the face, but the man withstood his gaze.

'Calm down,' the journalist said. 'Think about it: if this man goes to prison, you are going to have to take us too. It'll make our country stink. Don't you see, man? Everyone in the world will get to hear about it.'

The police chief hesitated for the first time. Indecision flickered across his face. He very slowly came off the boil. And the room took a deep sigh of relief.

I spent the next thirty minutes on the phone. Fortunately I had the home phone number of Sir Joseph Lockwood, the head of EMI, in London. After listening to my tale of woe, he arranged for EMI's main man in South Africa to come to the airport with a cheque for 40,000 SA Rand.

A deal was struck; they would confiscate my passport and put me under house arrest in a Johannesburg hotel (at my expense) until Monday morning, when EMI's cheque could be cleared.

As soon as I got to the hotel, I sent another telegram to Jackie.

'NOT GOING TO PRISON stop UNDER HOUSE ARREST IN JO'BURG HOTEL stop MORE NEWS LATER stop LOVE YOU stop'.

Maurice and I fretted about the £20,000 I was in danger of losing. We had to get out of the country, before that cheque was banked on Monday morning.

We talked to Arthur East, our lawyer in Cape Town, and outlined our concern about the money. The only thing he came up with was a plan that the 'Underground Movement' had put together. They would smuggle me out of the hotel in a laundry basket, take me in a fast car to somewhere out in the Bush near the border with Mozambique, and then point me in the right direction. Someone would be waiting on the other side to take me to safety.

I did seriously consider it, for a moment or two. Unfortunately, there was one problem. Apart from the worry about getting eaten by lions as we stumbled our way through the Bush, Maurice had a dodgy ticker. He'd had a couple of heart attacks already. I didn't want to be the cause of the fatal one as we vainly fought off the lions' jaws.

We told Arthur, 'Thanks, but no thanks!' As there was nothing he could do for us, legally, and eager to watch the pennies, we agreed his fee for services rendered, and said our fond goodbyes.

On the Monday morning the EMI cheque cleared. Maurice and I were escorted onto a plane by two security men. These two 'gentlemen' sat behind us during the flight. When we landed at the first stopover outside South Africa, they flashed their badges and left the aircraft. We never saw them again. They'd obviously been told to make absolutely sure we left South African territory.

First thing I did when the plane touched down at Heathrow was to kneel down for a second and touch the ground. England! Thank God.

The second was to send a telegram to Jackie.

'IN LONDON stop SAFE AT LAST stop MISS YOU stop HURRY HOME stop LOVE YOU stop'.

There was a trial later, in Johannesburg. I did not attend. Naturally, the judge decided in favour of the promoter, Mr R. Quibel, and I was found to be in breach of contract, and, naturally, Quibel kept the £20,000.

As for me? EMI deducted £20,000 from my subsequent record royalties, and Quibel never paid me a penny for the seven shows I had done.

A travesty of justice and a legal farce? Of course. But then if you were a sparrow in a cat kennel you wouldn't go looking for justice, would you?

ChapterNineteen

FTER THE SOUTH AFRICAN MESS WAS DONE AND DUSTED, LIFE slipped into a pretty comfortable routine.

By now Jackie and I were well ensconced in Tudor Court living as a couple. There had been one major blemish to disturb our idyll. A year after we started going out together, I got cold feet. I'd always reckoned that thirty-two was the ideal age for getting hitched. Yet, here I was still in my mid-twenties, staring married life in the eyes. Scared to death of total commitment, I kicked over the traces and nearly lost Jacqueline to a very nice man who raced motor-cars. It took some major waterworks and grovelling to get the relationship back on the right track.

We spent the next few years pursuing our joint interest of doing up houses. Our interest in old houses developed into full-blown property development. It was an old story, but one that could be very profitable, if you got it right.

Jackie was blessed with an amazing talent. She could walk into a derelict house and see in a flash the potential for rebuilding it into something wonderful. With my instinct for picking out the good deals, we had the wherewithal to turn our hobby into a business. With the help of a very bright estate agent, Andrew Langton, we made some great deals. Andrew, who is one of the finest brains in the property world, found half a street in Chelsea. Within days of us finalizing the deal, Andrew had found a buyer for our street and we spent the not inconsiderable profit on furniture and paintings. Antiques had become a passion and we were beginning to build up a wonderful collection.

What we really enjoyed, though, was the refurbishing of old houses. And then selling them on for a profit. But like so many of the business ventures I was to go into later, I was never able to commit myself totally. Show business was still very much part of my life. And even though my singing career was taking me down the road of cabaret and summer season which were totally unsuited to my temperament, my ambition to act was quietly working itself into a frenzy.

Eve Taylor was next to useless when it came to understanding my dilemma. She couldn't comprehend my attitude at all: there was still plenty of money to be made. A chain of very smart provincial night clubs had sprung up all over the country, and were becoming a lucrative home for rapidly fading pop stars. So what was the problem?

I tried for a while to fit into this set-up, but my heart wasn't in it. All the money in the world didn't compensate for the desolation I was feeling. I could see myself gently slipping into the undignified role of a geriatric pop singer living on past glories. Stumbling onto a stage, with my glitter-covered zimmerframe, croaking out 'What Do You Want?' in a voice beaten to the point of extinction by years of misuse.

Something had to be done. It was time to bite the bullet and fulfil my lifetime ambition to become an actor. But, saying good-bye to the trappings of pop singing was like giving up cigarettes: easy to talk about, flipping well nigh impossible to do.

Life had its distractions, though, and one of them was the Eurovision Song Contest.

Early in 1967 my voice was going through one of its periodic 'resting' periods – I'd murdered it on a short tour of variety theatres. The throat specialist had warned me in a weary voice that had seen too many torn-up vocal cords that if I didn't follow his instructions to maintain a complete silence of at least two months, I was in grave danger of no longer having a voice to abuse.

Sandie Shaw was chosen to represent us in the Eurovision Song Contest and as I was unable to work because of my sore throat, Jackie and I went along to offer our support. Well, that, and to take the opportunity to visit Vienna where the competition was being held.

It had been five weeks since I'd uttered a word, and to overcome the problem of communicating with each other, Jackie and I had learnt the basics of sign language. We managed fine until we needed to argue. Try having a row using sign language, and you'll see what frustration really means.

One night Jackie and I were having the mother of all arguments – probably about Eve Taylor's influence over me – Jackie hated Eve with a vengeance. It was an ongoing problem, and it was practically the only thing that Jackie and I ever had disagreements about. When we finally stopped arguing, more out of frustration at my not being able to talk than having resolved the problem, I found myself proposing to her.

It was the first time I'd ever proposed to a woman and here I was, making one of the most important decisions of my life, having to do it in sign language.

Jackie accepted, also in sign language. I looked at her in wonder for a moment, then I got my fingers going like they had St Vitus' dance: 'Why the hell are you accepting in sign language? You can talk, you twit!'

We fell on the bed in hysterics, an engaged couple.

After our engagement, the trip transformed itself into a pre-marriage honeymoon. Totally unplanned, that trip to Vienna turned out to be a romantic's paradise. Everything that was good somehow came to us.

The hotel got us two very rare tickets to the little chapel attached to the Spanish Riding School. When we got there, I thought it was all pretty run-of-the-mill stuff: some old priest swinging his smoking censer, mumbling ancient Latin phrases, a rather plain little chapel, nothing to write home about. And then quite suddenly, from above and behind us came forth the sweetest, most heavenly voices I'd ever heard. A pure clear sound wafted over the balcony. It was the sort of sound that sends a thrill right down your spine and then back up and across your scalp. We were listening to the Vienna Boys Choir. Hearing those kids sing, in the context of that plain little

147

chapel, is about as close as a twenty-six-year-old atheist could get to believing in the existence of God.

Jackie and I spent wonderful days sightseeing, taking in the best that Vienna had to offer; Mozart at the Vienna Concert Hall, the Schönbrunn Palace, the Spanish Riding School, chocolate cake and vodka in the amazing, beautifully preserved Sacher hotel. A dream start to our engagement. Romance, culture, heady love-making – wonderful!

But reality was waiting around the corner. There was my future career to sort out.

I got lucky. At a showbiz party one evening Eve Taylor met a young theatre producer called Martin Tickner. Like all bright young things, Tickner was out to make his mark. Within minutes, Eve had convinced him she knew the very thing that would help him make it: me.

Before he knew what he was doing, Eve had sent Martin down to Tudor Court. Before I knew where I was, I'd signed up with him to tour in the Emlyn Williams play *Night Must Fall*. I was beside myself with excitement. The first day of rehearsals couldn't come quickly enough.

But before that day arrived, there was the little matter of a wedding to contend with.

Jackie and I had decided on 19 August 1967 for the dirty deed. The announcement of the wedding date turned the publicity spotlight on us. Interviews, photos, radio, television. Jackie hated every minute of it all. Terry O'Neill – who'd been my best friend since we were kids of seventeen back in Acton – wanted to photograph me and Jackie in bed, being served breakfast by Vincente. All of Jackie's instincts were screaming at her to refuse. But Tel, who could talk Malcolm X into shaking hands with the Chief Wizard of the Ku-Klux-Klan, finally broke down her resistance. It is a decision she has regretted ever since, and triggered her ban on all photographs in our matrimonial home.

The press got wind of the time and place of the wedding ceremony, and the result was a near-riot outside the Caxton Hall Register Office in Westminster. The police had to help us get through the crowds, it was like being back in the early days of rock 'n' roll. It didn't faze me as much as it did Jackie. I'd grown used to dealing with crowds. In fact it was rather flattering that so many people were interested enough to show up and cheer us on. Actually there wasn't a whole lot Jackie did like about having her wedding splashed all over the papers. In fact it only reinforced her deep-seated fear that marrying me was all a ghastly mistake. Years later, she told me that on the way to Caxton Hall, she'd spent the whole car journey trying to think of an excuse to turn round. Finally she came to the conclusion that it wouldn't matter anyway. If she didn't like it after a few weeks, she'd just give the Big E to marriage; and *me*.

For weeks we'd agonized over what Jacqueline would wear for the ceremony. Then, at a party one night, she caught sight of Cat Stevens in a delightful little caftan number. It was 1960s Sergeant Pepper time, so flower power and dresses for men were very much the order of the day. We took the number of his dressmaker and Jackie got herself the most beautiful, long white caftan, lined in gold silk and embroidered in gold thread. Underneath she wore gold Paisley-patterned harem pants and a bolero top which showed off her wonderful figure, and on her feet were silver Turkish slippers. She looked like a princess from the *Arabian Nights*.

The ring I'd bought for her glittered on her finger a cabochon sapphire, encircled with diamonds. Fortunately, Eve knew of a jewellery maker in Hatton Garden and I got the ring made up at half the price it would have cost in Bond Street.

We had two receptions; one for the press to give them a chance to get their photos and interviews over and done with, and us a chance of having a second reception without press interest. After sharing a drink and receiving their good wishes, Jackie and I went off to our second reception.

It was probably the sight of Jackie being so happy that drove Eve Taylor to down more booze than an Australian rugby team. She distinguished herself by getting totally drunk. And proceeded to make an exhibition of herself by giving the bloke sitting next to her a tonsil inspection for most of the evening.

Jackie looked so dazzling that every man wanted to dance with her. Which was lucky for me: it meant I managed to avoid getting up on the dance floor all evening.

For some reason we didn't plan a honeymoon and spent the day after our wedding decorating the main bedroom. There was no way Jackie was going to tolerate sleeping in a white-and-purple room that would have done credit to a Hamburg brothel. We didn't need a honeymoon to celebrate our marriage. Jackie and I couldn't have been more content, covered in spots of white paint as we did up our little nest.

Chapter Twenty

MY STAGE ACTING DEBUT IN *NIGHT MUST FALL* BY EMLYN Williams was a fantastic experience for me. There I was pitched head first into a serious stage role opposite one of the greatest-ever icons of British theatre, Dame Sybil Thorndike. The fact that she'd agreed to act with me at all always struck me as nothing short of miraculous. We opened at the Oxford Playhouse thankfully to good reviews. On the opening night, I got a telegram from Noël Coward which read: 'At last you're legitimate; your mother will be pleased.' For the first time I could remember I was happy, truly happy, in my work.

When I met her, Sybil Thorndike was eighty-five years old. I can truthfully say that she was still one of the most charming, seductive and feminine women I've ever met in my life. She lived very modestly in Swan Court, looking after her husband, Lewis, who was in his nineties and unwell. To break the ice, we arranged to meet up for tea before going into rehearsals. Halfway through Sybil's ideas on the Ancient Greek language, Lewis, who'd put his legs a bit too near the electric fire, started to smoulder. Like an over-sensitive smoke-alarm Sybil picked up the scent. Without breaking her stride, she calmly reached for a glass of water, leaned over to Lewis, and put him out.

Spurred on by my minor triumph in *Night Must Fall*, Jackie and I decided to sell Tudor Court and move to London. We reasoned that as I wanted to be an actor and most good theatre was based in London, that's where we should be. Also it wasn't fair on Jackie to expect her to continue living in a house that had seen so much of my carnal mileage.

Our first real home together was a wonderful house in Cathcart Road, Fulham. Jackie worked with a lovely interior decorator, Christopher Rowley, and between them they turned our late-Georgian townhouse into a Venetian palace. A great sweeping staircase rose up to the first floor from a circular marble hallway. A glazed inner courtyard garden tinkled with fountains, and more fountains played on the outdoor patio. They had been installed by the last owners and were plumbed with copper, so that if the mood took you, you could run champagne through them for parties.

We used to sit with the big French windows open, listening to the gentle tinkle of water. And boy, did we think we were in heaven.

And we were. But the devil inside me was not a happy bunny. Discontentment with my career was threatening to turn me into a raging insomniac.

Sick of me whingeing about something I wasn't prepared to do anything about, Jackie finally grasped the nettle. One morning, she booted me out of the house with instructions not to come back until I'd been to the office and told Eve Taylor I was quitting my singing career.

Eve's reaction when I filled her in about my plans, told me better than anything that I was doing the right thing. She might be a monster, but she was no fool. She understood, perhaps even better than I did, that my career as a pop singer was coming to an end. My latest release, 'Cheryl's Goin' Home' had just managed to crawl into the charts at number forty-six, and had shot straight back out again after two pitiful weeks. It was to be my last.

Eve's ready acceptance shocked me for a second. It made me feel unwanted, and scared. This mummy-figure, who for so long had dominated my life, was saying that yes, I could come out

151

from under her wing, and run about in the sunlight all on my own. I'd been institutionalized and needed to get used to being responsible for my own actions.

But as I drove back across town to Jackie, the fear slowly dissolved. I'd made my choice and was ready to do battle on new ground. When I got home, I flung open the door. 'That's it!' I shouted. 'I've done it! There are no more dates in the book!'

Jackie and I had spent endless hours going over the ramifications of my quitting singing. We already knew that there was no way acting, at almost any level, could bring in the sort of lifestyle we were used to having. And anyway there was no guarantee that I could ever make it as an actor.

Also, being in *Night Must Fall* only convinced me that what I knew about acting wouldn't cover a postage stamp. I needed to learn. As that was likely to take a fair amount of time, and my immediate prospects as the bread winner were decidedly dodgy, we needed a plan. We got ourselves one. A five-year plan, to be precise.

We would give it five years for me to make it as an actor. And, so as not to wipe out our savings completely, we would sell up and move to a rented house. All the cars were to be sold and replaced with cheap bangers. We'd turn all our assets into cash and invest in 'safe' shares in the stock market. We would make a complete turn-about in our lifestyle. At the end of the five years, if I hadn't made it, we would give up show business, and buy a hotel in the country. That was our plan.

Without even a second's thought, Jackie was prepared to give up a wonderful lifestyle for a very uncertain promise, at the end of a very long and uncertain tunnel. I'd married a very special woman.

Getting people to take me seriously as an actor was not going to be a pushover. I needed to show them that I was serious about my new career, and was prepared to learn the trade properly, from the bottom up. So I wrote to practically every repertory company in the country, explaining that I was giving up pop singing on such and such a date to become an actor, and did they have any parts for me.

Slowly but surely, offers trickled in. The first was from the Citizens' Theatre, Glasgow, offering me the lead in Keith

Waterhouse's and Willis Hall's *Billy Liar*. What a fantastic start. The Cit's (as it is known in the trade) was, along with the Nottingham Playhouse, one of the most prestigious rep theatres in the land.

Jackie and I stayed with the Davidsons, friends of mine from my pop-singing days. Harvey and I had played at starting a business in office furniture and computer paper. Harvey was a great salesman, and I found I could get us into almost every boardroom in the country. But we didn't make a good partnership, we both suffered from the same flaws: an overactive desire for fun and a chronic aversion, bordering on paranoia, to account books. At the first sign of a balance-sheet, we'd be off to the nearest club to revive ourselves. We just didn't possess the focus and concentration required to make good businessmen. Our business went down the old plug-hole, taking our investment with it. Happily we stayed friends throughout the whole sorry saga.

Once *Billy Liar* came to an end, everything went very quiet. It gave me the willies to be out of work. The old working-class work ethic stuff, I suppose. But at least it afforded us some time to sort our lives out. The Sale of the Century got under way.

Our house in Cathcart Road sold for £42,500, all the cars and most of the antique furniture went as well. Then we bought a second-hand Mini for £200.

We no longer had Vincente and Angelina with us. Sadly, the year before, Vincente had been killed in a car-crash in Spain and Angelina had taken their baby daughter, Rosemary, back to their village to mourn him.

Our new home was the wing of a ramshackle old Georgian house at the top of Weybridge High Street. It had enormous rooms and the world's most atmospheric conservatory, which held an incredibly old and beautiful magnolia tree. The place had been empty for years, and the carpets were threadbare, but the whole mansion oozed its own unique shabby-genteel character. The rent was sixty pounds a week. We loved it.

I then discovered the reality of an actor's life: you have plenty of time to become an expert in your chosen hobby – so long as it's a cheap hobby.

After weeks of sitting around chewing my blankets, convinced I would never act again, I decided to stop being an armchair worrier and find something positive to do. It couldn't be karate, one of my earlier passions – I'd already tried that and had given

153

it up as soon as I'd reached black belt. To go on and become really good demanded more time than I was prepared to give it. So karate bit the dust.

Golf got the vote. I'd messed about with the game when I was pop singing, but had never had the time to play it properly. Well now, unfortunately, I did have the time, more than I wanted, so I went at it like a military operation. As usual, I probably got a little too obsessed, but I needed a challenge to keep the old grey matter from sinking into terminal laziness.

First thing I did was to book a series of lessons with John Jacobs, considered to be one of the best golf teachers of his day. He had a driving range in the middle of Sandown Park racecourse, just up the road from Weybridge. Every day, for months on end, I hit hundreds of balls, spending four or five hours practising.

Going into the sand is a hacker's nightmare. So to overcome that fear, I excavated a sand-bunker in the back garden. I built it facing the house. I got to be a dab hand at bunker play, once the glazier had been a couple of times.

All the practice did pay off. Before, when I'd played golf, I'd struggled to break one hundred, but after months of unemployment, I eventually got my game down to a nine handicap.

Golf is such an obsessive game that once I'd reached the goal of single figures, it was either give up normal life and get my handicap down to scratch or try to earn a living as an actor. I gave up golf and waited for my next job in rep.

Not long after moving to Weybridge, my mum died. She hadn't been well with diabetes, but she was only sixty, and we had taken it for granted that she would live for ever. So it was a shock when she went. Dad had left her in bed where she'd died and we all trooped into the bedroom to see her. When it came to my turn to kiss her I couldn't do it. I was too scared to touch a dead body, even that of my mum. Her skin stretched like parchment across her face frightened me.

I'd only seen one other dead body and that was one of my uncles. He was laid out in the front room and us kids were dragged in to pay our respects. My aunt thought that we hadn't paid our proper respects if we hadn't touched him. With my head hardly coming up to the top of the table she pulled my hand up and over onto my uncle's face. The moment my

154

fingers touched his skin my arm recoiled as if I'd been stung. The stiffness and coldness startled me so much I screamed my lungs out. Nell rocked with laughter. We weren't welcome back there for a while. My aunt took the demise of her old man very seriously.

There was a great emptiness in my life when Mum died. She'd always been my backstop if I felt burdened by life. She was my mum and she would look after me if I was in trouble and now she was gone. It was hard losing her. I miss her even now.

We took her ashes back to the house in Weybridge, giving the urn pride of place on the mantelpiece. To keep ourselves from falling into terminal depression we took ourselves off to lunch at a local restaurant. All of us that is except my younger sister, Christine. Always very close to Mum, she wasn't feeling very good and decided to stay behind in the house.

When we came back from the restaurant, we found Chris at the end of the long, elegant drawing-room, slumped across the sofa in front of the French windows. She was pale, and her face was streaked with tears. The vacuum cleaner was lying on the floor at her feet, and she was gazing down at it with an expression of misery on her face.

She looked up at us, and then dropped her gaze sorrowfully to the Hoover. In a voice breaking with sobs, she mumbled, 'Mum's in the Hoover.'

We all stared down at her.

'I've sucked Mum up,' she whispered in a quiet, hurt, little voice, 'in the Hoover.'

She'd been frantically cleaning the place, trying to take her mind off Nell's demise, when she'd accidentally knocked the urn off the mantelpiece with the tube of the vacuum cleaner. The urn had smashed into a dozen pieces on the carpet, spilling Mum's ashes all over the place, and in her panic she'd sucked them up in the Hoover.

Sometimes, when you're in the middle of tragedy, it only takes the slightest thing to tip you the other way.

Someone smiled. That was enough. A giggle followed. Next thing, we were all on the floor helpless. Mum had hated house-work. A vacuum-cleaner bag would have been the last place she'd have chosen for her final resting place.

We couldn't leave her in the vacuum cleaner, it wouldn't have been respectful, so we did the decent thing and emptied Nell, along with the rest of the contents of the cleaner bag, under the rhododendrons.

Much later, Donald Sutherland and his wife invited me and my personal assistant, Melanie Green, to have dinner with them at their Bel-Air home in Los Angeles.

We got on to talking about the saddest thing we'd ever known. When it came to my turn, I told them the story of Christine and the vacuum cleaner. I laid the misery on thick, keeping my face absolutely straight. Eventually, I got to the punch-line: '. . . and Christine said, "I've just sucked Mum up in the Hoover." '

I stopped and looked around the table. Donald was staring at me. His face was going a strange purple colour, as he tried desperately to look sympathetic. He took a deep breath, and laid his hands flat on the surface of the table. His eyes began bulging slightly, like a bullfrog's, and the purple flush spread right across his face. It was like watching a dam that was cracked and about to burst, trying to resist the huge weight of water pent up behind it.

In the end Donald's self-control gave way. He jerked to his feet. His whole body was shaking and trembling. Pushing his chair back from the table, he grabbed his napkin and stuffed the whole thing into his mouth. Then putting both hands over his face, he shot into the kitchen and exploded. We sat there, listening to this hysterical whooping and snorting coming from the next room, in complete silence. It took him a good fifteen minutes to calm down enough to rejoin us. To be fair to him, he did try, a couple of times, to bring himself under control. But the minute he opened the kitchen door, and saw our faces, off he'd go again. When he finally composed himself enough to come back into the dining-room, we all took one look at each other, and the whole silliness started all over again.

My last job in rep was at Northampton Repertory Theatre, as Feste in Shakespeare's *Twelfth Night*.

For my first entrance in the play I had to lie on a stone bench reading poetry as I was revealed to the audience 'on the revolve'. One curtain-up near the beginning of the run, I was lying there, listening to this 'Act-tor', who was playing Orlando, droning through his speech. Of all his many gifts, his voice was obviously the one he'd been most admired for. It was one of those deep, rolling bass voices that a certain kind of old-school thespian is inordinately proud to own. My man certainly seemed to be having an affair with his. The speech seemed to go on for ever.

I could feel my eyelids getting heavier and heavier, and I kept thinking that he must finish soon, because he'd been speaking for an hour, at least. Even Shakespeare didn't write speeches that long.

The next thing I knew, something sharp was prodding me hard in the ribs. I brushed it off. It dug into me again. Then there was laughter. Loud laughter. I sat up and rubbed my eyes. The whole of the audience, in front of me, was rocking with laughter. I had been dead to the world. It got the biggest laugh of the night, and Orlando sent me to Coventry for the rest of the run.

After Northampton, we moved home again. We were itching to do up another house. As we wanted to be near some new friends, who lived in Brighton, we chose Sussex. We'd met Alex and Kate Cohen through their son Dave, who had been the drummer in my backing group. And we'd all become inseparable.

Alex found us a very nice house in Henfield, a small village ten miles north of Brighton. We took to the countryside like we were born of the sod. Of course, I had the advantage over Jackie because I'd been listening to *The Archers* since the first episode. So I knew all about country folk.

Jackie and I had found our natural habitat and the countryside was to dominate our choice of homes from then on.

As well as moving house, there was another matter to be dealt with. My years in rep had convinced me that the time had finally come to part company with Eve Taylor.

There were still a couple of months left on my contract with her and she was already sharpening her pen for another five years. After all the humiliation I'd suffered at her hands, I was looking forward with great satisfaction to leaving her. I had the confidence, at last, to get out of her clutches. And the reason I had that confidence was very simple: creatively I was now on solid ground. I no longer believed the myth she'd carefully woven into my mind over the years, which said that it was Eve Taylor or artistic wilderness. I no longer cared where I went, or what I earned, all I wanted was to act. For the first time, I was confident about where I was going.

However hard I worked at it, regrettably I could never be a

great singer. But if I worked really hard at acting, there was a good chance I'd get up to a reasonable standard.

I'd found my vocation and it was stronger than Eve Taylor.

When I hit her with the news that it was all over, she sort of convulsed. Her body went rigid like it had just had 50,000 volts shot through it. Then suddenly she burst into action. She ranted and shrieked, her eyes bulged with fury. Her body twisted and turned and twitched like a shark tearing chunks out of its prey.

Using her tongue like a blunt instrument, she pounded me with insults, telling me how ungrateful I was. I'd never work again, if she had her way. On and on she went and I felt *grrreat*!

Eve dogged my footsteps all the way down the four flights of stairs that circled the lift-shaft, yelling invective with every step.

When I reached the bottom, I stopped and looked back up the stairwell. By now her ravings had brought people from their offices and they peered over the banisters like spectators at a cock-fight. Eve stopped for a second, took in the audience, drew in a huge lungful of breath and let fly with one final volley of spite and hate.

As I walked down Regent Street, an idiotic grin on my face, I felt light-headed. Free at last! This had to be one of the happiest days of my life.

Chapter Twenty-one

W E'D BEEN TRYING TO HAVE A BABY SINCE WE GOT MARRIED.
Jackie was unlucky in being built in such a way that her
womb couldn't support a baby once it got beyond a certain weight. She'd already lost twins, but we hadn't known when
it happened that this was due to anything other than a natural
accident of a first-time pregnancy. It had happened at such an
early stage of their development that the loss was just about bear-
able. But the second time was unbearable.

A couple of years before Jackie and I married, I was doing a
summer season on the South Pier, Blackpool, when we decided
to get a dog. Jackie had her heart set on an Afghan which was
a rare breed at the time. The idea that they were trained to hunt
snow-leopards in the mountains of Afghanistan touched a
romantic chord in Jackie; or maybe she wanted it to go with her
coat.

True to form, I rang up the Afghan society: if we were going to
get a dog, it had to be the best available. 'You're lucky,' they told

159

me. 'The best breeders of Afghans are right there, where you are, in Blackpool. Wilson's Kennels, North Shore.'

Jackie and I went round to Wilson's, determined to come away with a dog. Ian, their young helper, paraded their prize dog, Shan, in front of us. He was a champion and he wasn't for sale, but they wanted us to see an example of what a proper Afghan hound should look like. Tall and elegant, he looked magnificent. Long, soft white hair falling over his deep, intense brown eyes, like a coy starlet. One look at Jackie's eyes wide with admiration was enough for me. I had to get this dog for her.

I immediately offered the boys £25 if we could take the animal home with us. Roy Wilson nearly had an apoplectic fit. Wally Walker (Roy's partner), closed his eyes in resigned exasperation, Ian laughed like a hysterical chipmunk. A king's ransom couldn't have prised that dog away from the lads. This was their famous champion, it was worth a fortune. Apparently the only thing that stopped Roy from ending my life prematurely was that Wally didn't care for the sight of blood.

Fortunately they calmed down enough for us to order a puppy from the next litter. Over the next few weeks Jackie and I spent a lot of time chatting to the boys about Afghans. And when the great day arrived, it wasn't only our puppy that had been born: so had a marvellous friendship.

It was just one of those odd meetings in life between people who seem on the surface to have little in common, but by chance get on stupendously well. Wally, sadly, is now dead. But Roy and Ian their 'young helper', who eventually became a partner in the business, are still like family, and whenever either of us feels like winding down, we go and stay with them. Their kennel complex is a haven of peace from the outside world: everything you might want is laid on – tennis, badminton, snooker, a swimming-pool, the works, all set in thirteen acres. Sometimes, when we were there, we'd simply play football all day long, or just read the papers and talk.

A couple of years after we'd first met the boys, Jackie and I – now married – were staying with them for a few days. Jackie was pregnant for the second time and we'd figured that a few days at Roy's and Wally's would be a good break for her.

The baby started coming there in Blackpool, at seven-and-a-half months. By this time, the doctors, having done some tests, had told us Jackie would be lucky to keep any child. They were right, the baby was leaving her and she could feel it going.

They rushed Jackie off to hospital. I followed, both of us in a terrible state of fear and worry. We knew that in Blackpool there were none of the highly specialized facilities the child would need in order to survive. I blamed myself for letting Jackie make this trip, when she should have been in London where the facilities for premature babies were so much better.

It was a boy. He lived for one-and-a-half hours.

Because he had lived, even for so brief a spell, I had to go and register his birth at the Register Office. Jackie had always wanted to call our first son 'Heathcliff'. I'd steadfastly refused to accept this on the grounds that the poor boy's life wouldn't be worth living from the first moment he stepped through the school gates. But now, with him lying in the morgue dead, it didn't seem to matter any more. Standing in this bitterly cold Register Office, I named him Heathcliff Nelhams-Wright, our son who'd lived and died on the same day.

Up until that moment, I'd managed to stop myself thinking too deeply about what had happened by throwing all my energy and feelings into comforting Jackie. I suppose this was a way of blocking my own anguish. But when the registrar looked up at me and asked, 'Name?' it was all I could do – really all I could do – to open my mouth and speak the terrible words. My son, as I spoke his name, became a living human being. His life, as much as his death, was a fact. I went out into the hallway, leaned my head against a pillar, and cried my grief.

'Our son' was all I could think. 'We've lost our son.'

Losing that baby was like a black smoke rolling in on our lives, a thing of bitter depression that seeped into every cavity of being, every thought. There was nothing left inside us, we were hollow people – the grief and the loss ate up everything. It was years before either of us started getting over it.

I still wonder what our son might have grown up to be like, and whether I'd have been a good father to him.

Chapter Twenty-two

EVERY SO OFTEN, SOMETHING MIRACULOUS HAPPENS IN SHOW business that makes up for all the rejection, disappointments and unemployment.

Denis Van Thal, my new theatrical agent, came to Northampton for my last performance in *Twelfth Night* and decided that it was time for me to do a television series.

I went along to his office on the following Monday. He made one phone call and put together a lunch for me and Willis Hall. Along with Keith Waterhouse, Willis had written *Billy Liar*, the play I'd been in at the Citizen's in Glasgow.

Meeting the man who'd written *Billy Liar* was the most enormous thrill for me. What a play! Sometimes I'd enjoyed performing it so much, I'd wished I was in the audience watching it. As I stepped into the hushed, darkened atmosphere of the White Elephant restaurant in Curzon Street, I felt like a village priest getting a personal audience with the Pope.

Willis turned out to be a Yorkshireman with a slightly dour air about him. At first sight he didn't look as though he could write a funny line to save his life; he was more like a book-keeper, slightly dissatisfied with his lot. I liked him the minute I shook his hand.

For three years Willis, and his writing partner Keith Waterhouse, had been storing an idea under the bed about a crooked Soho porn-king and gang-boss called Charlie Endell. His little sidekick was a totally amoral wastrel, whose name was Budgie Bird.

Willis went on to weave the magical low-life world of Budgie. A seedy small-time crook, Budgie was a danger to himself because his ambitions exceeded his wit. As a result of his un-authorized freelance activities always going wrong, he was constantly in danger of getting kicked by Charlie's heavy-mob.

On top of that, Budgie had a kid by his live-in girlfriend, a prostitute girlfriend on the side, and a wife who was a feckless nymphomaniac, always running off with other men. It sounded like nirvana to me. I wanted to live in Budgie's world.

'We're calling it *The Loser.*' Willis raised his voice, to compete with the sound of my heart pounding. 'Do you fancy playing Budgie?'

I stared at him, taking in his face. He's asking me whether I fancy playing the part which could make the last four years on the road in rep worth every minute. He was asking a question with only one answer. *Of course* I fancied playing Budgie!

Willis and Keith had a meeting with Stella Richmond, head of London Weekend Television drama, and six months later we were filming the first episode. It couldn't happen that quickly in these days of audience research and committees. In fact, it's rare now to get a series idea on the air in less than two years.

I'll always be indebted to Stella Richmond for having the courage to take an untried TV actor – me – and give him a chance in a show that was trillions of years ahead of its time.

A television series. It was a dream come true. I couldn't believe it. It validated everything. It's a great sense of achievement when a business plan works out. This was the pay-off for all those years in rep. For all those years of patience and support. Our gamble had paid off. I couldn't wait to get home to tell Jackie.

All the way home I stewed on my exciting news. I planned to break the news of Willis's offer gently, cool and sophisticated. But it was hopeless. I spotted her walking back from the paint shop in our village, opened the car window, stuck my head out and screamed up the high street. 'Jack, I've got it! I've got the bloody part.'

We lived on tenterhooks, waiting to hear that the contracts for *The Loser* had been signed. Talk about a watched kettle. My life went into a state of suspended animation, waiting for the call to tell us the ink was dry. It was agony. All our hopes and dreams were invested in that one phone call.

Luckily, something happened that was probably the only thing that could have taken my mind off playing Budgie. Jackie got pregnant again.

We'd been trying like mad since Blackpool to conceive again, and now at last it had happened. We had decided that no matter what the result, this was going to be our last attempt to have a kid. Losing babies prematurely was far too upsetting for Jackie and me. Anyway, even at the best of times, Jackie's pregnancies were very stressful. Morning sickness, dizzy spells, eating coal with mustard; and that was only me.

At last we got the big phone call. My agent Denis Van Thal, the man who had started all this six months earlier, called to say he'd signed the contract on my behalf.

The Loser was go!

Rehearsals for *The Loser* started in December 1970. With Jackie getting more pregnant by the hour. We worried like hell about it. Seven months was getting close to the danger zone. This time there'd be no travelling, and no getting caught far from a special baby unit. Jackie had been advised that for the latter part of her pregnancy she should rest as much as possible. With her penchant for being a brickie, labourer and carpenter all rolled into one, it was a hell of a job to get her to put her tools away and concentrate on helping me through our pregnancy.

By the time the first day of rehearsals arrived, Jack had about eight weeks to go.

She pushed me out of the door, with my script under my arm and my heart in my mouth. I was petrified. When I finally got to the rehearsal room in the King's Road, my knees were knocking faster than a woodpecker on speed. I felt like a new boy on his first day at school and I was frightened to death. I wanted my mum.

After the initial embarrassed introductions, I settled in. Being at rehearsals, meeting new people, reading a script, clothes, hair, was all so exciting, my concern over Jackie's pregnancy was temporarily relegated to second place.

On the fourth day of rehearsals I got home to find Jackie sitting upstairs in her dressing-room wearing her fur coat and nothing else. Standing beside her was a bloke of about thirty-five who I'd never seen before. He stood looking at me. In his hand he held Jackie's suitcase. We stared at each other. Jackie broke the uneasy silence.

Quietly she explained that while she was shopping in Brighton her water had broken. Thank God, Kate Cohen was with her and had immediately called David Evans, their family doctor.

The gods must have been watching over Jackie because we'd been lucky to get a very special man to come to Jack's rescue. Dr David Evans sat me down and tried to calm my fears. Jackie was all right and he'd stabilized her enough to risk getting her to St Theresa's in Wimbledon. We'd prebooked Jack into St Theresa's the minute we knew she was pregnant; the hospital was reputed to be the best around for maternity. After all our previous unsuccessful attempts to extend the family, we hadn't wanted to leave anything to chance.

After grabbing a bag of things for myself, I followed David and Jackie to the hospital. It was a hell of a job trying to keep a grip of myself, I kept getting fits of the shakes on that journey up to Wimbledon.

'Not again, please, not again.'

Chapter Twenty-three

THE DOCTORS WERE HOPING TO DELAY THE BIRTH BY REST AND quiet. But on the fourth day, it became obvious that Jackie wasn't going to be able to hold on to the baby. It was on its way. At seven months it was unlikely that the baby would be able to survive. David gently prepared us for the worst.

I spent the night at the hospital, trying to grab a few minutes' shut-eye between worrying about Jackie. Typically, it all couldn't have happened at a worse time. I was scheduled to report for the first day of filming of *The Loser* the next morning.

At six o'clock on 19 December 1970 our daughter Katya arrived in the world – we called her Katya because Jackie happened to be reading *Anna Karenina*. Shaking, watching this tiny thing coming out, I stood in the delivery-room gripping Jackie's hand hard – not just for her benefit, but to stop myself from fainting. All I could feel was fear. More than two months premature, Katya looked for all the world like a little pink gold-fish. So tiny, so vulnerable. Looking down at her, I reckoned her chances of survival must be almost nil.

They let Jackie have one fleeting glimpse, then whipped our baby away to an intensive-care unit in Clapham. I stood stroking Jackie's hair and still gripping her hand like a vice. We could hear the sound of the siren fading as the ambulance carried Katya away.

Jackie, exhausted by the stress and effort of giving birth, settled down with a couple of Mogadons to sleep off her weariness.

I went off for the first day of filming *The Loser*.

The location was a transport cafe on the A1. Most of the time between takes was spent in the telephone box up the road. 'Is she all right?' I'd ask for the twentieth time. 'Will she live?' All I wanted was some small glimmer of hope that there was a chance of our baby surviving.

We knew Katya couldn't be in better hands. Dr Stroud was respected all over the world for his work on premature babies. And his staff matched his dedication. They were kindness itself. Their gentle handling of all the highly distressed parents that came through their ward was so sensitive and supportive. What they couldn't do, though, was to tell us for certain that Katya would live, because they didn't know. All they could say was that for each day she stayed alive, her chances of living improved a tiny bit. This terrible suspense went on for five weeks, with us never knowing whether she would live or die.

One evening I was looking down at this tiny little mite in her strange little plastic box called an incubator, set about as she was with feeding pipes and breathing pipes and goodness knows what. With her spikey white-blond wisps of hair and pale blue eyes, when you were lucky enough to catch them open, she looked like a baby chick who'd lost its mother. I wanted to pick her up in my arms and protect her from the world.

I called a nurse over and asked if I was allowed to touch the baby.

She nodded and I gingerly threaded my hand through the covered hole in the side of the incubator. Petrified of breaking her in two, I delicately brushed Katya's face. Instinctively she raised her hand and caught hold of my finger, gripping it with a determination that showed how strongly she wanted to live. No matter what anyone thought, this little thing was not about to give up the fight. Tears pricked the back of my eyes and I sat there, petrified to breathe, in case she let go and went back to sleep. As long as she had hold of my finger, I could feel the life in her.

After a couple of days' filming on the A1 we moved into the King's Road rehearsal rooms. Later in the week Terry O'Neill arrived a few minutes early for our lunch date, and stood watching the end of a scene that I was doing with Lynn Dalby – who was playing Hazel, my live-in girlfriend.

Five minutes later, as we were walking to the restaurant, Tel launched into a whole diatribe on where he thought I was going wrong with my playing of Budgie.

It can sometimes be a very small thing that gives you the key to the personality of a character. Laurence Olivier would say that something as seemingly irrelevant as a pair of shoes could work the trick, or it might be the way someone lights a cigarette. For me, the trigger was walking along the King's Road watching Tel's shoulders shrugging. The cheekiness of it was the essence of Budgie. On that short walk, Tel had given me my character.

That evening Jackie and I sat in the kitchen of a friend's house and talked about the realistic possibility of giving up smoking. The doctor had told me that if Katya did suffer any complications later in life as a result of her premature birth, they'd most likely be respiratory. So it wouldn't do to encourage her to smoke.

I hadn't caught breath for half an hour, piously spouting on about the horrors of smoking, when Jack called my bluff. Without a word, she very deliberately withdrew her Peter Stuyvesant from between her full pouting lips. Holding my gaze through the mist of smoke, as she let it spill languidly out of her mouth, she slowly ground the filthy weed out in the Casa Pupo ashtray.

It was a magnificent gesture. Jack needed nicotine like a car needed petrol. She couldn't move in the mornings until she'd had a lungful of smoke. And here she was, making the ultimate sacrifice for the sake of her daughter. There was nothing for it, I had to rise to the occasion. My half-smoked Gitanes tipped found its final resting-place in the ashtray beside Jackie's king-size.

Four days later, she was back on the cigarettes. I'm still off them. And Katya smokes like a steam train. So much for sacrifices.

After five weeks in the incubator we were allowed to take Katya home. Life was not at all bad. We had a healthy baby, and the filming for *The Loser* series was coming up to everyone's expectations. Which was just as well, because after we'd finished five or six episodes, ready for transmission a few months later, a buzz went round the studios. London Weekend Television, the company we were making the show for, had been taken over.

The new owner was a mysterious Australian tycoon. His name was Rupert Murdoch. A shiver of apprehension went through us when we heard the news. Supposing he didn't like the show? If he didn't, that was it, *finito*. He could pull the whole series and Jackie and I would be buying our country hotel and I'd be doing a Basil Fawlty five years before he'd been thought of.

When this Australian arrived, he immediately sent for Stella Richmond. He wanted to look at all the programmes they were producing. For several days on end, they sat there in the viewing-room. Fortunately, we passed muster, but our title didn't. Murdoch insisted that no-one would want to watch a show called *The Loser* and ordered it to be retitled *Budgie*. Verity Lambert had misgivings about reshooting the titles, but under pressure she came up with the idea for Budgie to be chasing money. As for me, the change of title could hardly have been better: right out of the blue it had become 'my' series.

It was a little disappointing that, after the six episodes, *Budgie* still hadn't caught the public's imagination enough to put it in the TV charts. After being out in the cold for three or four years, with people thinking that I'd died, I was looking for this major new television series to launch me back into the sunshine. And here it was creeping out like a hedgehog at dusk.

Then, quite suddenly, right after episode six, *Budgie* came into the charts at number seven. It had been taking its time, building its audience by word-of-mouth. It was such an unusual show for its day, bearing on things like sleaze, prostitution, theft and punishment beatings – and yet managing to be funny about them. It wasn't that surprising if people were taking a little time getting used to it.

Now, when you look at it with the benefit of hindsight, you can trace a whole strain of British television drama back down the line to *Budgie*. It was no coincidence that Verity Lambert went on to produce its greater and even more successful offspring, *Minder*.

It's not often writing of that quality comes to an actor, and I couldn't wait to get each script. Many's the hour I spent parked in a lay-by, too impatient to wait until I got home, reading the next episode.

Everybody who watched *Budgie* was convinced that because the dialogue was so authentic we actors were making it up as we went along. But in all the twenty-six episodes we made, I doubt there were three words that we changed. Keith and Willis were at the height of their writing partnership and we all benefited from their genius.

Chapter Twenty-four

OBSESSION IS A TERRIBLE BURDEN. I DIDN'T WANT TO DO IT, I didn't go looking for it, I didn't have the time for it; but once I was in it, there was no getting out. As far as I was concerned, the amazing voice I was listening to was the business, and sitting there in my drawing-room, I knew I wasn't going to rest until the whole world agreed with me.

Just after filming started for the second series of *Budgie*, my mate Dave Cohen had been holding auditions in Brighton and felt he'd come up with rock's next superstar. He'd managed to negotiate a recording contract for the group and wanted me to give it the once-over.

Reluctantly, because I was in the middle of learning lines for the next episode of *Budgie*, I agreed to look at the contract and listen to a tape of songs he'd written with the singer in the band.

This is usually the sort of situation that people in show business hate. I'd listened to thousands of tapes of would-be stars, and been decidedly underwhelmed by every one. And here was my friend all excited with his new discovery about to be disappointed by my inevitable response. Talent being so thin on the ground, it would have been a miracle if this was the one in a thousand that had potential. I didn't want to deflate my friend too much, so as I read the contract I was trying to think up ways to soften the blow. Dave put the tape on.

As I listened, the small hairs on the nape of my neck began to rise. It was magical! A couple of days later Dave and I had a joint company recording, publishing and managing the newly named 'Leo Sayer'.

Between rehearsals for *Budgie* I spent most of my time on the phone negotiating deals for our new singer. We set up a recording contract with Warner Brothers; that didn't work out. Then we did a record deal with The Who's management, Chris Stamp and Chris Lambert, and that was an even bigger disaster. It went so badly wrong that Chris Lambert and I almost had a stand-up fight in Baker Street, outside the recording studios.

It was difficult to get someone to part with a huge pile of dough without them wanting a say in how it was spent. But already the 'obsession' was on me, like a witch-doctor's spell. I was more and more convinced by the minute – and the bank overdraft – that Dave and I were the only people on earth who knew what Leo Sayer needed.

I'd heard the magic on the original demo tape of Dave's. It was a fresh original sound that Dave with his tunes and Leo with his lyrics had created. Coupled with Leo's amazing voice, they were an unbeatable creative force. I wasn't going to allow anyone to undermine that. To keep total creative control, I decided to finance Leo Sayer's first album myself.

Big mistake.

I had been out of the recording world for so long, I had no idea what it cost to make a modern rock album. Even without the promotion and manufacturing costs, I found myself staring at the thick end of £70,000. Within a short space of time, I was in so deep that Leo Sayer's recording career either became a huge success or I was in grave danger of visiting Carey Street.

Apart from recording costs, there was stuff like sound equipment, instruments, transport, etc., to contend with. I got it into my head that Leo Sayer was the best, and I wanted him to have the best. It was spend, spend, spend.

I dived in with both feet and ended up in quicksand. The more I struggled to keep the costs under control, the more I sank up to my armpits in bills. It took every spare minute I had, and every penny I didn't have. It ate money and time. It became a gamble that had to pay off.

Jackie thought I was insane. Not because of the money I was getting through, but because managing a rock singer was interfering with my acting career. She was right. I was so bogged down by the constant demands of this new career I'd got myself into, I was in danger of letting it encroach on my acting. I was determined to keep both activities separate, but with the financial burdens bearing down on me it was sometimes difficult not to take Leo Sayer into rehearsals. There were times when I didn't know who I was, Budgie or Colonel Parker. The two lives were in danger of bashing into each other and it was getting far too much for me to cope with on my own. I needed help.

Dave couldn't spare the time to organize things at the office we'd got ourselves in Brighton, he was needed to write the melodies to Leo's lyrics. We employed a secretary. She was a terrific girl called Paula Warren. She got us organized but couldn't help with management decisions.

When I look back now, I find it difficult to believe that I'd spent four years and a large chunk of Jackie's financial security working towards my big acting break, and here I was letting my obsession with an unknown singer threaten that chance. I must have been two sandwiches short of a picnic. What I should have done right there and then was to forget management, forget Dave, and forget Leo Sayer and get on with my acting career. It had turned out just how we could've imagined it. What did I need all this nonsense for? I've had a go at analysing my actions and motives for abandoning a flourishing acting career to manage an unknown singer. The only answer I've come up with is that it's typical of me. Once I put a foot on the mountain I have to climb it, and there's no stopping until I get to the top, or fall off in the attempt. If I'd wanted to avoid this chaos I'd got myself into, I should have stopped listening to Dave's tape after the first four bars. But as I hadn't there was no other route open to me, I had to see my new challenge through to the end.

Jackie wasn't best pleased with me in these Sayer days. Not only was she angry at me for threatening to sabotage my acting career, her patience was wearing thin because she and Katya had hardly seen me for weeks. I was spending all day on the *Budgie* set, and all night in the recording studio with Leo and Dave. I didn't suspect it, but I was about to get kicked into touch.

One morning around 5 a.m., Dave brought me back from Olympic Sound Studios in Barnes where we'd been putting some finishing touches to Leo's first album. As I walked up to the front door, I noticed a familiar object sitting on the top step – it was my suitcase, fully packed. Flipping heck, I was locked out. I rang the bell and knocked for half an hour, but it was no use: Jackie's patience had finally given out.

It's a tribute to Dave's generous and hospitable nature that for the next four weeks he slept on a makeshift bed in his box-room no bigger than a cupboard, and gave me his bed. I was comfortable enough in the master bedroom, but after a week, even I was beginning to feel guilty about Dave sleeping on a two-foot-wide camp-bed.

Jackie wasn't a vindictive woman, she was just firing a shot across my bows; it was no more than I deserved. I finally persuaded her to meet up and talk. If I promised to mend my ways, I reasoned, she'd let me go back and everything would be back to normal. I prepared the argument for my defence as I drove to meet her, even though there was nothing much I could say, except 'Sorry'. In spite of, unjustifiably, suspecting that my nocturnal activities were not all confined to the recording studio, she let me say sorry for my unsociable behaviour and allowed me once again to share the matrimonial bed. For the first time in a month, Dave got a good night's sleep.

Things settled down, and for a while I tried to be a good lad and live a normal life. But Leo's career was demanding more and more of my time. His first single was almost ready to be released, and there was a lot of work to do with our new record company. I'd gone to the States to make a deal with the head of Warner Records, Joe Smith, for them to take the American market, and for Chrysalis to have the European side. I'd already had experience of Warner's operation and I wasn't impressed. Now that Leo's record launch was imminent and there was a lot to do, we knew we had to find help. But that was easier said than done. Then, quite by chance, Dave and I bumped into a man on the train.

We had been commuting up to London so regularly that we'd got on talking terms with some of our fellow commuters. One girl we became particularly friendly with was a call girl who worked from a service flat in Kensington High Street. One morning on the 9.20 to London Dave and I were chatting to our lady friend – probably about how her kids were doing at school – when the compartment suddenly went dark. It was as if there had been a sudden eclipse. Instinctively, we all looked up. Bending his head to get into the compartment, this immaculately dressed, folically embarrassed, tower of a man filled the doorway. He'd spotted Dave, an old acquaintance, as he was passing up the carriage, and had come in to say hello.

Very occasionally in life, you meet someone who almost at once seems like a friend you've known for years and years. Andrew Tribe was one of those people. Andrew had been on the Deep Purple management team, helping to get Purple Records up and running. We exchanged notes about the rock business and by the end of the train journey he'd agreed to talk about coming on board. His function would be managing those little incidental details of an up-and-coming rock singer's career – like getting him around the world on a major tour and making sure we lost as little money as possible.

Having Andrew on board took some of the pressure off Dave and me, but it didn't cure our money worries. In spite of Andrew's efforts to keep spending under control, the expenses kept building up relentlessly. To finance it all, I was slowly stripping my house of its treasures. In the first three years of managing, publishing and recording Leo Sayer, I spent the entire sum of Jackie's and my savings, including the nest-egg we'd put by in case we wanted to run away and start a hotel. I took Impressionist pictures off the wall and sold them, I sold all the Georgian silver we'd collected – the whole thing took over and nigh-on cleaned me out. I learned the hard way that nothing uses money faster than launching a rock act from scratch.

But quite soon, even though I had promised to calm down and delegate more of the Leo Sayer business to Andrew and Dave, and generally to buck up all round, I found it impossible to do so. I was like a greyhound in a field full of hares, chasing everything and anything that moved, and in severe danger of a nervous breakdown.

Something had to give, and sure enough, something did.

ChapterTwenty-five

I HIT THE TREE AT ABOUT THREE-TWENTY IN THE MORNING.
The second series of *Budgie* had been completed and I was
working full time on Leo's management. We were doing a
gig in St Albans and my mission that night was to sack Leo's
group. In the time that I'd been managing him, Leo had moved
into a different league from the people he started out with. I
didn't feel that the band were up to his standard any longer, and
as his manager it was my job to deal with the difficult bits. Firing
people is the worst job on earth. Anyone who enjoys it should
seek professional help. I hate it.

The group-members were naturally very upset, Leo was very
upset, and I was very upset. I drove Leo and his wife, Jan, back to
Victoria Station, so they could get the last train back home to
Brighton. As she got out of the car, Jan bumped her head. 'Oh,' I
said, 'be careful!' That was the last thing I remember with any
clarity, until two weeks later when I found myself being driven in
an ambulance through the Sussex countryside.

I'd spent fourteen days in ward G4 of Crawley Hospital,

176

About to get duffed up on *Budgie* (note the 'Budgie jacket').

Getting duffed up... by John Rhys Davies.

And getting told off by Ian Cuthbertson.

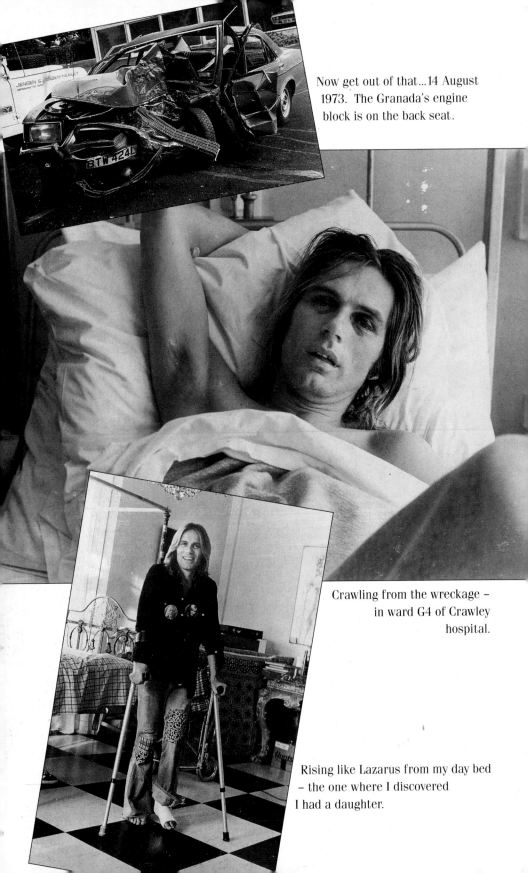

Now get out of that...14 August 1973. The Granada's engine block is on the back seat.

Crawling from the wreckage – in ward G4 of Crawley hospital.

Rising like Lazarus from my day bed – the one where I discovered I had a daughter.

Don't mess with me, kid... Katya, tender in age, but not in will.

Katya with Jackie in bed.

I survived the cemetery –
just. Post-crash, 1974.

On the set of *Stardust*
with David Essex.
That's me sitting right at
the back.

A scene from *Stardust*:
Mike Menary rolling up with
Jim Maclaine.

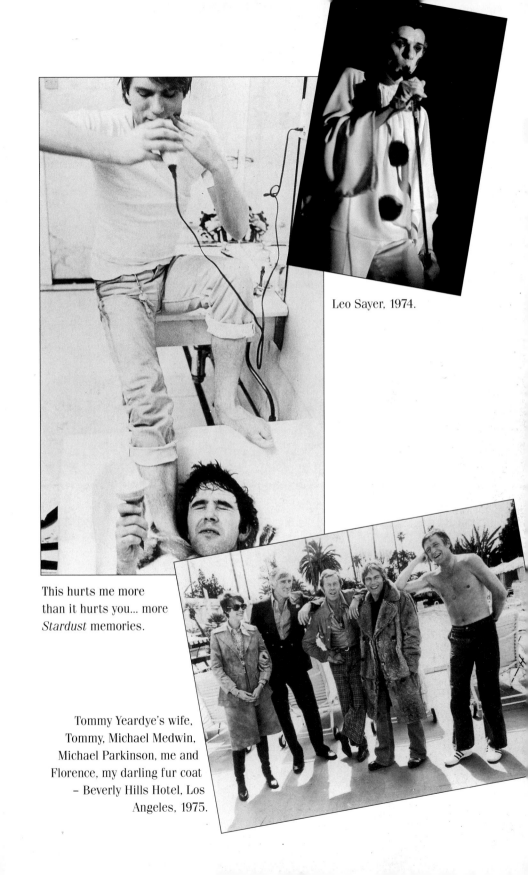

Leo Sayer, 1974.

This hurts me more than it hurts you... more *Stardust* memories.

Tommy Yeardye's wife, Tommy, Michael Medwin, Michael Parkinson, me and Florence, my darling fur coat – Beverly Hills Hotel, Los Angeles, 1975.

Seventies Man – there's Florence again.

Crowhurst Place, 1979

At home with Paul and Linda McCartney plus children, Michael Jackson, Jackie, Angelina and Katya and the boys from Blackpool – Wally Walker, Roy Wilson and Ian Hodgson.

With Paul McCartney, 1980.

Jackie's riding instructor, Paul Redmond, with Jackie, Katya and me, 1980.

Working hard at my desk in Fortnum & Mason's, 1980.

This is what the helicopter
looked like before I bent it.

With Roger Daltrey and John McVicar, Cannes 1980.

Rehearsing *Alfie* with director
Alan Parker, Liverpool Playhouse,
October 1983.

No such thing as a private life?

CHRISSIE LOVES ADAM FAITH

Chris Evert, 1984.

THE MAN who designed tennis ace Chrissie Evert's wedding dress revealed last night that former pop idol Adam Faith broke up her marriage to John Lloyd.

Tennis fashion king Teddy Tinling said: "Chris and Adam are infatuated with each other.

By PETER BOND
and MIKE ATCHINSON

"I'm afraid poor John is out of the game."

Mr Tinling 73, said 43-year-old Faith had been secretly dating Wimbledon star Chris, 28, for more than a year.

The couple are now believed to be togther at the tennis ace's home in Fort Lauderdale, Florida.

John Lloyd, who wed Chris in 1979, is also in America preparing for a big tennis tournament in Memphis, Tennessee, next week.

American Chris — three times the Wimbledon ladies champion — and Briton John shook the tennis world at the weekend by announcing they had started a trial separation to try to save their five-year-old marriage.

But Mr Tinling said: "Their life together is now over.

"The relationship between Adam and Chris

Continued on Page Two

Tennis tycoon tells of affair

With Elton John, 1985.

DID OVERWORK BREAK ADAM'S HEART?

Fighting back ... after his crash

He put faith in his fitness

HE IS tanned, trim and fantastically fit for 47. And only last week Adam Faith was pounding round London's Hyde Park on one of his regular seven-mile runs.

Now the Sixties pop idol turned actor and businessman is recovering from major heart surgery in a £345-a-night room in the exclusive Wellington Hospital.

Faith, in hospital under the assumed name Terence Wright—his real name is Terence Nelhams—went for a routine medical check-up on Friday.

He was admitted for heart surgery the same day.

A business contact who saw him just beforehand said: "There was no clue that he might have been ill. He looked in great shape—as he always did.

Fight

"He doesn't smoke and ̶doesn't drink and he's ̶̶̶ and fit."

̶ wife, Jackie, ̶̶̶ancer, was by ̶̶ the hospital ̶̶ next door to ̶̶cket Ground.

̶ only allowed ̶̶itors in the first ̶̶s—hospital staff ̶ to turn away ̶delivered by a ̶̶̶er.

̶ be the second ̶ has had to fight ̶̶ back to health ̶assive surgery.

̶bad car accident in ̶ he broke every ̶down one side of ̶dy. Surgeons took ̶urs just to put one ̶s ankles together

By ROSLYN GROSE

to myself I could do it again."

Faith was due to go on holiday this week after starting gruelling rehearsals for a new musical based on his hit telly role as Budgie.

He has been learning tap dancing and taking coaching to polish up his singing style.

But that was a doddle to the man who helped launch a Sports Council campaign to encourage people to take up regular exercise.

Even when it is raining, Faith clocks up his daily jogging miles on a £2,500 electric treadmill installed in a corner of his luxurious Knightsbridge office.

Smart

Before hitting the headlines, the Cockney teenager sold them—in his first job as a £3-a-week newspaper boy.

Now he is a millionaire who made his first £100,000 at 19 with the No 1 hit What Do You Want If You Don't Want Money?

His latest venture is Faith, a financial management company set up to help rich stars get richer by shrewd investment and smart career moves.

Faith says: "I'd have

now! I've had to wait till 47 to own the world."

A workaholic, he has had to turn down an American film offer, is considering a TV detective series, making Budgie, as well as running his company.

"There aren't enough hours in the day," is a favourite Faith saying.

Now it looks as if he might have over-stretched himself—though Adam denies that his over-achieving style puts any pressure on him. He says:

"Part of the reason I stay fit is so that I'm mentally and physically on' top."

But being fit is not enough to save anyone from heart disease, according to a top British expert.

Professor Desmond Julian, medical director of the British Heart Foundation, says: "The sad fact is that heart disease can strike anybody.

"But it is more likely to strike if you don't keep fit."

The *Sun* breaks the news of a 'broken' heart.

Budgie the Musical, first-night party with Seb Coe, 1988.

With Don Black, Ronnie Corbett and Jimmy Tarbuck at the same bash.

Linda Agram, me and Helly (Helena Sykes, Kat's best friend) in the Serengetti, 1988.

Morning ablutions, Jackie and Katya, Sand River, Masai Mara, 1988.

En famille, Budgie the Musical, first night.

With the then chancellor, Nigel Lawson, his wife, Thérèse, and Jackie, after a party in aid of Great Ormond Street Children's Hospital.

The *Daily Mail* heralds the 'Faith in Money' column, 25 November 1988.

The old proverbial hits the fan – and I come out covered in it. The Levitt débâcle, January 1991.

CRASHED · 'LUCKY ESCAPE' · LOST £2.2m · SPORTING LINK

End of an empire: Levitt is charged with stealing £665,000; Winner got £1m back; Forsyth lost £2.2m; Coe introduced celebrities

Adam Faith under fire for link to failed tycoon

by Maurice Chittenden and Jeff Randall

ONE of Britain's leading film-makers has accused Adam Faith, the 1960s pop star turned financial adviser, of persuading friends and associates to invest in the financial empire of Roger Levitt, which has since collapsed.

Michael Winner, director of Death Wish and Bullseye, agreed to hand over £1m to be invested by the Levitt Group, one of Britain's leading financial services companies until it crashed with debts of more than £35m last month.

Yesterday Winner, who

wealthy celebrities as potential clients. "I was lucky to escape," he said. "I deeply regret not going public on this before because it might have helped others to save their money."

His criticism follows the downfall of the flamboyant Levitt, who once boasted of being the City's top financial salesman, selling insurance, pensions and investments to

business friends. He has managed Leo Sayer, the singer, and acted with David Essex and Anita Dobson. Until shortly after the stock-market crash of 1987, Faith ran a Knightsbridge-based investment company that helped sports celebrities including Sebastian Coe and Tessa Sanderson.

Winner, who lost £50,000 on Faith's previous venture, said the former singer — whose first hit in 1959 was What Do You Want If You Don't Want Money? — should

£40,000 a year from The Mail On Sunday, writing a weekly column called Faith in the City.

His job with Levitt was to introduce wealthy individuals who needed advice. They were offered a range of financial services, with promises of a return of up to 25% on their capital.

Winner said: "Adam Faith rang me in late 1988 or early 1989 and told me how he had met this genius. According to Adam, he was the most wonderful thing since sliced bread.

With my oldest friend Terry O'Neill in 1991.

Well, it seemed like a really good idea to start with... The fateful 'I can make you into a millionaire' headline.

The Mail on Sunday, April 19, 1992

FAITH in the City

How to turn £6,000 into ONE MILLION!

RIGHT folks, hang on to your proverbials. I have something absolutely sensational to tell you.

I've found a bloke in the City who reckons it should be possible to turn £6,000 into a MILLION in ten years.

That's right, £1,000,000 —

a cup of Darjeeling at the Savoy last week. But this idea comes from a very credible source — he is a top-rated technical analyst.

According to him, it involves aiming to double your money each year.

Scheme

After a couple of hours with him, I am just as convinced as he is. And I am going to give him his chance to show Faith in the City readers how to become

weeks to give you time to get your act together.

In the meantime, if you fancy having a go, there is work to be done.

1 Find £6,000 before May 18: Raid granny's mattress, pawn your Sony camcorder, but please don't get carried away and borrow the cash. The Number One rule when buying shares is: The your own money.

2 Start a self-select PEP: (ask a bank, stockbroker, independent financial adviser) If

fair amount of buying and selling, the cost could be prohibitive through a normal share service.

So you might want to take advantage of The Mail on Sunday cheap share-dealing service, using a self-select PEP.

Get on to them pronto, because you will need to set up an account. Phone 0891 123891 (36p a minute cheap rate, 48p other times).

OK! It's 21 days to lift-off. From May 10 you will be

Love Hurts, Zoë Wanamaker and 'our' baby, 1992.

Hard at it filming *Love Hurts* in Israel.

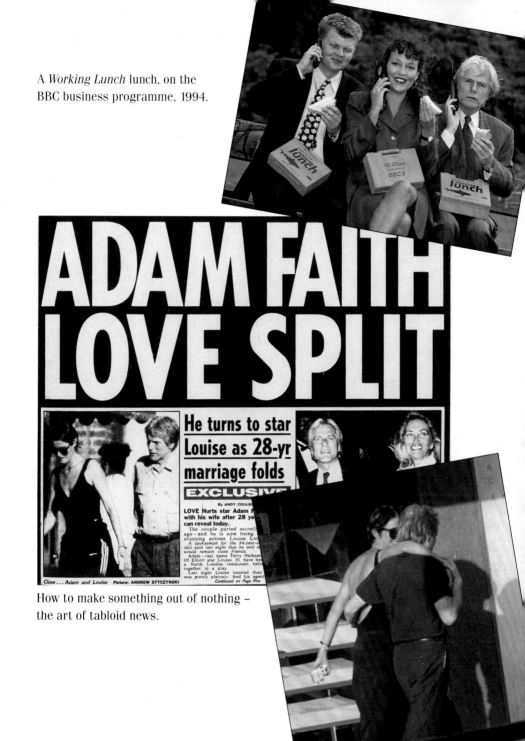

A *Working Lunch* lunch, on the BBC business programme, 1994.

ADAM FAITH LOVE SPLIT

He turns to star Louise as 28-yr marriage folds

EXCLUSIVE

By ANDY COULSON

LOVE Hurts star Adam F[...]
with his wife after 28 ye[...]
can reveal today.

The couple parted secretl[...]
ago – and he is now being [...]
stunning actress Louise Lo[...]
idol said last night that he and [...]
would remain close friends.

Adam – real name Terry Nelham[...]
Of Elliott star Louise, 25, have be[...]
a North London restaurant befo[...]
together in a play.

Last night Louise insisted their [...]
was purely platonic. And his agent[...]
Continued on Page Five

Close...Adam and Louise Picture: ANDREW STYCZYNSKI

How to make something out of nothing –
the art of tabloid news.

Just good friends...with Louise Lombard.

Katya graduates from Harvard
University – I broke through
security to sit behind her, hence
the astonished look on her face.

My all-time favourite
photograph of Katya
and me.

covered from head to toe in pipes and blood-transfusion bottles. To this day, I still don't know what happened that night, and the facts of the accident told me very little.

At 3.20 a.m. on 14 August 1973, four miles from home, passing through a village called Cowfold on the A21, I'd suddenly veered off the road and driven smack bang straight into a tree. The car had folded up like a concertina, with its engine-block coming to rest on the back seat, crushing everything inside the car on its way through, including most of my left side.

Although, in those days, seat-belts weren't compulsory, the ones on the Ford Granada Hertz rental car I'd been driving were very comfortable; so I'd fallen into the habit of putting mine on. That belt had undoubtedly saved my life.

The engine pushed my left ankle up into my lower leg, splitting the shin and crushing the ankle joint; it broke all but one of the ribs on my left side, smashed my left arm, ruptured my spleen, and perforated my bladder. Oh, and part of the lining of my abdomen disengaged from the muscle wall. My face was smashed up, with two great big black eyes, cuts and bruises all over the place, and some of the windscreen glass had taken a fancy to my face. I also had severe concussion from a blow to the head, resulting in my loss of memory. I can't say that I had a particularly bad time at the hands of that accident. As I couldn't remember anything about it, I breezed through the recovery without a worry in the world. Jackie told me that I must have been in considerable pain, because my craving for morphine got to be so bad, the hospital decided it was a wise move to wean me off it. Better to live with the pain, than turn out to be an opiate junkie.

I spent eight hours in the operating theatre, five of which the surgeon devoted to rebuilding my ankle and leg. Afterwards, he said he'd never seen such a bad crush injury to a leg, and had at first thought he'd have no choice but to amputate. I asked him why he'd gone ahead and tried to save it.

'Well,' he replied, 'I looked down and thought, I've got Adam Faith here on the slab; I'd better do a good job, because he's going to be a walking advert for my skills ever after, and I don't want him to be a bad one.' Painstakingly, and with infinite care, he'd screwed all the shattered splinters of bone back together.

That crash knocked me right off my perch, bringing my whole life to a complete halt for about four months. Despite my efforts to sabotage my acting career it had, up to then, been showing every sign of taking off. The second series of *Budgie* had been more successful than the first and offers were rolling in, but there was no way I was going to be ready to work for some time.

After disrupting the hospital for two weeks with my fussy eating habits, they released me early on the condition I employ a twenty-four-hour nursing service.

One strange and wonderful thing happened to me as a result of the accident: I discovered that I had a daughter.

Although Katya was already about three years old by then, I hadn't built up much of a relationship with her. By this, I mean I didn't tell her at least once a day that I loved her and was glad to be her father. I didn't take her on my knee and read to her. I didn't play all those rough-and-tumble games all small children want to play with their parents and that mean far more than anything you can ever buy them; and I didn't swing her up into the air or tickle her until she was helpless with laughter. Like many men, and perhaps nowadays many women, I convinced myself I didn't have the time for that kind of thing, and that in any case it didn't matter. Wasn't earning lots of money the best way of showing that you loved your kid?

When I arrived home, encased in my plaster shell, I couldn't get up the stairs; so Jackie and the nurse made up a bed for me in the drawing-room. I was slowly getting better, but the pain kept me awake much of the time, despite all the powerful analgesics I kept stuffing down my throat. I lay there, most of the night, staring at the ceiling, unable to move, just thinking.

As the morning light started to filter into my temporary hospital ward, on my first morning home, I was staring blankly up at the ceiling wondering what it would have been like to have no leg and therefore no pain, when I heard a pattering sound. I turned my head to the side and was amazed to see this small figure padding towards me.

Katya had woken and decided to explore.

She hadn't seen me much in the three years since her birth. What with *Budgie* and Leo Sayer I hadn't spent a whole lot of time getting to know her.

Her tiny bare feet padded over the black-and-white tiles and up to where I was lying. I looked down, and there was this scrap of a child with a great big grin of welcome and pleasure all over her face, her head just about up to the level of my own. This was my little girl.

I hauled her carefully up onto the bed, pausing only to groan a bit, and she sat there happily in my arms, chattering away until the rest of the house came to life.

This early morning meeting became a ritual and was the high-light of my recovery. I have absolutely no idea what we talked about. I was just happy to lie there and let her voice tinkle over me. She'd climb all over me as if I were a playframe, curious about my plaster. I had a knitting-needle, which I used to shove down under the plaster when the itching got too bad. When she found out what this was for, Katya would slip her skinny little arm down beneath the casing on my arm and scratch away with her tiny fingernails.

As the days went by, I gradually got to know this precious thing that had had such a struggle to survive. I slowly began to appreciate and to understand what it meant to have a child. Up to then, I think I'd treated my daughter pretty much as my parents had treated me: you've been born, now get on with your life.

Those weeks with Katya taught me different. She was my company, my entertainment, and my official scratcher-in-chief. We'd sit and chat, she'd sing me a rhyme or a song she'd learned, get me to read her a little book, and I learned that with children as with other things in life, you get back what you put in. It was worth going through that accident just to find my daughter.

Once they'd let me out of the wheelchair and cut off some of the plaster, the doctors told me I'd better come to terms with the fact that I'd never walk again. If I did walk again, they said, it would be with a pronounced limp. As soon as I heard this, I made up my mind that not only would I walk again, but I'd walk normally – exactly as I had done before the crash. There was no way in the world I was going to walk with a limp.

While I was still on my crutches, I hired a local physiotherapist to visit me before and after her work. Her way of getting me walking again was very simple: 'However much it hurts,' she told me, 'walk as you walked before. Whatever you do, don't limp.'

Whatever I did hurt like hell – but I walked.

Chapter Twenty-six

I'D COMPLETELY LOST SIGHT OF WHO I WAS AND WHAT I WAS supposed to be doing. I'd let myself get swept right away by Leo Sayer. At the very time I should have been building on the success of *Budgie,* I was doing anything and everything but acting.

I wouldn't talk about the fact that I was no longer acting, not even with Jackie. But the truth was I'd just gone through a battering in the car crash, and I didn't want to expose myself to the possibility of getting hurt again. It wasn't Adam Faith who was in the car crash and it wasn't him that was hurting. It was me, Terry Nelhams, and I needed time to repair. Adam Faith was going to have to take a backseat for a while.

If I hadn't had that car crash, I wonder if things would have been different. Might I have gone on to build on the success of *Budgie*? Could I have been so besotted with another man's talent that I would subjugate my own career to promote his? Or was I just using Leo Sayer's career to throw a smoke screen around my own reasons for not wanting to act? It took me over twenty years to start dealing with that conundrum.

Sometimes, after the accident, I'd get our driver to take me up to the crash-site at Cowfold. I'd sit in the car for hours on end, staring at the tree, willing my memory of that journey to come back. I'd keep asking myself what had happened? I thought if I could remember it, and relive it, that would eventually lay it to rest. But I never remembered.

Jackie probably thought about divorce as a serious option during the early part of my recovery. Now she had two children to look after. It's amazing how quickly your bones heal up and that fools you into thinking that you're getting back to normal. But underneath my mind had been through a scrambling and although I was totally unaware of it myself at the time, it was going to take a long time to unravel itself.

On the surface I seemed perfectly normal, I felt normal, but my behaviour wasn't normal. All the least likeable traits in my nature became highlighted. If it was possible I became more obsessive, manically convinced that I was the only one who had any answers.

After *Budgie*, offers started coming in. Before the crash, I'd waited eagerly for each one. After the crash, I refused to read a single script. I started piling them all the way up the staircase. Each script having its own little step. They sat there, week after week, month after month, gathering dust. We even cleaned round them.

I suppose this bizarre behaviour was me saying, 'I don't want you, but I want to be reminded that you want me.' I left those scripts there on the stairs for two or three years. They were a symbol of something inside me I couldn't bear to look at.

There are some individuals in life who just won't take 'No' for an answer. I should know, I'm one of them; and David Puttnam is another. He brought Michael Apted, the film director, and Ray Connolly to the studios one day in 1974 when we were in the middle of recording Leo Sayer.

David had a project he wanted me to act in called *Stardust*. I refused point-blank even to think about it. He said he'd already sent me the script, and had I read it? I hadn't, but I promised him I would.

I wasn't in any hurry to start exposing my emotions on a film set. Acting is about expressing and using your feelings, and of all things now I had a horror of putting my feelings on the line again.

181

I felt battered, physically and mentally, wrung out, unable to do anything except survive from day to day. I just wanted to live as Terry Nelhams for a spell, and let Leo Sayer's career take my mind off the crash.

The more I kept saying 'No,' the more David kept calling.

Finally, he phoned me up on Christmas Day.

'Look,' he said, 'at least just read the script. If you read it, you'll want to do it. If you read it, and you still don't want to do it, I'll buy you a case of Moët & Chandon.'

I don't like Champagne, but I didn't have the heart to tell him that. Still it was very flattering to have Puttnam interested in me as an actor, and as a courtesy I felt the least I could do was read the script.

I went downstairs, made some tea, picked up the script, and came back to bed. After four pages, I put the script down, phoned David and told him to forget the Champagne. If he still wanted me I was in.

It had been sixteen months since the accident and I don't suppose I was really ready to do the movie, but I loved the script so much I would have acted on crutches if necessary. I certainly didn't want to leave the house but once again Jackie was behind me threatening to kick me out bodily if I didn't get a move on.

A great joy about doing the film was getting to know David Essex. A gentle lad, he dealt very well with the fact that he had to get used to a new actor in a role he'd been used to seeing Ringo Starr play. Ringo played the manager in *That'll be the Day* – the forerunner to *Stardust*.

With one week's shooting in the can, I was called into a meeting at Lee Studios, near Paddington. Puttnam, Apted and Connolly were all sitting round a long table, with grim, determined looks on their faces. I felt like a naughty schoolboy going in to see the headmaster. They explained that they were very worried about my performance. 'We're very concerned,' began Puttnam.

'Oh yes?' I asked. 'What about?'

There was a silence while the three men in front of me fiddled with their pens. Nobody wanted to come straight out with it. Then one of them blurted out, 'Nothing's happening. You're not doing anything with your performance. Nothing's happening on the screen.'

Nothing was going to shake my belief in my method of acting.

I'd watched too many American movies not to know what film acting was all about. It's all in the eyes. Think it and the audience will see it. Do as little as possible, and say as much as you can.

Stardust was the first big film I'd done and it was a wonderful part; I wasn't going to blow it. This was what I'd dreamt about doing right from the first moment I saw James Dean. I wasn't going to make a mess of it now.

A story I'd heard years earlier about Gregory Peck put acting in a nutshell for me. Peck was making a movie and got called to the set. In his haste he'd forgotten his script. Waving a second assistant over he asked the kid to go to his mobile-home dressing-room and fetch his script. When the kid picked up the script he noticed that the initials N.A.R. were written in the corner of some of the pages.

Unable to contain his curiosity, the second assistant asked Peck what N.A.R. meant. Peck smiled and quietly imparted the greatest bit of acting advice ever. 'No Acting Required.'

I tried to calm their worries. 'What do you want?' I asked. 'Do you want me to do the whole film in every scene? Please be patient, and let me do it my way, I promised them it would turn out all right.

To their credit and my relief, they agreed to give me some more time. Fortunately it turned out well. *Stardust* was a huge success.

Despite all the back-slapping I got for the part that I played in *Stardust*, by the end of it I felt that nothing had changed. I was still sick at heart. I still didn't want to be Adam Faith any more. I wanted to carry on festering.

I found out just how true this was later in 1974, when I was going up the escalator in Charles de Gaulle Airport, outside Paris. I was sailing along, in a daydream, when an American voice I didn't recognize boomed out from just behind me, 'I've just seen *Stardust*, and I thought you were fabulous in it.'

I looked round to find this bearded bloke standing there, beaming at me. I was sure I'd never clapped eyes on him before, but there was something vaguely familiar about him for all that.

'Excuse me?' I replied.

'May I introduce myself,' he went on. 'I'm Francis Ford Coppola – I've just seen you in *Stardust* – and I thought you were really great.'

Out of embarrassment, or diffidence, I made some remarks to the effect that what I'd done wasn't that great an achievement, that being on stage was much harder than being in films – ridiculous and stupid comments of that kind. I could hardly have said anything more crass to this man, in this place, at this time. At the flick of an eyelid, Coppola could have given me parts in films that any actor would have crawled over rusty knives to be in, regardless of their success.

Before that smash, Francis Ford Coppola wouldn't have stood a chance. I'd have moved into his hotel suite and slept in front of his bedroom door until he'd given me a part in one of his movies. But there I was, giving this great director the brush-off when he was coming at me. We hadn't heard much about post-traumatic stress syndrome in those days, but looking back now, that can be the only explanation. I was like a dog that had been beaten about the head with a stick. I was cutting life off.

Chapter Twenty-seven

LEO'S CAREER STARTED TO TAKE OFF IN A BIG WAY AND ALTHOUGH I'd always wanted huge success for him, I hadn't foreseen how much work it would involve, nor the effect it would have on Dave Cohen and me.

Dave had been writing much of Leo's material, but wasn't receiving the credit or recognition he felt he deserved. He wanted to pursue a solo career and had changed his name to Dave Courtney and signed a record deal.

The first I heard of the deal was after it had been signed. I was disappointed that Dave hadn't told me about it, but arranged to meet him at my local pub to discuss our management of Leo.

Leo's success and Dave's plans brought home to me the danger of my own career being foreshadowed. After the crash I'd more or less shut off from acting, but now I started to feel uneasy and frightened that my acting career was receding. I wanted Dave to assume more responsibility for Leo so that I could get back to acting. But Dave was having none of it. As he sat there telling me 'I've got my own career to think of,' it suddenly struck me: What about my career? More out of anger than common sense I told him that it was all or nothing: either he took over completely or I bought him out. It was an out and out ultimatum and in the event Dave stuck to his guns and we parted company.

Another factor that contributed to the split between Dave and I was the appointment of Colin Berlin – my old pal from the Eve Taylor days – as Leo Sayer's agent. In the early Seventies Colin had helped Gordon Mills turn the income of Tom Jones and Engelbert Humperdinck into a public company called MAM, and I wanted him to do the same for us with Leo. Dave had been dubious about the appointment from the start. He felt that because Colin was from the old school of variety, rock music wasn't his bag. Dave was right really, but whatever Colin was or wasn't, he had a reputation for being one of the best operators in the game and we needed a business head to make this thing earn its keep. Having had a working relationship with Colin previously, I found myself, insensitively, talking more and more with Colin than with Dave, which made Dave feel that he was being left out in the cold.

With Dave gone I went solo to produce Leo's third album. Fortunately we had a big hit single in the UK. Which was a relief for me. But it wasn't the same. I missed Dave's creative input, both from a writing and producing aspect. I missed him.

The album didn't impress the Americans and I worried that without Dave we had lost the magic formula. Dave and I had talents that complemented each other, and had produced financial, as well as creative, success. Apart from two very well-received albums, we'd also produced a hit solo album for Roger Daltrey – lead singer with The Who.

The Daltrey album had come about when Dave and I were having our third try at recording Leo's first LP. We hired Roger's recording studio which he had set up in a barn at his East Sussex home. Roger spent a lot of time in the studio with us and liked what he was hearing. After a few weeks he asked us to produce his first solo album for him. Leo and Dave wrote most of the songs, I collaborated with Dave on a couple of little ditties. I'm happy to report that all went well and we got Roger a hit single with 'Giving it All Away'.

That was an idyllic time. Dave and I built a couple of low-slung missiles from Lotus Europa car-kits, and spent all summer tearing around the narrow country lanes of East Sussex doing a fair imitation of James Hunt and Niki Lauda.

How we didn't kill ourselves on our daily trips to Roger's studio I'll never know. You'd think that with my experience of car mishandling I would have known better. Do we ever learn?

After getting three successful albums with two different artistes, it was difficult to go it alone. I'd only really got involved in this whole diversion from my acting career because of my friendship with Dave. And now he was gone my heart wasn't into producing anymore.

We'd forged a great friendship before all this stuff had come between us, I really missed him. The daft things we used to do. One summer before *Budgie* we decided to become used-car salesmen.

Dave's father Alec owned a big garage in Brighton and was always on the lookout for good-quality second-hand cars to display in his showroom.

Armed with *Glass's Guide*, the bible of the second-hand car business, Dave and I wandered round Sussex looking for bargains. If we bought, Dave would drive our new purchase home to Brighton, and I'd follow in our car. We spent a very happy few months that year; a couple of likely lads without a care in the world.

Still life had to go on and there was Leo's American record career to think about. In the end, I chose to get him hooked up with American producer Richard Perry. He made a wonderful album, which produced two number one hits for Leo in America. But for all its brilliant success, it wasn't really him. LA music didn't fit Leo, it turned him into an upmarket pop singer, when his real talent lay nearer Van Morrison, or Randy Newman.

Unwittingly, I'd steered Leo away from the more serious music he wanted to make, and encouraged him into the sugar-candy pop market. I put success before creative direction and I should have known better. This was exactly what Eve Taylor had done to me.

It's a constant dilemma that artists have to face. Financial security or creative satisfaction? Not an easy choice if you've spent the best part of your adult life trying to get a break.

Having told people over and over that this boy was the greatest thing since sliced bread, I was desperate to break him into the American market and prove to them all that I was right.

* * *

As the 1970s progressed, in a blaze of orange-and-brown carpets, flared polyester trousers, tank-tops and *Starsky & Hutch*, we sold our house in Henfield. The not inconsiderable profit went (on orders from Jackie) straight into cold storage. There was no way we wanted to let that money go anywhere except on another house. We had rebuilt the inside of the Henfield house and Jackie was dying to get her teeth into another one.

While we were looking for our next dream purchase, we rented a lovely Georgian village house in Lindfield, Sussex. At the north end of the village, Lindfield Place was a crumbling Jane Austen type of house. It had its own stables, which was fatal. The second I saw those empty stalls I could see a little pony making itself at home. Christmas was on its way and I commissioned Jackie's riding instructor, Paul Redman, to go looking for an old campaigner that could teach Kat to ride.

When Paul rescued Mikey he was an emaciated little thing scrambling around on top of a scrap-heap and living on potato peelings. He'd taught half the kids in Kent to ride. Paul and Jackie hid him in a local riding stables while they got him in shape for Christmas Day.

On Christmas morning we led Kat down to the stables for her surprise. Her face was a picture when we took off the blindfold. Her little eyes screwed up in excitement, she couldn't contain herself. After drowning Mikey in hugs and kisses, she was plonked up on top of her new friend and we took a stroll through the village.

I looked at Jackie across Mikey's bobbing neck, his long mane swaying with the movement, as he carried his new mistress for her morning ride. Jackie didn't have to say a word, I could see what was going through her mind. So often she had talked about her childhood and the dreams she'd had for herself.

Growing up as she did in the backstreets of Manchester, hers was a dream plucked from the storybooks she'd read as a small child: about girls at lovely schools, whose parents came to pick them up in shiny cars laden with picnic hampers. Girls who had wonderful clothes, and *ponies*, and scrumptious midnight feasts in the fourth-form dorm.

Katya was living the life Jackie had dreamt for herself.

My own vision of the perfect childhood was taken straight from the pages of Enid Blyton, in particular the *Famous Five* books. The gang would be packed off on holiday to stay by the sea with a grumpy uncle (who turned out to be not so grumpy) and then they'd crack a smuggling-ring that had been going on the whole time right under the noses of the semi-comatose adults.

I didn't want midnight feasts – I wanted adventure.

I laid out a mini-motorbike scramble course across the fields and up through the woods. We would race each other on our motorbikes. Kat, being so young, had to make do with a 50cc Suzuki, which she complained about bitterly because I was astride a 195cc Kawasaki and therefore had the power advantage. But somehow or other she always seemed to end up in the lead. If I found myself getting too far in the lead, I'd run off the track, or pitch the bike into a ditch. Then secretly smile with delight as I watched her serious little face, determined to win, race by me.

There was one time I could have lived without being father of the year. Kat had been reading *Swallows and Amazons* and decided she wanted to camp out for the night.

If there's anything more uncomfortable than spending a night, fully clothed, with two overcoats for extra warmth, squeezed up with a kid who's practising the Booga Loo in her sleep, in a tiny two-man tent, pitched on a freezing lawn in the middle of winter, then I don't want to know about it.

What a night. It was cold enough to freeze the 'whatsits' off a grass-snake. A slab of marble in a morgue would have seemed like a suite in the Savoy compared to that ice-hard lawn. But I did get a pile of brownie points from the daughter after that ordeal. It was fun giving Kat the life we would have liked.

We stayed at Lindfield Place for just over a year, before we found a house that suited us.

Then we met Perry Press. One of the boys in Pink Floyd had recommended him when they knew we were looking for a house. An estate agent, Perry Press specialized in finding 'great houses' for the rock industry. Perry took Jackie and me all over Sussex looking at houses. Owners of these august piles didn't know sometimes whether to call the police or a priest to have their houses exorcized when Perry turned up. He wore nothing but black. He was obsessed with black. His car was black, his sitting-room was black, his cat was black.

Owners would visibly recoil when they opened the door to Perry. But a couple of minutes in the presence of the master charmer and they were eating out of his hand. He also, in spite of his appearance, knew his onions when it came to houses, and eventually came up with a most stunning Georgian mansion on the Ashdown Forest. It was being sold by John Paul Jones, the bass guitarist from Led Zeppelin.

Sitting on the side of a hill, Warren House was full of big beautiful rooms. The first thing I did was fill one of them with a snooker table. And not just because I wanted my mates round to play. It was the cheapest way of furnishing a room. The place was huge and it was going to cost a bomb to fill it.

The gardens were something else; they seemed to go on for ever. Years earlier they'd been open to the public. They were divided into individual 'rooms' and Kat and I had great times playing cowboys and Indians, hiding from each other in this stunning garden. I got us water pistols, so at least the plants got the benefit of a drink while Kat and I tried to plug each other. You could go for hours without getting caught.

Rhododendrons and azaleas flourished like weeds on the clay soil of the Ashdown Forest, and Warren House had an amazing display. Over the years it had become especially well known for its rhodies. They were a sight to behold when they were in full bloom. Great banks of blazing colours, they towered sixteen-feet high, like a giant Impressionist painting.

No wonder people travelled from all over to see them when they came into full flower around the middle of May.

The circular azalea room was at the end of the games lawn, with its entrance facing the house. Sitting with a good book and an ice-cold can of the old 'American champagne', I spent many a happy hour staring back at the house and wondering how I got to be so lucky. Although, if there's one thing you learn over the years, it's that success owes more to sweat than luck or talent.

More recently, I was having dinner with Sir Rick Greenbury (Chairman of Marks & Spencer) and Sir Harry Solomon (Chairman of Hillsdown Holdings, a huge food conglomerate) – I was writing a financial page at the time for the *Mail on Sunday* and I wanted to get their take on success.

Rick very deliberately reached into his jacket and brought out his wallet. In it he kept a piece of paper with a quote that he'd read in Ray Kroc's autobiography (the bloke who took McDonald's from a hamburger joint to the massive empire it is today). He read it out:

'Nothing in the world can take the place of persistence. Talent will not; nothing is more common than unsuccessful men with talent. Genius will not; unrewarded genius is almost a proverb. Education will not; the world is full of educated derelicts. Persistence and determination alone are omnipotent.'

Rick had read it years earlier and kept a copy of it on him at all times. I keep a copy on me now.

There was one point where I got really worried that my obsession to give Kat a perfect childhood would spoil her. We wanted her to have a childhood full of wonderful memories but we didn't want it to ruin her. We needn't have worried because in actual fact, you can't spoil kids with love. Kids are only spoilt when you try to buy them off with material things. Tell them you love them every day, and you'll have your child as a friend for life.

What was far more worrying to Jackie and me was the hype that surrounds show business. I'd already seen what this could do to my younger brother, Roger, back in 1960. The minute I'd become famous, some sabre-toothed manager had got hold of Roger, and encouraged him to believe that he could become a pop singer.

I was against it from the start, and refused to help. I thought this shark was only out to exploit him, and that Rog would end up looking silly and humiliated. I'd seen what had happened to the relatives of other big acts – like Tommy Steele's brother Colin. I didn't want someone exploiting Roger.

At the time I was doing it to protect my younger brother, but I wonder now if I did the right thing. Who was I to judge Roger's chances? I'm about ten years older than he is and, naturally, he looked up to me as a role model; I didn't really understand that then. Perhaps I should have helped him have his crack at the big time, and given him a leg up. Maybe he could have made it.

I talked about fame driving a wedge through our family, and what happened to Roger is the best example you could get of that. Roger found it difficult to cope with what had suddenly happened to his older brother. The first thing he did was run away from home, at the age of thirteen. The shock of that turned my mother's hair white in a night. Roger, her youngest, was the one Mum loved most of all.

It got worse. Roger spent his youth going in and out of prison for all kinds of minor offences. I used to dread the phone calls coming from the police. I used to dread the phone calls coming from anywhere, if they were to do with Rog. One night I got a call from a very well-known film actor who also lived in Acton. He'd been burgled and had heard a rumour that my brother was involved. He promised to keep the police out of it, if I could recover his stolen goods. Roger never admitted to the crime but promised to help me.

Two days later I found myself at two o'clock in the morning, sitting in my car at the back of a local pub. The headlights flashed twice as the Cortina pulled into the car park. I returned the signal. The mystery driver swung his car in a wide arc and reversed towards me until our boots were almost touching. The stolen treasures were dumped into my boot and my money disappeared for ever into his. I returned the goods and the matter was dropped.

Experiences like that drove a wedge between Roger and me for years, but the story has a happy ending. We've recently found each other again, as friends – which for me has been a great thing. He's married and living in East Anglia.

All my worries about exposing Katya to Adam Faith came back to me one afternoon when I was listening to Radio 4. I'd switched on to catch the afternoon play and instead caught the end of *Woman's Hour*.

Sheila Hancock was talking about some publicity photographs she and her husband, John Thaw, had agreed to do, with their kids. Sheila had caught sight of her daughter actually enjoying the attention and posing for the camera. From that moment on, she told the *Woman's Hour* presenter, she and John decided to keep show business away from their kids until they were old enough to make up their own minds. It bothered them to see their children being swallowed up by their parents' show-business personas.

That struck a chord with me. Jackie and I didn't want Katya to grow up as an appendage to Adam Faith. We wanted her to grow up in her own right, as Katya Nelhams-Wright, not as 'Adam Faith's daughter'.

We made a pact that day that we would do everything we could to keep Adam Faith away from our home.

As usual I went overboard with obsession. I knew that if we let Adam Faith creep in quietly by the side door, he'd be there, and he'd take everything over, including Kat's life, so we really went for it: photographs, old records, newspaper and magazine articles, the memorabilia, everything to do with show business was taboo. We never mentioned Adam Faith in the house.

This strategy was so successful that for many years Katya had no idea what her dad did for a living. As far as she knew I went off to some mysterious place of work in the mornings and came back in the evenings like a normal dad.

Because we always lived miles from civilization, Kat had to be ferried to and from school. Jackie, never at her best in the morning until after three fags and a gallon of Nescafé, would do the picking up, and whenever I was in England, I took the morning shift. It was our time to talk together, and I wouldn't take a business appointment if it clashed with my school run.

It was inevitable that sooner or later she would find out what her dad did for a living. One afternoon, when Katya was six, Jackie was driving her back from school. Kat turned to Jackie and asked her in all innocence, 'Are we famous?' Jackie stalled. She knew what was coming.

'Why?' she asked.

'Well, when Daddy dropped me off at school this morning, one of the teachers said that he's famous. She said he's called "Adam Faith". Is that true?'

Jackie had to sit her down and explain about this monster we'd kept locked in the attic all these years, and who we were now going to have to let out.

Towards the end of the Seventies I was spending more time in LA than I was in England. It was beginning to get ridiculous. I was commuting sometimes twice in a month. One weekend I came home from LA just so I could spend a night in my own bed. Although none of us was particularly enthusiastic about living in LA, we decided we should give it a go.

We took a fantastic house way up Sunset Boulevard in Manderville Canyon. It was about halfway from the beach at Santa Monica and the Beverly Hills Hotel. Kat lived in the huge pool that snuggled up to the back of the house. Each bedroom had its own private patio. Ours had a lemon tree in the corner and I picked a fresh one every morning for my tea.

Poor old Jackie tried to fit into the *Stepford Wives* lifestyle, but she was like a young puppy going to a new home, and spent most of the time silently crying inside for her English way of life. She missed Sussex.

It was Katya who finally broke the proverbial straw.

She'd been going to a summer school with the daughter of the manager of the Beverly Hills Hotel. One afternoon she was dropped off by the yellow school bus and rushed into the house. Wearing her LA Bruins cap and her Mickey Mouse Disneyland sweatshirt, she called out in a perfect American accent, 'Hi mom, I'm home. Got any cookies?'

That was it!

The next morning I was preparing breakfast – hot pancakes with maple syrup – when Jackie, who'd been sitting in unusual silence, surrounded by the morning activity, suddenly flung her face into her arms, resting on the kitchen table, and burst into uncontrollable sobs. She wanted to go home. Well, in the face of this outrageous bit of overacting (she always should have been an actress) there was no other choice. No debate. Two minutes later we were packing. She'd lived in America for three weeks!

Chapter Twenty-eight

'YOU *MUST* SEE THIS HOUSE!' DAVID JOYES, AN ESTATE AGENT friend from Tunbridge Wells, was on the phone from England. I was having my usual breakfast in the Polo Lounge of the Beverly Hills Hotel.

'I think I've found "the" house,' David Joyes shouted down the phone. 'You should come and look at it immediately.'

Oh sure, drop everything and traipse back to England on a fool's errand. I'd seen too many houses in my time to think that there was any such thing as 'the' house.

Anyway we'd not long sold our house on the Ashdown Forest and were living in a small farm that we'd bought from Geoff and Marcia Jacques – friends of ours that we'd met through their young daughter Sophie, who was at infant school with Katya.

How we came to get the money to buy the farm is a story that could only have come out of the madness of Los Angeles the Seventies.

I was in LA when the negotiations to buy Heaseman's Lodge Farm were being finalized. I'd just got off the blower to the

195

Jacques' estate agent, arguing for the umpteenth time about the price, when I was joined by Artie Mogel, President of Capital Records. He had finished his breakfast meeting and had spotted me on his way out. After exchanging the usual show-business banter, he asked if I'd like to make an album for him.

Making another album was the furthest thing from my mind. Since the débâcle of the *I Survived* album, I wasn't exactly champing at the bit to repeat the experience. Laughing off Artie's offer, I ordered him some coffee and we settled down to talk over old times. A few months earlier he'd visited us in Warren House, which he loved, and was aghast when I told him that we were thinking of selling up and were trying to buy a small farm.

Artie sat there listening to me going on and on about the sensational farm I was negotiating to buy. Then when I finally stopped for breath, he leaned back into the banquette, and casually dropped a real biggie in my lap: 'Make me an album and I'll buy the farm for you.'

Artie had a reputation for acting on his instincts, but even this was too mad to take seriously.

'I'll buy it for you.' Artie persisted. 'Make me an album and I'll buy the farm for you. How much is it?'

Not believing a word he was saying, I slowly took a sip of my juice. Did he mean it? What did I have to lose? I told him the price of the farm.

Without flinching Artie extended his right hand to me, offering me the deal. And that is how we came to live in 140 acres of sheer heaven in the Ashdown Forest.

And now, six months after moving into Heaseman's Lodge, I wasn't in the mood to listen to David going on about a fabulous new house. Kat was only five and she'd already lived in four houses. Enough was enough, we needed to settle for a while. We weren't in the mood to move twice in the same year. But David had caught Artie's disease of refusing to take no for an answer.

'Terry, Terry, are you listening,' David was still on the line. 'You *must* see this house.'

Quite a shy, diffident kind of man, I was unused to this rush of emotion from him. The urgency in his voice startled me.

'Terry, please listen to me. I'm telling you. I think you ought to look at this property right now. You'll love it. It's a medieval moated manorhouse near Lingfield racecourse. It's one of the finest houses in private ownership in England – no exaggeration. I've been to see it: this is *your* house. Did I mention it's got a moat?'

He didn't need to labour the point. At the very mention of a moat, I was mentally making plans to cancel my skiing weekend in Mammoth Mountain, which is just north of LA.

A house with a moat, how fantastic!

After booking a seat on the evening flight to Gatwick, I called the wine lodge on Rodeo Drive to order my wine for the plane journey. On the whole, airlines serve reconstituted battery acid with their food, so I'd got into the habit of travelling with my own wine.

Mike Caine was on that flight, as was Chris Wright, owner of Chrysalis records, Leo Sayer's UK record company. My bottle of 1961 Château Montrose made the journey go that much quicker for the three of us.

David Joyes met me off the plane the next morning. Unbeknownst to me, David had put an advert in *The Sunday Times*: 'Wanted: Medieval manorhouse, isolated, with land, south-east, prefer Surrey/Sussex.' And the owner had responded with a photograph of *the* house.

Crowhurst Place sat in twenty-six acres of park and gardens. Its current owner was a man called Sir John Davis, the very same frightening John Davis that I'd worked for as a messenger boy all those years ago at Rank. This was going to be interesting.

We approached the house through a tunnel of ancient stone, formed by the gatehouse that met above our heads. A long straight drive arrowed forward, bounded on one side by tall hawthorn hedges, on the other by open farmland. My stomach started churning with excitement as we went through the lodge-house archway. We passed a crumbling, ancient, wooden bridge, which spanned the moat. I got ready to leap out, expecting David to pull up. But David informed me that this was only the trades-man's entrance, and swung the car round to meet the front of the house. The drive curled around a thirteenth-century tithe barn, built in the same period as the core of the house; next to that was an enormous Elizabethan barn.

I've complained about my lack of education once before in this book when trying to describe Jacqueline the first time I saw her. But Shakespeare, Wordsworth, even Pam Ayres would have had a job to do justice to what stood in front of me.

197

The house opened up its true and beautiful face to you in muted shades – the oak half-timbering grey-brown with age, the irregular-shaped grey Horsham-stone tiles overgrown with dark-green antique moss, the colours mellow, blending together in the warm sunlight. There were red-brick Tudor chimneys, their exuberant tall stacks topped with stepped overhanging capitals, or twisting cleverly through flamboyant runs; the bricklayer's trade turned to art.

The years had put their sinews into the manor, stretching and bending its original lines into funny curves that murmured its age. Lead-latticed windows with poured glass panes reflected back the thick shrubbery swarming across the façade.

We parked, and walked across the stone bridge that lead to the front of the house. The whole place smoked and perspired and sweated with its history. I wanted this house; it was like a fever in my blood. With every roll of the tyres down the drive, with every step I took across the bridge, I wanted this house. I wanted it, and nothing on earth was going to stop me getting it.

The housekeeper greeted us at the imposing front door studded with hand-beaten iron nails that had seen comings and goings since Robin Hood pranced around Sherwood in his little green suit.

We followed the housekeeper along a narrow flag-stone passageway, very plain, very downbeat. A most disappointing introduction to the interior, after the overwhelming fanfare of the approach. She made a sharp turn to the right, and we stepped into the great hall.

If I'd dropped dead at that second, I'd have died a happy man. I'd stepped back five hundred years. The atmosphere took hold of me, lifted me right out of the present. One side of the hall was almost entirely composed of windows, the main oriel window soaring thirty feet, ceiling to floor. The fireplace was so vast we could have quite happily set up home in there. The floor of massive oak boards, polished to the colour of a shining chestnut racehorse, swept across to a massive bookcase that practically covered the wall facing us.

Above the bookcase, two storeys up, there was a little window. Peering down on us was a ghostly face that immediately jerked out of sight when it caught me looking up. It was my old boss. While we waited for the great man to appear, David Joyes and I drank in the rest of the hall. The carved wooden medieval ceiling, forty feet above us, was magnificent. The housekeeper, in hushed tones, confided to us that it was the finest example of a medieval wooden ceiling in private ownership. After imparting a few more little titbits about the house, she quietly faded from the room, like a wisp of smoke disappearing into the air. Sir John had arrived.

I felt sick – physically sick; I had to live in this house. Please don't let the fact that I had been his messenger boy deter John Davis from letting me become a part of the history of this house, I pleaded internally.

In the event Sir John, who had a reputation for being a hard man, was charm itself. He took me slowly around the house, and each room was more stunning and beautiful than the last.

For the first time ever, in all my experience of property, I liked every single room. Perry Press always said that if there was one 'great' room in a house it's enough reason to buy it; if there are two 'great' rooms, offer whatever they are asking. This house had at least five *great* rooms and that was only on the ground floor. What on earth had David stumbled on?

The house was split in two by the great hall. Off to the south side a doorway led to the great parlour, a wonderful room that went all the way from the front of the house to the back. The muted light that settled on the room gave it, in contrast to the magnificent boldness of the great hall, a soft and mellow, almost Jacobean atmosphere. Adjoining the parlour was a cosy snug (only eighteen by twenty-two feet) with a beautifully painted ceiling. The soft Elizabethan cobalt blues, red and yellow ochres, created a masterpiece that carried you back on a romantic journey to times gone by. Sir John used this room as his winter study.

We then turned our attentions to the east side of the house. Sir John led us through the great hall and into the dining room. It was the sort of room that could encourage you into obesity. One look at the prettiest of Elizabethan linen-fold panelling and you could have stayed gazing at it all day long. Apparently, rodents were in the habit of 'meeting their maker' in the space between the panelling and the wall, which gave the room a certain raw pungency.

Next on the tour was the kitchen, a great cavernous place, with an open log fire that stretched half the room it was a working kitchen that had only played host to staff. I could already see Angelina, who had returned to us from Spain, stirring the sponge-mix for my syrup pud.

After showing me and David every nook and cranny of the interior, John Davis led me round the grounds. Opposite the kitchen bridge there was a small lake running away from a manicured lawn. On its banks towered a huge dovecote, handsome and warm with history; I could happily have lived there. A score or more doves fluttered round their palace, flirting.

Behind the massive barn complex of garages and stables there was an open-air Elizabethan theatre. Its thick yew hedges formed wings behind which the actors could change, then make their entrances and exits. In front of the grassy stage a small open area of lawn had been terraced for the audience. You couldn't help but wonder – did Shakespeare give Elizabeth and Essex a quick preview of his latest offering, *Twelfth Night*, here at Crowhurst?

For two hours, John Davis courteously introduced me to the rest of Crowhurst Place bit by bit, he opened up the history of the house. It had been laid down in the eleventh century and had been refurbished and added to over the centuries.

I was faint. All I could think of as I walked round the grounds was what Jackie and Kat would say when I showed them their new home.

After two hours John Davis and I hadn't exchanged a single word of a personal nature: he was the seller, I was the buyer. But right at the end of the tour of inspection, we stood by the little waterfall running into the top end of the moat. Looking out across the lawns sweeping up to the rear of the house, with the big fat Koi carp swimming lazily at our feet, he turned to me and said, 'So you've done well for yourself then?'

'I suppose so,' I replied. 'Well, I'm here buying your house, aren't I?'

We made no other reference to those early days at Rank.

His asking price was £250,000. After a short discussion we settled with a handshake on £235,000.

It was a long time before we exchanged contracts. Nothing is more stressful than waiting to exchange contracts on the house of your dreams. Jackie and I bit our nails down to nothing in those tense days.

Perry Press heard through the estate agents' grapevine that when Knight, Frank & Rutley, the estate agents, had got wind of this private sale, they threw a very polite fit. 'Let the hounds see the hare,' they pleaded with John Davis. They were sure it would

200

go for double the price he'd asked, if only he'd let them market the house.

'I can't,' he told them. 'I've shaken hands on the deal.'

Without any contract John Davis kept his word and lived with our handshake. And that says a great deal about Sir John Davis.

Eventually the great day arrived for us to move into this wonderland. All the furniture we'd amassed over the years didn't even begin to fill it. We got onto a friend, Pam, who owned Great Brampton Antiques up in Herefordshire. She came down and looked at Crowhurst, sighed a bit, and then smiled reassuringly.

'Don't worry,' she told us. 'I'll lend you some furniture.' She sent down two removal vans stuffed to the gills with her finest Elizabethan stock: there were whole sets of a dozen dining-chairs, long refectory-tables, miles of old books for the empty shelves, chandeliers, court-cupboards and pictures, acres of pictures.

'We'll leave it in for a year,' she said, 'and see what you want at the end of that time. Then we'll agree a price.'

Everything needed doing to the house – and everything cost so much to do. It was Grade I listed, which meant that all the materials and workmanship had to replicate the original. It needed rewiring, new plumbing, a new roof, the moat needed relining – it was like shovelling money into a bottomless pit. It sounds like it was falling down, but everything worked well enough, it just needed a bit of a push now and then.

To save costs on the heating we used the north wing in the winter and moved over to the south side of the house when it was casting clouts time at the beginning of June. All the bedrooms had titles. Our winter bedroom, which had a bower that sat over the front door like a maiden's bonnet, was the Henry VIII room. Apparently Henry had wooed Anne Boleyn in that room, hence its name. Our summer bedroom was named after the Duchess of Marlborough who had done a lot of restoration on the house and gardens in the Thirties.

The top floor of both sides of the house were consigned to Kat. She found a secret passageway that led from one of the bedrooms down to a cupboard door set above the kitchen fireplace. This became her secret camp. She was told that if the house was ever invaded by burglars, she was to hide there until the police arrived. Kat was now six, and Crowhurst Place was her fifth home.

It cost us about £1,000 a week to keep Crowhurst Place open, even before we ate. We had to have two full-time gardeners, one of whom doubled as a handyman, a daily woman to clean, and Angelina to cook. It took a petrol tanker of oil every week just to keep the house above freezing point. With the top rate of income tax at 83 per cent in the pound, and investment income being taxed at 98 per cent the house was killing us.

There were moments of light relief. A few weeks after we'd moved in a lady came to the door. She was from the Lingfield Silver Band. It had been a tradition of the house that every Christmas Eve the band played Christmas carols for the family. She wanted to know if we wanted to keep up the tradition. Of course we did!

For our first Christmas, we invited the Jacques family over.

With Katya and all the other children spread around us in the porch, we listened and sang along while this wonderful band played Christmas carols to us – it was like a scene out of *The Pickwick Papers*. Kat and Sophie Jacques provided us with the snow by tipping torn-up bits of paper from the Henry VIII bedroom window that overhung the porch.

It was indescribably romantic. We had, for a short moment, stepped back in time.

Our guests were required to help serve the band with refreshments of mulled wine and mince pies. Michael and Judi Williams (Judi Dench) and their daughter Finty, who had become regular guests, did everything to dodge serving duties. The bigger the star, often the shyer they are.

We spent nearly three happy years at Crowhurst. But at the end of that time we came to the dismal conclusion that we couldn't afford to hang onto the place.

Although Leo Sayer was at last making us money and our property portfolio was piling up considerable capital, without a substantial and regular income, which I never had, Crowhurst Place was financial suicide.

Every time Alan Shalet, my accountant, came round, he'd say that we had to sell the house. We'd found the house of our lives only to lose it for lack of a weekly income. If Jack and I had been the kind of people who inherited their own furniture, we'd have known what to do when the shoe started pinching: turn the heating off and put on an extra sweater. But we had no idea.

Selling Crowhurst Place is one of the few things I've really regretted in my whole life. I never once walked down the main staircase into the great hall without catching my breath. Crowhurst Place was a house that was beyond even my wildest childhood dreams.

To this day, the biggest incentive I have to work, is to earn enough money to buy Crowhurst Place back, and die in it.

We asked Perry Press to find a sympathetic buyer.

Rod Stewart came to see it and complained that it was too small for his taste; which tells us a lot more about Rod Stewart than it does about Crowhurst Place.

Ridley Scott (the film director) came to see the house and immediately put in an acceptable offer. We exchanged contracts, but for some reason Ridley never completed. I never questioned him about this, but it had to be something very serious for him not to buy it.

Ridley got in another buyer, a French-Canadian property-dealer, and Crowhurst Place fell to him. I made around half a million pounds on the deal but the profit tasted like sand in my mouth. £500,000 was no compensation for losing the house of a lifetime.

Until I drove through the gatehouse for the last time, it didn't really hit me what a dreadful thing I'd done by selling Crowhurst Place.

Chapter Twenty-nine

'DADS, CAN WE GO DEEP SEA DIVING? THERE'S A MAN AT THE hotel who gives lessons.' Katya came running up the beach.

As a relief from LA, we'd taken a house in Barbados for a month, just up from the Sandy Lane Hotel. Built in the wooden colonial style, the house was right at the water's edge, with a magnificent view of the ocean.

I was sitting in the shade of the patio when Kat joined me. I'd been in the shade for over two weeks and I was fed up with it. As bad luck would have it, since we'd booked this trip I'd agreed to do the *McVicar* film. Roger Daltrey, who'd put the movie together, had asked me to play the part of Wally Probyn, John McVicar's mucker in Durham high-security nick.

Making a movie at Pinewood with a good friend didn't seem like a bad way of passing the summer, so I agreed. But old lags weren't meant to look like they'd been on holiday. So I promised myself, for the sake of art, that I would stay out of the sun.

But I was getting bored watching Jackie and Kat – not to

mention Paul Redman, Jackie's riding instructor, who'd joined us for the holiday – playing around on the beach, while I hid from the sun. So Kat's idea of deep-sea diving came just at the right time. I was ready for a bit of excitement but if only it hadn't involved swimming. Even with all the lessons I'd had in the South of France, swimming and I were deadly enemies. I hated the water and like a mad dog it sensed my fear. Still, what could I do? My darling daughter wanted to go diving, so diving it was.

Jackie wouldn't entertain the idea. She suffered from chronic claustrophobia. So I trotted up the beach with Kat and Paul praying that the aqualung instructor had decided to take a few years off for lunch.

The Jacques Cousteau of the Sandy Lane Hotel beach turned out to be a twenty-eight-year-old white Barbadian lad who seemed to float a few inches off the sand on a cloud of spliff smoke.

His long blond hair hung in limp strands like dirty white string. Deeply tanned, he lounged on the sand and shielded his eyes from the sun as we made arrangements for our lessons. He was a beach bum with expert knowledge in aqualung diving. In spite of his dream-like condition he managed to come down to earth long enough to tell us that at seven years old Katya was too young to go diving. This was a major blow to me, as I'd been hoping she'd be around to save me if I got into trouble. Unfortunately, the fact that Kat couldn't go was no let-off for me. I'd stepped on the mountain of fear and now it had become another challenge to overcome. After a bit of persuasion the Barbadian agreed to let Kat join us for the first lesson which was to be held in the hotel swimming-pool.

After showing us a few basics, the Barbadian announced that Paul and I were ready for our first dive.

He anchored the boat just off-shore, where the water was about fifteen feet deep. Paul and I waved to the girls as we got into our gear – flippers, weights, airtanks, mask.

Paul, who was a great swimmer (in fact he'd taught Kat to swim), put his mouthpiece in and slid gracefully over the side. One flick of his flippers and he somersaulted in the water and disappeared from sight, leaving a small whirlpool twirling behind.

With a final wave to the girls, I – well, I sort of fell off the side of the boat. Arms and legs thrashing about like a neurotic windmill, I hit the water. Spluttering from the half-gallon of sea-water I'd taken in, I somehow managed to bob back to the surface and grab the side of the boat.

Eventually, calling on enormous reserves of courage and determination, I managed to get myself submerged.

We swam around. It was pleasant enough, lots of sand, shells and fish. Sunlight pierced the surface of the sea and filtered in long golden fingers down towards us. It was sparkling and, for a while, I was lost in its magic.

But that old enemy 'fear' started playing with me and I used up my air far quicker than I should, finishing my dive in record time.

That night Paul and I told, and retold, every moment of our adventure to the girls. And we laughed at my running out of air because the fear made me breathe so quickly.

But secretly, I was quite pleased with myself. I'd confronted a fear and had spat in its face. I went to bed that night actually looking forward to the next day's lesson.

Next morning, Jackie and I were lazing in bed in that lovely state between sleep and waking when the most horrific scream rocked the house. Up like a shot we were at the door in less than a second. Kat was already peering out of her room. At the same time the bathroom door burst open and a blurred screaming vision flashed by. Is it a bird? Is it a plane? No, it's Super-Paul, screaming like a banshee, heading for the ocean, shorts at half mast, desperate to bathe his bum in salt water. A pincer where it hurts most, when you least expect it, is enough to ruin your enjoyment of natural functions for life.

Somehow or other a crab with, according to Paul, twelve-inch pincers had got into the sewer system and decided to visit our loo at precisely the same time as Paul. When it found someone else trying to horn in on its territory it did the only thing possible: it pinched Paul's bum.

Joseph, the wise old maître d' of the house, advised us to bang the loo seat with Kat's spade before we ventured to sit down. Trouble was, we got to know each other's toilet habits better than any of us cared to. It got so you couldn't get within a mile of the lavatory without hearing the chorus, 'Don't forget the spade.'

Diving lesson number two went well enough. It was pretty much the same as the day before. We were still moored just offshore, only this time we were to go down to thirty feet. Before we dived, we had strict instructions from the Barbadian that we were not, *not*, to go over the edge of the coral reef. Just to convince us, he added that it was very dangerous and there might even be sharks and barracuda. He didn't have to lay it on thick for me. Wild seahorses couldn't have dragged me over the top of that underwater cliff.

Down a little deeper we saw a few more fish, the odd bit of coral that was quite pretty, a few more shells, but to tell you the truth after twenty minutes I found it all a little bit tame. As usual, I was the first to run out of air, which was the only exciting thing that happened. When we convened in the hotel beach-bar I suggested that we look for a wreck to dive. Our Barbadian nearly swallowed his cocktail stick. There was no way we were qualified to dive a wreck and in any case the only one that was close enough was, at 130 feet, far too deep for beginners.

I argued and he said no. I argued some more and still he refused to consider the idea. Somehow or other I managed to wear him down and he finally agreed on the understanding that we kept quiet about it. He was fearful of losing his licence if anyone found out that he was taking novices down that deep.

Twenty-four hours later, Paul and I were on a boat with the Barbadian and a driver who looked the spit image of Quarrel in *Dr No*, heading for our wreck.

About a mile offshore, a freighter that had gone down years earlier was sitting on the sea-bed, waiting for the intrepid adventurers to pay it a visit.

We were hardly out of the shelter of the reef when the beginnings of a storm hit us. The wind came searing across the surface of the sea, whipping up the waves into an angry swell. Each wave bigger than the last, they rolled towards us, bouncing our little boat about like a child playing with her ball.

Now, if there's anything I hate more than being under the sea, it's being on it. I love the sea and boats – when I'm looking at them from the safety of the shore. But put me on them and it's instant seasick. I can't think of a more magnificent and exciting sight than the sea in full storm. Just leave me off it.

Up and down, up and down. We rolled up to the top of the waves and then pitched down the other side. It was agony. Why hadn't I listened to Jackie when I told her I wanted to dive a wreck. She was furious, incensed that I should take this terrible risk for nothing other than what she saw as a weird psychological quirk. But it was my quirk, and I was stuck with it.

'How dare you do this to us?' she berated me. 'You're just going to leave Katya and me on the shore, with no idea whether or not you'll be coming back? How dare you?'

But there was no going back – it was the old stepping foot on the mountain again. I'd got it in my mind that I was going to dive that wreck and I wouldn't be able to look in the mirror again if I didn't give it my best shot. What I hadn't figured in the equation was a battle with the elements. I never thought I'd ever be saying it, but I couldn't wait to get underwater. Twice I emptied my stomach over the side. The first time into the wind. Being seasick is probably the worst feeling you can have as a human being and not die. I sat there, green in the cheek, thinking that death would be an attractive option. I clung to that tossing boat like I was a survivor from *The Cruel Sea*.

'We should go back,' the Barbadian said, looking for a last-minute way out. 'You're ill. There's no way you can dive in that condition.'

'No!' I grunted. 'We're here. Let's do it.' But then a terrible thought occurred to me. 'It won't be like this all the way down, will it? I mean rough like this?'

'When we get twenty feet down, it'll get calm,' he said. At that I reached for my waist-belt and began feverishly strapping it on, ramming the lead weights into it as fast as I could. If it meant the end of my seasickness, the sooner I went in, the better.

The huge metal buoy marking the spot where the wreck was loomed up out of the waves ahead of us. 'This is it,' our Barbadian said tersely. 'Get ready.' Then he went through a list of last-minute reminders and instructions, a list we'd already been through twice onshore. The plan was to follow the chain from the buoy, down to the wreck, where it was attached to the deck of the ship. Pick up a souvenir for Kat, and then straight back up to the surface, holding the buoy chain all the time. And he reiterated firmly that we were to stop every thirty feet for one minute to decompress. Suited me. The state I was in, all I wanted was to get the whole horror story over and done with as soon as possible.

I was very afraid and sick by now, and the worst thing was waiting and sitting there in this horrible little boat, getting tossed about.

Paul Redman, all cocky because he swam like a fish, jumped in. But because he wasn't wearing enough lead weights to give him negative buoyancy, he bounced straight back up again and whacked his head on the underside of the buoy. Not an auspicious start.

We revived Paul and tipped him back in the sea, then it was my turn. Because the boat was pitching so much in the wind, which was getting stronger by the minute, I mistimed my jump. Instead of stepping off the edge of the boat when it was at the bottom of a swell, my fear made me hesitate a second too long and I found myself being pushed bodily off the boat by the Barbadian just as the wave reached its highest point. I hit the water in a huge belly-flop that nearly tore my mask and air-tank from me.

Our instructor followed us in and we assembled at our meeting point, which was twenty feet below the surface. A few last-minute equipment checks and we started our descent. Pulling ourselves hand over hand down the thick rusted iron rings, we descended into the gloom. I was absolutely petrified. What on earth was I doing? After a short while the blackness deprived you of all your normal senses. It got like you couldn't tell what side up you were. Wishing I'd kept my mouth shut, I clung to that chain like a lifeline.

The descent seemed to take hours and I now had a crushing pain running up from my eyes into the front of my head, caused by the pressure in my sinus cavities.

Then, quite suddenly, I felt an incredible rush of excitement. There, in the gloom just below was a massive manmade shape, looming towards me like a steel cliff. It was the ship. In the half-light it was indistinct, like a Turner seascape. I had the sense of it without being able to distinguish the details.

I was down; but once again, the fear was making me breathe too fast. It was so deep. If something did go wrong, it was Davy Jones's locker for me. I would most certainly drown. If I could have sweated at that depth I would have done. Instead, I hung in the water, rigid with fear.

At last we pulled ourselves down onto the deck of the ship. It was all grey, shades of grey with long reddish streaks of rust. The Barbadian signalled that we should find something at hand, and then he jerked his thumb upwards. He waited for us to confirm, we understood it was the signal to make our way back up the chain. Then he paddled around looking for a souvenir for Kat.

But now I was down, and standing, a little of the fear ebbed away. I managed to clear my sinuses, which helped me to see, and the ship was an amazing thing, spreading all around us. She was a huge bulk carrier. Looking over the grey deck, I made out the rust-streaked superstructure. Weeds and molluscs clung to her. Fish flashed in silver shoals around her in the gloom, and moved away in orchestrated waves, as you glided towards them. It was remarkable, and the thing that struck me most was the silence. It was eerie being on a boat that had once been so full of life and now lay like a silent rotting corpse, home to the fishes and crabs.

The Barbadian flashed his right hand at me three times, to indicate that we had fifteen minutes before we needed to surface. Plenty of time yet, no need to panic. I was down there, and as Nelson had more chance of getting his eye back than me coming this way again, I figured we ought to look around. What would Kat say when she asked me what it was like down here if all I could reply was we came straight back up? Ten minutes isn't long, but it's just enough to do some exploring.

I signalled to the Barbadian that I wanted to go inside the hulk. His reaction was instant and furious. He wagged his finger wildly at me, then tapped his watch: 'No, no, no. Up.'

I wagged my finger back at him, nodding, 'Yes, yes, yes. Inside,' and started swimming towards an open hatch.

He couldn't leave us, so he shot forward and led the way. As we swam through the dismal corridors, the soft swell of the sea down there occasionally rocked one or other of us up against a bulkhead. A dull 'Clang!' reverberated through the surrounding iron as an air-tank banged up against it. The first time this happened, I just about did a back somersault, the noise so terri-fied me, like the knell of my doom. I stopped and looked wildly around, trying to work out where that terrible ringing had come from, breathing super-fast. Paul Redman's teeth flashed at me in the darkness, as he tapped his tank. It only served to make me more neurotic. I had another thing to be terrified of. Supposing I hit my tank on the bulkhead and it severed my air-line?

We swam down a stairway, pulling at the steps, sidled into cabins, surging along until we'd gone right through the ship. One thought kept driving me on: I'm not ever going to do this again. I'm never going to do this again. It's too frightening. Over and over it pulsated through my brain. But now that I was there, better see everything I could.

We swam up out of the cabins and emerged back onto the foredeck. The Barbadian tapped his watch. 'Time.' I ignored him and swam to the guardrail and looked down. The sheer steel side of the freighter plunged away from me to meet the sandy bottom. It seemed like a hundred feet more. Hey, what the hell, let's take a look. I signalled that I'd like to go right down to the sea-bed.

The Barbadian was not a happy diver. He was going to give me an almighty bollocking for going inside the ship against his will, so I might as well go for the full Monty, and be done with it. To finish the finger-wagging, I turned, put both hands on the guardrail, and pulled myself forward as hard as I could. I fell over the edge of the ship towards the bottom in a vertical plunge.

The Barbadian came after me like Johnny Weismuller saving Jane from a marauding croc. We hit the sand at the same time, sending clouds of it up and around us. Still wagging his finger in disapproval he reluctantly led me down the side of the ship to look at the propellors.

By now, the Barbadian had had enough. He came up to me, held his big diver's watch to my face, and banged on it, over and over, until I nodded my consent. What was his problem? Somewhere I'd temporarily laid aside my fear. Still tapping his watch, he grabbed my arm and pulled me sharply.

We reached the main deck. 'Up,' signalled the Barbadian. 'Now. Up.' I shrugged my shoulders – 'No souvenir.' With that he bent down and began scrabbling around in a pile of old debris and muck on the deck at our feet. A slow mushroom cloud of dust particles rose and built around him as his fingers moved through this junk, clouding the water all around us. It was surprising, I thought, how quickly you could lose someone deep in the water, even when you knew they were there.

At last he found something, a bolt, there on the deck quite close to the anchor chain. He rubbed at the bolt with a gloved hand, and flakes of rust floated off in the gloom.

Waiting for the Barbadian to finish cleaning it, I started to feel as if I were breathing through a handkerchief.

At first, I didn't realize what was happening. I felt the air-pipe at my throat, then bit at the mouthpiece. There was something in the way of my air. It was as if someone had hold of the pipe, and was twisting it to stop the flow. I sucked at it desperately, but the

211

more I sucked the less air I got. An invisible cloth was clamping down across my mouth, a wet cloth that was choking me. At last, through the icy chill of the panic gripping at my chest and gut, I realized what was happening: I was running out of air.

My chest felt as though a giant had hold of me and was squeezing my lungs. All I could hear was the hammering of my own pulse. My left hand scrabbled frantically for the emergency lever that would give me another five minutes of air. I couldn't find it. My right hand was at my throat, clawing at the breathing-pipe, trying to stop it from sucking shut. The Barbadian was still standing there, rubbing the bolt, gazing down at it. Time had stood still. He hadn't noticed me and I was dying. I was out of air, now, sucking with long hard useless whoops at the empty tank. I started to writhe. The silt on the deck clouded up all around me as I kicked, one hand clamped at my neck, the other flapping use-lessly in front of my face. I was wriggling about like a newly gaffed fish.

The professional kicked in. The Barbadian turned and in a flash was on me. He spun me round, pulled the lever. A great Whoosh! of bubbles burst out into the water all around us, enveloping and blinding me. That terrified me even more. I'd lost touch with what was happening. All I knew was that very shortly I was going to die.

Paul saw what was happening and he was off. Straight up and as fast as a Polaris he headed for safety.

My emergency air cut in. I could breathe again, but in my terror I was hyperventilating. At the rate I was breathing, I'd be lucky if I got an extra minute out of it, never mind five. I was in the worst state of fear I'd ever known. All sense left me. I floun-dered on the deck unable to think clearly. I felt helpless. This time I'd overstepped the mark. Why didn't I listen to the Barbadian when he pleaded with me not to dive the wreck. I cursed myself for being so persuasive.

I peered out of my mask, pleading with the Barbadian for help. In a second he was beside me holding my shoulders to comfort me. We both knew this was serious. There was only one way I was getting out of this and that was to put my life in his hands.

Slowly we started our ascent. Hand by hand I pulled myself up the chain with the Barbadian in attendance. He was good. He was trying to keep me calm. He knew that all my sinews were fighting to leave all common sense behind and strike out for the surface. He slowed me down and stopped us at our first decompression point thirty feet up the chain. We were only there for a minute but every second seemed like a year. We set off again and everything was going swimmingly. Halfway through our second stop my emergency air ran out. I'd run out of air for a second time, only now I didn't have an emergency supply to call on.

Panic consumed me. It wheeled up from my boots like a boiling pan of milk threatening to overflow. Here I was over a hundred feet underwater with no air. The claustrophobia was overwhelming. It crushed me.

The Barbadian took control and saved my life. I was about to get another lesson in life-saving techniques, only this was no lesson, this was the real thing.

He took a long deep breath, then, in what seemed like the slowest of slow motion, handed me his mouthpiece. I grabbed at it, stuck it in my mouth, and gulped greedily. My life now literally depended on that mouthpiece. The Barbadian pointed to it, wanting it back. I couldn't give it to him. I just couldn't bring myself to hand it back. My teeth had clamped around the rubber as though I were hanging from it over a long drop. I didn't think that he might die, it didn't occur to me. Nothing occurred to me except getting out of this alive, and that mouthpiece was keeping me alive. The last thing I wanted to do was to give it away.

The Barbadian had other ideas. He got himself off to one side of me, and hit me as hard as he could on the back of the head. The rubber shot out of my mouth, and I almost gulped seawater down into my bursting lungs. Three times on that long journey back to the surface we repeated this procedure. Each time it got more difficult to hand back the mouthpiece.

At last we broke surface. Something slapped me hard in the face, and now I did swallow salt water, at least a pint of it. The squall that had been blowing up was right over us. We'd come up into a storm. Great waves were crashing at the buoy, which tore at its chain, swinging wildly in all directions like a huge hammer wielded by some drunken giant. I was petrified and exhausted.

Where was the boat?

Before diving on the wreck I'd told Quarrel to keep the boat right by the buoy. I'd explained that I could hardly swim. I remembered him nodding at me enthusiastically as I'd told him this. So where was he? Where was the bloody boat? I swivelled my head, blinded by the spray. Nowhere in sight. A big swell tossed me up high and I saw the Barbadian treading water about twenty feet away. But no boat.

The only thing I could think of was to grab hold of the buoy. It was plunging up and down, tossing me this way and that. I hung on for dear life, but the barnacle-encrusted iron tore at my skin. I thought that at any second this great plunging thing above me must dash out my brains. I was going to have to let go of it.

Then I felt an arm on my shoulder. The Barbadian shouted something, but it was lost to me in the wind and waves. He took off his own tank, with its remaining air, and strapped me into it. Taking my empty tank he shouted at me to go down below the waves and wait for him to come back with the boat.

The last thing I wanted to do was to go back under, but if I held onto the buoy it would kill me. Calling up every last dreg of courage, every scrap of remaining energy, I stuck the mouthpiece in and pulled myself down under the sea. As I went down I saw him strike out for the wayward boat.

I'll never forget the wonderful shape of that small boat's keel overhead with its screw churning through the water. I struck out for the surface. Paul and the two islanders hauled me up and dropped me into the bottom of the boat.

I lay there limply, like a small pile of wet rags, moaning quietly from time to time. It felt as though every bone in my body had been broken. I was too exhausted even to feel seasick again.

I never went down again and Kat never got her souvenir. In the rush to save my life, the Barbadian had dropped it.

Chapter Thirty

I MUST HAVE HAD A SORT OF DEATH WISH IN THE LATE SEVENTIES, early Eighties. I'd no sooner escaped from the jaws of death on the deck of the wreck than I chanced my arm on a windsurf board.

In the middle of the latest Leo recordings in LA, I realized I was missing everybody, so I took a flight to join Jackie and Katya on holiday in Antibes with our Blackpool friends, Roy, Wally and Ian. They had a flat on the top floor of a villa right on the beach.

The boys had already got Kat and me interested in windsurfing, in a minor way: I didn't go that much on it because it involved being on – and often in – water. I wasn't that confident on the board, but on the afternoon I arrived in Antibes it just so happened they were going out for a surf in the bay between Antibes and Juan-les-Pins. I rented a windsurf board on the beach and caught up with the others. Wally and Jackie sat on the balcony of the apartment waving to us from time to time.

The wind was moderate, but Kat got tired after an hour and Ian towed her back to shore. After another twenty minutes Roy and I decided to call it a day. It was late in the afternoon, and a sharp wind was sneaking its way into the bay, chilling the air.

We turned to the shore and headed back. After a few minutes of this, I started to notice that instead of getting closer to shore I was getting farther away from it. With each new tack, the shoreline, and Roy, were getting smaller. The wind, I realized with some horror, had moved round, and instead of coming *in* off the sea, was blowing, with increasing strength, *out* to sea.

The clammy word *mistral* reverberated in my brain like an old-fashioned fire-engine bell. If that dreaded wind was blowing up, I was a gonner. There was no way I was going to be able to pit myself against it. I wasn't skilled enough to fight anything more than a force 3.

As the minutes passed, I tried more and more desperately to find any tack at all that would save me, even if it meant sailing sideways right across the bay to some other point of land. But I just kept going in reverse. It felt as though I was on a long piece of elastic, which was pulling me farther and farther out to sea. I waved at the increasingly miniature figures of Jackie and Wally on the balcony of the villa, sipping, no doubt, some exotic cocktail and having a warm and pleasant chat – and they waved back.

The disaster that was about to befall me unfolded in my mind's eye: I was going to drown, or die of hypothermia, waving frantically to my nearest and dearest, who'd wave gaily back at me, not understanding I was slipping backwards to my doom.

The long arms of that wind dragged me nearer and nearer the mouth of the bay. Suddenly the sea hit me square in the face with its full might, and the mistral set about me with a vengeance. At once I lost control of the sail. The wind snatched it away and threw it on the sea. With the wind whipping the sea up into a frenzy it was impossible to stay on my feet, so I sat down astride the board and wrapped my legs tight around it.

Over to the right, I was passing some rocks off the headland about eighty yards away. For one mad moment I contemplated leaving the board and swimming for it. Some hope. I had difficulty reaching the other end of the bath with a weak breaststroke, I don't know how I even dared to think I could have swum to that headland. Even with a buoyancy belt on, with the wind and the current against me I'd be swept out to sea. In my swimming-trunks and life-jacket, there'd be no chance at all of being spotted. The board meant I was visible, up above the waves at least.

I'd been waving like mad at the shore, and they'd all been waving happily back to me. And here I was, clinging to my board like a baby monkey to his mum's belly, heading straight out to sea; next stop Corsica.

Bad weather clouds came rolling up, and with the afternoon worn away, darkness was only a short time coming. My legs and arms began to go numb as the cold crept into them.

I knew that at any minute my arms would let go of the board, I'd slip into the choppy sea and that would be it. I was going to die. Oh, God! Here we go again.

Then I saw a sight that gave me a rush of hope: a great yacht, running for cover before the storm, was bearing down on me under full power. I waved at it frantically for help. It altered course slightly. They'd seen me! I was saved. I started screaming at the top of my voice, 'Help! Help!' But the yacht was travelling at such high speed, and it was so big, that it simply charged past me, unable, or unwilling, to heave to. I watched it rocket away into the spume, kissing my life goodbye.

As I watched helplessly, the yacht heeled sharply over into a U-turn: it was making another pass! There was still hope. As it came plunging at me for the second time, carving spray from its massive bows, I saw someone standing with a coil of rope in the waist, ready to fling it at me. At once, I understood: I was to grab the rope, and they'd haul me in. But the yacht was racing in that wind, really flying along. The arm went back and the line snaked out through the intervening air and spray towards me. I heard the hiss of the keel going by. By some miracle, I grabbed the rope. The line went taut, and before I knew it I was bouncing stretched at full-length across the surface of the sea, face-down, smashing from wave to wave.

I held on for all I was worth, but that was all I could do – my arms were coming right out of their sockets. For a few seconds longer I managed to cling to the rope, then I realized it was hopeless and let go. Slowly, shivering with cold and despair, I turned around and swam back towards the safety of the now-distant board.

It was pitch-black, I couldn't even see the shoreline. I lay down, gripping the board with my arms and my legs. The sea, getting stroppier by the minute, had tipped the board over a couple of times already and I was getting too tired to face another dousing. My strength and courage were being drained out of me by the buffeting waves and the numbing cold.

I started to hallucinate. A strange noise, like castanets, clacked in the dark: it was my teeth chattering. At this rate, the freezing cold was going to get me before the sea could lay claim.

At the very last moment, as I was preparing to sink beneath the waves, I heard a French voice bellowing something out of the gloom. I speak Spanish, but hardly have a word of French. I think it was shouting, 'Allo, allo? Il y a quelqu'un?' and it didn't really matter. I bawled back, 'Ici, ici! Help!' at the top of my lungs. There was a second shout in return. I heard the roar of an outboard motor. I was saved.

I don't know whether it was the yacht skipper or my family and friends back on shore who called the coastguards. But there they were, my two brawny saviours, in a little rubber inflatable.

I wanted to climb straight into the boat with them, ditch the board and pay for it later: it was only a rotten piece of fibreglass; but the laughing coastguards wouldn't have it. Instead of hauling me into their happy little rubber boat, wrapping me up in a mountain of blankets and giving me cognac to swig, as was surely their duty – they flung me a rope. I shouted and protested in my best cod French, but to no avail. They towed me slowly and painfully all the way back to shore.

Does a Frenchman need any reason to humiliate an Englishman?

After we left Crowhurst Place we moved to a farm. And Kat, at seven years of age, had got herself her sixth home.

Old Shoyswell Farm, near Tunbridge Wells, was four hundred acres of bliss. A black-and-white timber-framed five-bedroom Elizabethan house stood bang in the middle of the land. You approached the house down a half-mile-long drive, which curved away to the right and along a valley, right up to the front door.

We'd gone for a farm because the way taxes were you couldn't be sure what was coming next. We figured it was time to dig in and hope for better times. At least with a farm we could get ourselves into a position to be self-sufficient. We'd do a *Good Life* on a slightly bigger scale. Jackie set about rebuilding the interior of the house, while I tried to get to grips with farming.

By pure coincidence, Roger Daltrey's farm was just a couple of villages away. Roger had been farming for some time, and was appalled when we told him what we were planning.

218

'Penny in. Pound out,' he told me. I didn't realize how true that was. Another favourite of Roger's was: 'Farming is paying for someone else's view.' It turned out he was right; we wasted a fortune getting the farm into shape. Miles of fences had to be rebuilt, thousands of pounds' worth of expensive chemicals were needed to put life back in the soil, farm buildings were screaming out for care and attention, all demanding a fortune. Being an amateur farmer is just about the quickest way to lose money.

Reality is a cruel companion at times. It's hard being in a business when even the most junior employee knows more than you do. We paid to learn but while we were doing it we had a lovely time. We built a lake and merged the garden into it. As Jackie was now competing at medium dressage, which is quite demanding, we built an indoor riding-school near the stables so she could train all winter. We were swept along with the farming dream. Homebred meat, milk and cream from the Guernsey house cow, Angelina baking homemade bread with flour milled from our own wheat. The lifestyle was wonderful and Old Shoyswell was just the place to entertain friends.

Paul McCartney says I'm responsible for Michael Jackson buying the rights to the Beatles' music. Paul, Linda and the kids were coming over for lunch, and on the way they rang to ask if they could bring someone with them.

'Sure,' I said, 'bring who you like . . .'

They walked in with Michael Jackson and his roadie.

Michael was the sweetest, kindest boy you could ever wish to meet; he spent most of his time playing football with the kids in the indoor riding-school.

We were sitting around the dining-table after lunch, when Michael, who was the smallest eater I have ever seen, suddenly started going on about all the money he was earning, and what should he do with it? I piped up that he should sink it all into music publishing. The rest is history: Jackson made a small fortune out of buying the rights to the Beatles' songs, and then selling them on to Sony. He'd snatched them from under Paul's nose.

Mind you, I never got any commission.

ChapterThirty-one

YOU'D THINK THAT BY THE AGE OF FORTY, AND ESPECIALLY AFTER the diving saga from hell, *and* my windsurfing adventure, I'd have learned to control my urge to self-destruct in the name of conquering fear. But no, not a bit of it. Fed up with challenging the sea, I turned to the air.

Ken Lyndon Dyke, an old friend, called me one day and told me he was going hang-gliding on the Sussex Downs, near Westerham.

I'd seen gliders off the Devil's Dyke near Brighton and always gazed in awe as they went soaring like giant seagulls on the thermals. But even in my most lyrical of moments, it had never occurred to me to have a go. I'm not keen on flying even when you've got four Rolls-Royce jet engines to keep you aloft, never mind strapping yourself to a couple of bits of metal tubing and a sheet of canvas and flinging yourself off the edge of a cliff.

But Ken has the gift of the gab and before I knew it I was hanging underneath an oversized kite, competing for airspace with the local sparrows. An instructor on the ground was shouting orders to me through a radio link.

On my second lesson I misunderstood his instructions and instead of turning right into the wind, I pulled left and ended up having a confrontation with the side of the hill.

While I was hobbling around on crutches, Andrew Tribe, my old rock manager friend, persuaded me to give up flying things with no engines and have a go at helicopters.

I'd had a go at flying small one-engine planes some time before, but I'd never really taken to it. Trouble was, I hated flying. In fact that's what made me have a go at single-engine planes in the first place. My logic was that if I could learn to fly myself, I would stop being scared because I'd know what was going on. But on one particularly bumpy ride, after filling the cockpit with last night's dinner, I came to the conclusion that flying single-engine fixed-wing planes was most definitely not for me.

But helicopters – now that might be interesting.

Andrew took me to see Alan Bristow at Redhill aerodrome. Bristow's is one of the leading companies in commercial helicopter-pilot training. At first they weren't too keen on adding an amateur to one of their courses, but after I'd pestered them for a few days, they agreed to let me join the end of a forty-nine-week Bristow's cadet course.

From the first second you start out to get a private pilot's licence, one thought occupies your mind to the exclusion of everything else: the *solo* flight. Climb into that plane or that helicopter for the first time, and you know that in a very short time indeed, maybe as little as ten or eleven hours, you're going to be up there, entirely alone, flying this incredibly complicated machine with your life depending on your ability to get it right. I didn't want to get into a helicopter on the ground, even while it was in the hangar, in case something terrible happened. The idea of flying one on my own frightened the life out of me.

I staggered through the early lessons and the day came round for my first solo flight. I had a fast car, but I drove it up the hill overlooking Redhill aerodrome extremely slowly. If there were no helicopters on the tarmac outside the hangar, relief! That meant, for whatever reason (probably low cloud-base), there would be no flying. I could spend a cushy day in ground school. Infinitely more preferable to taking your life in your hands by flying an overgrown mechanical daddy-longlegs two thousand feet up.

No such luck: shining in the morning sunlight, looking like a refugee from M.A.S.H., was my little Bell 47. Chris Cane, my instructor, was waiting for me and hurried me into the helicopter.

On the edge of the airfield was a practice hover-square. 'Just take it out to the perimeter track,' said Chris, 'and hover over the square until I tell you to move.' We hovered over this helipad for a minute. So far, so good; but then so long as he was with me, ready to take the controls in case anything went wrong, I could manage.

'All right,' he said. 'That's fine. I tell you what we're going to do now. We'll do a circuit together, with you in control of the machine, and then land. When we've done that, I'm going to get out, stand in front of you, and raise my hands. When you see me do that, lift off and come to the hover. When I'm satisfied that you can hover and land, I'll raise my arms towards the sky, and that will be a signal for you to do one circuit of the field. You know the routine by now, we've done it a hundred times: take off, climb to five hundred feet, turn right when you reach five hundred feet, turn right again on the downward leg, right again for one last time, and complete the rectangle. Then return here to the hover. I'll be watching, and waiting. Don't worry about looking behind on take-off, I'll make sure you're clear. Just go on my signal. All clear?' I swallowed, hard, and nodded.

We did the circuit together and then he jumped out and stood in front. He raised his hands. I put the helicopter into the hover about twenty feet off the ground, and held it there, steady. He dropped his hands. I landed it.

The moment had come. The helicopter was thumping and vibrating all around me, but still the shaking of my hands on the controls, the quivering of my knees, seemed greater.

Chris raised his hands. I went into the hover. He stepped to one side, and flung his hands up at the sky. I pushed the cyclic (joystick) forward a little and the machine began picking up speed. When it was over runway zero-eight, I started to climb.

I was halfway along the first leg, at about three hundred and fifty feet and climbing, when I noticed the carburettor heat gauge warning me that the carb temperature was falling. Because of the pressure change, the carburettor can ice up. If this happens, you will lose engine power and you can crash. It is therefore in your interest to sort out the carb heat immediately, if not sooner. You pull a little lever, hot air goes into the engine, the temperature comes back up to normal, and life goes on. Simple; some adjustment to engine temperature is necessary on almost every flight. It's just about the only routine drill that has to be done on top of the basic flying. It's a dead simple 'S.O.P.' – standard operating procedure. No big deal.

But this was my first solo. It wasn't like the lessons, where I could take a minute or two to make the adjustment. This was life or death. I thought that if I didn't adjust the carb heat immediately, I'd crash. In my highly fragile state, brought on by muck fear, I wasn't thinking clearly.

In fact there was plenty of time to deal with the situation. All I had to do calmly and deliberately was to pull the carb-heat control lever, and let the warm air solve my problem. Despite hours of perhaps the best professional training available in the UK, I could not, for the life of me, keep a grip of myself. I felt the first tricklings of an awful panic.

Flying helicopters, both hands are occupied: the right hand is on the joystick between your knees, which controls the direction, the left hand on the collective, which makes the chopper go up and down. On the end of the collective is the throttle, which naturally controls your revs.

On the Bell 47, flying solo, you sit in the left-hand seat of the helicopter. The instrument pedestal is about one foot across, on the aircraft's centre-line, and thus to your right. The carb heat lever is in the top left-hand corner of the pedestal. It's got a knob on the end of it.

I looked at this lever. It was roughly level with my chin, at about one o'clock from where I was sitting. All I had to do was reach forward and pull it down a bit from the 'normal air' position towards 'fully hot'. But to do that, I'd have to use my right hand, which meant letting go of the cyclic. This is not recommended. The Bell 47 is a very unstable flying machine. It's a bit like trying to balance a pencil on its point – easy, as long as you're holding it; impossible if you let go. I knew I had to use my left hand – but that meant letting go of the collective – also not recommended. What was the solution? What had they taught me to do? I knew what to do, why couldn't I remember? What was the matter with me?

I glanced at the needle of the carb heat gauge. It had definitely moved further over towards the icing-up end of the scale. Oh my

223

God. The carb heat! Fix it! Don't just sit there, you idiot. Do something!

What they'd trained me to do was: put my left knee up against the collective, thereby temporarily jamming it in position; take left hand off collective, reach forward, and pull down carb-heat lever. Nothing could be simpler – as long as you remember the crucial bit about the knee.

I took my right hand off the cyclic. This you should never do – it's just like letting go of the steering-wheel in a car, only a helicopter is far less forgiving. This one didn't forgive me. I lifted my left hand up off the collective and grabbed the cyclic with it. Then I adjusted the carb heat. In my panic to get my left hand back on the collective I inadvertently knocked the throttle off.

I immediately and dramatically started to lose height. My mouth went dry. The engine note died right away, increasing my fear 100 per cent. I saw that the needles had split on the tachometer gauge, indicating that the throttle was closed. There was no power driving the rotors. I looked down and saw the M25 coming up fast, between my feet.

Panic and fear flooded through my body, immobilizing me.

I should have just got a grip and told myself what a silly idiot I'd been, brought the throttle back up until the engine revs matched the rotor revs, pulled on the collective, then climbed back up to height and completed the circuit.

I was way past calming down.

I saw the ground coming up at me. It seemed to be coming even faster. I sat there, rigid with fear. Tears of panic pricked at the back of my eyes. All my responses had frozen solid. Only my eyeballs were still working. Through the tears of fright, I noticed that I was through three hundred feet and still falling. Then, in my headphones, I heard a voice, stricken with terror, shouting, 'Mayday, mayday, Mike Yankee going down, north of the field. Mayday, mayday, mayday.'

I sat there listening to this. Whoever that was, he was making me feel much, much worse. Then I snapped awake. 'Jesus Christ,' I thought, 'that's me! I'm a mayday!' All my resistance drained away. I wanted to throw the controls away and pray I'd come out alive. Then a weird logic took over: 'That can't be me. I can't be a mayday. No,' I thought. 'It's him, on the ground, that sadistic instructor. He's got a remote control. The bastard! It's his fault the controls are all going wrong. It's just part of the test.'

Whilst this rigmarole went through my head, I was staring mesmerized at the altimeter. The pointer was winding back furiously as I watched. But why would he want to frighten me like that? It wasn't fair. Please, I thought, please switch the engine back on. Don't play with me like this! Don't frighten me. Let me get out of here!

Every time I'd been up, every single lesson, the instructor had made me practise an 'engine-off' landing. At fifteen hundred feet, he would cut the engine, and shout, 'Engine failure!' Again, this is a S.O.P. – it's quite straightforward landing a helicopter with its engine off, and perfectly safe. It's called 'autorotating'. I'd entered this interesting condition without really meaning to. If I was autorotating, all was not lost. All I had to do was to pitch the aircraft straight down and 'spin the rotor up' – let the airflow make the rotor go round faster and faster as the Bell 47 glided down, and then, about fifty feet from the ground, 'deny the aircraft to the ground', that is raise the collective to make the rotors bite the air with increasing pitch and force, and feather it gently onto terra firma.

Passing one hundred and fifty feet I started pulling myself together. That insane voice was still shouting, 'Mayday!' in my ears, but my brain had started working again.

The last fifty feet, I thought. It's all about the last fifty feet. That's what he'd taught me. But you mustn't whack on all of the collective at once – little by little, watching the effect, leaving some in reserve if possible. It was all done in the last fifty feet.

The other essential thing, I recalled, as the Bell went through one hundred feet, was choosing your spot for landing. I'd forgotten all about that. Avoiding the M25 would be a good idea. A nice empty field – that was the thing. Was there one of those around? Did it matter any more? I looked through the windscreen. A row of trees was rushing up at me. Oak trees. No, it was too late to worry any more. I was definitely going to hit the oak trees. Too low and too slow to get over them, too close to pull up in front. My optimum glide-path for an engine-off landing under my present circumstances was straight through the middle of those trees.

I had to get over those trees. Just before I ploughed into them, I yanked on the collective stick. Trouble was I was still at about eighty feet – thirty feet too soon. But there was no option. The thing helicopters hate most of all are trees. I pulled, hard.

It almost worked. The helicopter heaved itself up and for a moment it looked like I'd got away with it. Then the tail rotor took a shine to the top of the nearest tree and crashed through it. The chopper pitched forward and ended up nose down in the field on the other side of the oaks. I'd landed – well, crash-landed at least.

I was left hanging nose-down from my harness-straps, staring at the ground. Lifting my eyes I could see the main rotor, still swishing round in a big lazy arc above my head, the blade-tips just missing the grass below my nose. By craning my head right back, I could just make out a herd of cows, wandering up to see what had crashed into their field.

I hung there for a few minutes, with my eyes crossed, unsure as to whether I might be alive or dead. There was a horrible smell of fuel in the air.

All of a sudden, I heard the sound of helicopters. It sounded as though there were dozens of them, thundering everywhere around me. All the Bristow's cadets had jumped into the other machines and flown over to see what had happened. Then I heard the engines of large trucks and jeeps – the crash tenders. They were coming to rescue me.

Someone flung open the door, and a face appeared in the opening. It was one of the other instructors. After checking that I was still alive, he grinned at me. Then he looked at the instruments.

'Who's a naughty boy, then? Who didn't do his emergency drills?' he said.

'Me,' I replied weakly.

'Who didn't put out a mayday?'

'Me,' I croaked.

He reached across and flicked up a switch alongside the collective.

'Who didn't switch off his fuel cock?'

'Me,' I replied meekly.

'And who didn't turn his magnetos off?' (These are the helicopter's spark-plugs.)

'Me,' I mumbled.

'And the battery master-switch?'

As he recited the litany of my failure, he kept flicking off switches, doing the things that I should have done to prevent any further disasters – like a massive explosion.

'It's an official crash,' he told me, 'so we're getting you into an ambulance.'

226

By the time we'd got back to the hangar the newspapers had already called for news of the accident. Someone at the aerodrome must have put in a call to them the minute they realized that I was a mayday and a potential story. I phoned Jackie immediately I wanted to get to her before the newspapers did.

I told her what had happened.

'I'm going to have a cup of tea, then take a slow drive and come home,' I said.

'Oh no you're not,' Jackie told me. 'You're going back up again. Look,' she said, 'you're not coming back home here tonight unless you get straight back up in the air again. I know you. If you don't do it right away, you'll never go up again.'

She was right. I flew one circuit round the airfield with Chris my instructor by my side and escaped to the safety of my car.

That crash gave me nightmares for months. It took me an extra ten lessons before I plucked up the courage to fly solo again.

Chapter Thirty-two

DEBT IS A FEARSOME THING.
It's frightening how quickly things can go wrong for you financially. One minute you're sailing along, blissfully certain that you can pay the milk bill, and it will always stay that way; the next – crash! Staring you in the face is bankruptcy.

When we bought Old Shoyswell Farm, instead of taking the money from the sale of Crowhurst Place and buying it outright, we embarked on a whole series of property deals, borrowing more money on the strength of that half-million profit from the sale of Crowhurst, and putting as little down on the farm as possible. With £500,000 as a deposit, the banks were bursting to lend up to ten times that much. Mrs Thatcher had made buying property an adventure, and everyone was going for it.

We'd had a good run investing in property since the middle Seventies, and while prices kept booming, the banks were quite happy to go on shovelling money at us. But now we were coming up to the start of the Eighties and all of a sudden property prices had started to drop. With the rough edges of that boom

228

beginning to show, we suddenly found ourselves the proud owners of a property that had a negative equity to the tune of £1.3 million.

Banks that had thrown money at us the day before were suddenly gripped in terminal panic. I spent more of my time running around keeping them at bay than I did working on my acting career. At one time we had nine banks to deal with simultaneously. But now, with the property crash hitting prices, we were no longer dealing with our nice local bank manager. Head office took control and turned their guns on the poor old private customers.

One bank manager actually admitted to me that he wasn't keen on lending money to customers. He preferred to put his allocation of money each month into the money markets. That way, he was sure to meet his targets set by head office. In their panic to make up for their own mistakes – bad loans to Third World countries and buying overpriced American banks – they took to calling in loans indiscriminately from their private customers (you and me), and in the process drove many people into unnecessary and premature bankruptcy.

I kept juggling the loans, but the pressure from the banks to clear up the situation was getting stronger and, with interest piling up, a decision had to be made.

Should we give the debt up as a bad job, and dump all our creditors right in the dirt, or should we try to fight our way out of it? Bankruptcy was very tempting for about two seconds, but hey, we'd borrowed the money and it had to be paid back, simple as that! After a series of meetings with my accountant, Alan Shalet, we all agreed the debts had to be met. We would fight.

We started selling while there was still a market to sell into, and we were not alone. People everywhere were trying to dump property. Jackie and I sold everything we could get our hands on. Our commercial property portfolio was the first to go. A factory here, a small row of shops there. A farm complex in Hartfield, Winnie the Pooh's home on the Ashdown Forest. David Joyes had found us a complex of farm buildings and we'd obtained planning permission to turn the whole lot into a sort of mini Brookside Close. That went. We had, in effect, a private boot sale, but even with all our property sold off at much reduced prices, we were still a long way short of clearing the debt.

Our own home was next to come under scrutiny. Because of the extortionate interest rates – at one time they were over 25 per cent – the debt was rising so fast that we were having trouble keeping up with it. We reluctantly decided that to reduce it by a substantial amount, Old Shoyswell Farm had to go. When at last everything was sold, we came out of it with a debt of just over a million pounds.

While Old Shoyswell was being marketed, we did what we should have done at Crowhurst Place and moved out of the main house. Three of the farm cottages were in a terrace and Jackie had turned them into a wonderful five-bedroomed house, so we decamped there while we tried to sort out our lives.

Jackie was fantastic about the mess my shenanigans had landed us all in: 'Why worry?' she comforted me. 'Let's just go and live in a caravan somewhere.' I'd taken her secure comfortable life and thrown it in the waste-bin, and not a word of recrimination from her. What an amazing girl.

Living with debt is absolutely terrible. You wake up every morning feeling sick in the stomach. All day the debt ulcer eats away at your guts, and when you go to bed, that sick feeling keeps you counting bills all night. I walked around in a coma, numbed by debt, unable to laugh or even smile, hardly able to eat. It changes the way you look at things, it even changes the taste of food – when you can bring yourself to eat, which is hardly ever.

I think that debt can have the effect many drugs have: it can turn you paranoid. I felt hunted, cornered, cutting myself off from everyone, even from Jackie and Katya, the people who loved and supported me the most. Like most men in that position, I tried to keep the worst of the problem from my family – what was the point of worrying them unnecessarily. But keeping your family at arm's length is absolutely the worst thing you can do in that pass. If there's one thing you need, when you're staring into that black hole, it's love. All the cherishing and affection the people closest to you can give, and only they can give, is your lifeline.

But you feel such a failure – that you've let them down. What a fool you've been. Many, many times, all I felt like doing was shutting myself away in a dark room and hiding until the storm passed over.

But there was no point in wallowing in self-pity, there was a job to do. The debt had to be managed and ultimately cleared. What we didn't know then was that there was even more trouble on the horizon. There would be an expensive and messy divorce from Leo Sayer to go through. That whole débâcle dragged on until the middle Eighties, ending in an out-of-court settlement, the details of which none of us is supposed to talk about.

Then there were the growing problems of Lloyds insurance. Back in the golden days of the early Seventies, I'd been introduced to a Lloyds agent called Christopher Moran at a party in LA. Christopher and I got on well, so well that he convinced me that Lloyds was a good place for some of my spare cash. He was right: at the time, it was. I used the seemingly painless income from Lloyds to pay my taxes. It made a change from having to sell a house.

Now the rumour was that there'd be some 'cash-calls' coming in the not too distant future – and like everybody in Lloyds, my liability as a name was *unlimited*. That meant that they could take your cash, home and the shirt off your back if they needed it. The time was coming to pay the price for a decade's easy income. With all these factors coming into play, over the forthcoming years our debt mountain was to grow to over £2,000,000.

It was a difficult period, but it wasn't all doom and gloom. We went on the odd holiday and put Katya through Harvard. In some of the darker moments of the crisis it got to be almost comical. There were times when we were stuck at home because we didn't even have the cash to buy petrol. A Rolls-Royce outside the house and no petrol: what a joke!

Jackie's mum, Min (who was now living with us), came to the rescue on more than one occasion. If it hadn't been for her pension there were times when we would have gone hungry.

Alan Shalet, was a rock, a true friend indeed. Without Alan's help and financial support, sometimes – although he would never admit it – from his own pocket, we would never have got through the worst of the crisis.

Alan is a devout Jew and a strong supporter of Israel. Whenever he goes to Jerusalem his first stop is at the Wailing Wall for his bracha. For the past ten years he's added a prayer for me and mine. When Zoë and I were filming *Love Hurts* in Israel, I slipped away for a minute and, kneeling in front of the Wailing Wall, returned the compliment.

Debt is a hungry bed-fellow; it eats up every spare penny. It's taken us nearly fifteen years to see the light at the end of the tunnel, but by the time you read this page, hopefully, I will be getting a decent night's sleep for the first time in a decade and a half.

Chapter Thirty-three

S WILLING AROUND AT THE VERY BOTTOM OF THIS TROUGH IN 1982, not knowing which way to turn, I got a call from a friend called Paul Dainty while I was on business in LA.

Paul was promoting a women's invitational tennis tournament in Australia. He had a load of spare first-class tickets on Continental Airlines, who were bringing all the women tennis players to Sydney, and he invited me out.

During the many years we'd been friends and business associates, Paul Dainty and I had got into the habit of going to Wimbledon every year and watching the entire tournament. From the Björn Borg era onwards, it had become our way of taking our annual holiday. We block-booked a table at San Lorenzo's in Wimbledon, where we'd have lunch and dinner for the whole fortnight.

One of the women players I'd met once or twice around the players' lounge at Wimbledon was Chris Evert, and when I boarded the plane in LA I discovered that she had a seat just behind me. We didn't particularly seek each other out on the plane, but we were friendly enough, and passed some of the otherwise boring flight chatting about life and tennis.

After a few days in Sydney, Paul took half the girls, including Chris Evert, to Perth for an exhibition tournament. I stayed behind in Sydney to hang out with the rest of the women players for a couple of days until they left for Taiwan. When it came time for my lot to move on I was tempted to join them. Just before we were due to head east, Paul Dainty phoned me and urged me to join him in Perth. The bribe was that after the matches finished in the late evening we would get to hit with the women pros. That was enough of an incentive. I caught the next plane to Perth.

When I arrived at the hotel, I picked up the backstage passes that Paul had left for me and shot off to the stadium where the tournament was being held.

The first person I bumped into was Chris Evert. She was coming out of the physio's room after treatment and seemed surprised to see me.

'Where have you been, Adam?' She smiled. 'Haven't seen you around for a few days.'

'Why,' I retorted, with a devastating line of wit, 'have you missed me?'

We held each other's eyes for a second and, with a dismissive grunt, she walked on court for her next match.

In that brief moment something had happened. I hadn't anticipated it happening and I'm sure it was the furthest thing from Chris's mind. But by the end of the three-day tournament, whatever it was had gone way beyond a passing fling.

It seemed to have come out of nowhere, but when I think about it now, even though neither of us realized it at the time, it had been brewing from our very first meeting at Wimbledon a couple of years earlier.

Chris Evert was remarkable. How do you ever really know what attracts you to somebody? All I knew was that there was something very special about her. Michael Lindsay-Hogg, who had directed *Budgie*, always told me that if you want a girl to fall in love with you, take her to watch you work. Mike's theory certainly worked in my case as far as Chris was concerned. Everyone has their little thing that they're good at, but watching Chris move in her graceful feminine way around a tennis court sparked off an all-consuming desire. Talent is a powerful aphrodisiac!

We spent more and more time in one another's company, and pretty soon we didn't want to be apart – not for one second. We had a lot in common, which surprised us. Occasionally, when I could persuade her, we'd play tennis. We'd sometimes hit late into the night, to the sound of rock 'n' roll music, and I don't think I ever won a point unless she wanted me to. But I didn't care – I was just happy to be on the other side of the net watching her move about the court.

We kept the affair secret and travelled all over the world to see each other. Our cover was finally blown in Hong Kong. She'd been playing a tournament in Tokyo and afterwards we took off for a couple of days' fun. We were sitting in one of the floating restaurants moored in the middle of Hong Kong Bay. Chris and I were deep in some conversation, when she glanced up to a point just above my left shoulder. I felt a hand come down on my shoulder. It was Tina, Bobby Moore's wife.

'Hi, Adam,' she said, 'what on earth are you doing here?'

Looking as guilty as hell, I introduced Tina to Chris and we joined her, Bobby, Alan Ball and his wife at their table. After a couple of drinks we stood up and said goodnight and left the restaurant, trying desperately not to look like a couple. But, of course, they all knew.

Next morning there were photographers crawling all over the hotel. When I got back to England two days later, Terry O'Neill rang me and asked if I'd seen the *Sun*. Right across the whole front page of the newspaper was the headline: 'Chris loves Adam'. It was 30 January 1984. And that was the whole thing blown.

For nearly two years I'd kept the relationship with Chris a secret from Jackie – this headline was the first she knew of it. It blew her apart. It blew our marriage apart too. It broke up Chris and her husband John Lloyd, and in the end it blew Chris and me back to our own sides of the Atlantic.

Everybody has problems with their emotional relationships. Most people work these problems out between themselves, in private. But when you have to deal with a problem out in public, with the world watching your every move, it's just about impossible to resolve. Every da, there's a story there on the page in front of you to pick the scab off a wound just when it's beginning to heal.

It doesn't make me feel good to admit it now, but I'd left a long wake of unhappiness through the lives of at least four people. I'd been selfish and self-obsessed.

Jackie had shown me nothing but love, she'd cherished me, comforted and supported me in my worst moments and I repaid her by throwing her love back in her face. Over the forthcoming years I tried to make amends, and I was lucky – although I didn't deserve to be allowed back into her life, Jackie took me in.

But once you smash a house down, no matter how hard you try to rebuild it, it can never be the same again. It may, as it was in our case, be better and stronger, but it will never be the same. The affair with Chris was not just a fly-by-night thing, but obviously it wasn't to be.

Recently, when Chris was asked about our relationship by a journalist, she answered: 'There was an opportunity for us to go forward together, but unfortunately it wasn't taken.'

I can't put it any more eloquently than that. Why didn't I go with Chris? I suppose because I couldn't live without Jack and Kat. All through the affair with Chris, I never stopped loving Jack. The dream is and always has been to be content with one woman, but maybe if the dream came true I wouldn't recognize it.

After the Chris Evert affair, my life wasn't so much worn as threadbare. Not only did the pieces of my shattered relationship with Jackie need to be picked up and put back together, I still had to deal with the financial shambles that the debt had left me in. I had a lot to face up to. So I did what any normal red-blooded idiot would do, I went out and bought a nice new shovel and dug a big hole in the sand and shoved my head in it. I then proceeded to live my life as if nothing had happened. I did what I'd always done with problems, I pretended they didn't exist and convinced myself that if I gave them enough time they would simply resolve themselves.

With the collapse of our finances, cash was in very short supply. I'd done a major job of grovelling to a couple of our banks and had managed to squeeze £300,000 out of them to buy our new home. Crockham Grange was a pretty Georgian house in Kent, which we'd bought to be near Kat's new school, Croydon High School for Girls. With Angelina and her daughter, Rosemary, installed in the staff quarters and Min, Jack's mum, tucked away cosily in the attic, we settled down with our entourage ready to face whatever life had to throw at us.

Kat now had her eighth house and her sixth school. Although Kat was to live in two more houses before she finally got her own flat at the age of twenty-four, Croydon High turned out to be her last school. Kat had tried boarding at Princess Di's old school, West Heath in Sevenoaks, and hated it. On the recommendation of our friend Marcia Jacques, we enrolled Kat at Croydon High. It turned out to be one of our better decisions.

Croydon High was very proud of its sporting history and that suited Kat down to the ground. In no time at all she'd made both the netball and hockey teams. I loved going to watch her play for the school. In all her years there, I hardly missed a match. It was the highlight of my week standing on the sidelines shouting myself hoarse.

Kat also found herself a new friend, Helena Sykes. She captured Jackie's heart and mine as well and has become one of our closest friends. A beautiful girl, rather like a younger version of Ingrid Bergman, Helly, one of the most feminine women I know, is also one of the funniest people around. She came with us on holidays all over the world and would keep us in hysterics reading from her favourite Mills and Boon book. Her quirky way of looking at life is wasted on after-dinner small talk and it's my life's mission to get her to put her not inconsiderable talents into writing.

Although money was in short supply, somehow or another we scraped together enough for Jackie to do a course at the Pardon specialist painting school in Belgravia, London. She was going to learn how to paint wood and make it look like marble, or paint marble to look like stone, or paint stone and make it look like wood – you get the picture.

On the course with Jack was a girl called Karen Killik. Karen's husband, Paul, was a stockbroker with Quilter Goodison, whose chairman, Sir Nicholas Goodison, was also Chairman of the Stock Exchange. It was about as Establishment as you can get. Except for one element, Paul Killik.

Paul walked, talked and acted like a typical stockbroker, but he wasn't in the least bit typical. He was only pretending. Underneath he was the only broker I'd met from the City who understood and cared that ordinary people might want to deal in shares.

Paul and I hit it off at once. We discovered that when it came to the City we had a lot of common ground under our feet. I shared Paul's views about the need for the City to get into the lives of 'ordinary people'. We sat, late into the night, swapping ideas on how to make the City accessible.

Some months later I was in a play called *Down an Alley Filled with Cats* at the Mermaid Theatre. Paul called and asked me to lunch, he had a business proposition he wanted to put to me. Apparently he'd got his fellow directors at Quilter Goodison fired up about the idea of going into business with me. They wanted to start a joint company offering financial advice to high earners in the media and show business.

There's always been a gap, born of mutual suspicion and disdain, between the City and Celebrity. As no artist can relate to people in the 'boring' City, and City establishment folk have trouble relating to 'anyone', Paul felt that I might be just the person to bridge that gap. For once I didn't in my usual lunatic manner jump straight in with both feet. This took some thinking about. This was very grown-up. I didn't know whether I was ready to blow the cobwebs off the wedding suit and sit behind a desk in a 'real' office. After asking for time to think it over I retired to my old 'office' in one of the restaurants in Fortnum & Mason.

I'd spent the Sixties and Seventies doing business from the corner table in the Soda Fountain at Fortnums. There had been many times in the early Seventies when my personal assistant Melanie Green and I would arrive for breakfast and hold meetings right through until closing time at midnight.

Melanie had thick black luscious hair that hung in waves across her shoulders, and full sensuous lips and an even fuller figure. She had a body that men went to war over, and she was the first woman friend I ever had. Not only was she exceptionally efficient, she became my emotional guru all through the Chris Evert affair. For four or five years, there was hardly a place anywhere in the world that I travelled to without Melanie being by my side. We shared everything: thoughts, humour, aspirations, everything, in fact, except carnal knowledge of each other. Mel kept that part of her life strictly for her boyfriend.

Although Colin Berlin (Leo Sayer's joint manager) and I had a working base in nearby Berkeley Street, I hardly set foot in the place. Holding court in the stylish surroundings of Fortnum & Mason's Soda Fountain restaurant beat the formality of offices any old day. But there was one big drawback. Mobile phones hadn't yet been invented and there was a scarcity of public phones. I had to take all my business calls in the kitchen. It's not very easy to do business deals when you've got 'two poached eggs on wholemeal' banging away in your ear.

It wasn't an arrangement that suited the kitchen staff either. They got fed up with some self-important actor screaming at them to keep the noise down while he got on with his negotiations.

Eventually things came to a head and Gerry Hamilton, the Managing Director of Fortnums, informed me one day, that because of my overuse of their phone, the kitchen staff were threatening a mutiny. He'd considered the situation carefully (Uh oh, here it comes, I thought. The big E) and because I was a valued customer, he'd decided to get British Telecom to install my own direct line at the table.

Only in England!

Timing is everything in life, and Paul was spot on with his. My private life had taken a battering and the dreaded debt followed me like a black cloud wherever I went. I'd resisted being a grown-up all my life and this is how I'd ended up for my troubles. The more I thought about Paul's offer the more I thought that putting some responsible structure into my life was an attractive prospect. Perhaps it was time to start taking life a little bit more seriously.

No more using a teashop for an office, no more mad obsessions with helicopters, no more flitting around the world on the whim of a short skirt, it was time to grow up and deal with my responsibilities.

In the past I'd put Jackie's emotional and financial security at risk. Now I prepared myself to fight my natural instincts for having fun and bury myself in the grey boring world of business. With this offer from Quilter Goodison, I could see a chance – if only I could knuckle down to it – of at least rebuilding our financial security.

I discarded my jeans and T-shirt and forced myself into a pin-striped suit. I had a new role to play and I committed myself to it 100 per cent.

We called our company Faith and we had the best launch-party ever, thanks, not least, to the efforts of Juliet Parry my wonderful, voluptuous red-headed secretary and my new assistant, Jo Bowlby.

I'd first met Jo in the office of my Sixties estate-agent friend Andrew Langton. As part of my property dealings, I had a small flat in Kensington I wanted to get rid of, and one day after having lunch at San Lorenzo's, Andrew and I went back to his office to discuss how best to market the flat. As we were walking upstairs to his room on the first floor we passed the most stunning girl. It was Jo Bowlby.

At nineteen she looked like a Belgravia version of Mariel Hemingway, with dark hair. What I didn't know when I insisted to Andrew that this nineteen-year-old novice estate agent should handle the sale of my flat was that she was going to turn out to be one of the brightest people I've ever met. She has an incredible ability to turn the most complicated set of circumstances into clear and simple logic. Also, despite her Belgravia background, she had what the Queen Mother's famous for, the ability to move across all bands of society. Acton to Belgravia is only six miles by car, but by birth they're a million miles apart.

Jo's ability to mix with everybody came in very useful at the party considering it was like a who's who of politics, sport and show business. In her wonderful confident way she shared with me the burden of putting everyone at their ease. There was Ravi Tikoo, the shipping millionaire, scribbling mathematical equations on the back of his hand to show Tessa Sanderson how she could get an extra three metres out of her javelin throw, while Sir Nicholas Goodison swopped notes on music with Eric Clapton. It was an amazing night with a fantastic mixture of people, and with everyone congratulating us, it augured well for the future of the company.

We set up offices in Knightsbridge and slowly but steadily, over the next year or so, we began building our portfolio of clients. Seb Coe was one of the first names we took on. I'd become friends with him and his dad, Peter, through training at Battersea Park athletics track. Peter had put together a marathon training programme for me and very kindly monitored my progress.

By this time I was doing around forty miles a week and was on schedule for my first marathon. Because I didn't want our fickle weather interfering with my training I bought a running machine and installed it in my office. It was great – I could run and do business on the phone at the same time.

It was on one of these long runs that I first realized that I had a heart problem.

240

Chapter Thirty-four

IN JULY 1986 I WAS DOING A TWELVE-MILER ON THE RUNNING machine before getting down to work. It's a fact of getting fit that the more you train the fitter you get. After months of hard running you shouldn't feel after just a few miles that you're running through treacle, yet that day the longer I ran the thicker the treacle became.

By the time the twelve miles had gone by I was in a bad way. Sweating and dizzy, I staggered to the sofa in my office and fell onto it, exhausted. All my energy had been drained from me, making me feel like a dishcloth that had been wrung out and tossed in the corner. Something was wrong, very wrong.

I went down the road to my doctor, Michael Gormley, who had a practice in Basil Street. He was a sweet man and a very good doctor. I'd been going to him for years, and trusted him implicitly.

When I told him I had a heart problem he smiled kindly and stuck a thermometer in my mouth while he took my blood pressure. A prod here and a prod there and then an ECG – that's when they stick little rubber pads, with wires attaching them to a machine, all over your chest and monitor your heartbeat. Everything came out normal and Michael, who knew about some of my money troubles, felt I was probably suffering from stress. Nothing that my three-week holiday in Kenya, due to start in two days, couldn't cure.

But I knew different. When you are very fit, as I was, you get to know your body like a Grand Prix racing driver knows his car. There was something wrong with my heart and no matter what Michael said, even though he was a doctor, I knew my body better than he did. And anyway I'd had a warning. Over lunch one day, Michael Winner, the film director (who was a friend at the time), had told me that the only certain way doctors could diagnose heart problems was by giving you an angiogram. Winner once had a bit of a scare with his health, and being very meticulous had studied the different treatments. He told me that if ever I was to have a heart problem, I should demand an angiogram. This is when they stick a camera with a light on it into one of your main arteries – say in the leg or the arm – and then feed it up through your arterial system to the heart, where it videos all the clogged-up gubbins and faulty plumbing. So, armed with Winner's advice, no matter what the doctor said, I was in no mood to argue. I knew in my bones that I had a heart problem!

We politely argued the issue back and forth and at last, to placate me, I suspect, Michael sent me off to the Cromwell Hospital for a treadmill test. Once they'd wired me up to the monitor, I jogged away on the running machine. The test lasts for fifteen minutes and every three minutes the operator increases the gradient of the track, so that it's as if you're running up a gradually steepening hill.

I was trotting along happily on this machine, feeling fine and trying desperately to impress the comely nurse in charge of the test with my incredible fitness. But on the fourteenth minute she suddenly called me to a halt. I protested saying that this test could take the place of my evening run, but she was having none of it and warned me not to run any more until Michael Gormley had seen the results. When I pressed her to tell me if there was anything wrong she just clammed up. No matter how much I bullied and cajoled, she wouldn't tell me what she'd seen on the trace.

The next morning I was outside Michael's surgery the minute they opened for business. He told me there was a slight blip at

242

fourteen-and-a-half minutes, but that it was nothing to worry about and that I should go off on holiday the next day as planned.

Again I insisted on getting an angiogram, there was no way I wanted to go off to Kenya and be brought home in a wooden box after keeling over running on a beach in Mombasa.

We argued the toss back and forth, getting nowhere, until in desperation I threatened to sit in his waiting-room all day and all night if need be until he found me a specialist who would give me the test. I also told him that if he didn't help me, I'd tell all his patients that he was trying to kill me off. Two hours later I had an appointment with one of the top men in Harley Street.

The specialist did the same tests as Michael Gormley had done. He looked at the monitor trace from the running-machine and passed me fit. This was getting decidedly boring. What did I have to do to convince these people? I had a heart problem and I was going to get my angiogram if it killed me. The consultant prattled on about how they were intrusive into the heart, and that they didn't like doing them unless they were certain there was a problem.

'Look,' he said patiently, 'let me put it in perspective for you: if I were to go out into the street and interview 1,000 men of your age and size, with your test results, we'd be lucky if we found even one with a heart problem.'

'Well this is your lucky day,' I persisted, 'because you've found him, and he wants an angiogram.'

It's at times like this that you thank God for money: because I was a private patient I eventually got my way. I went home and told Jackie the news. She went berserk. 'Only you would do this to us on the day we're all supposed to be going on holiday. Why can't you behave like a normal person?'

Finally I calmed her down and we agreed that she should go to the airport the next day with Kat and Helly. She could check us in and I would meet them in the BA lounge once I'd finished at the hospital. Next morning I crept out of the house at 5 a.m. and arrived at the Wellington Hospital triumphant. At last I was getting my test.

Two hours later I was woken by the specialist shaking my arm.

'We've had to get you up early,' he murmured, in that quiet calm voice doctors use when they are about to hit you with the thing you least want to hear. 'I'm afraid you've got to cancel your holiday, all the main arteries from your heart are 70 per cent blocked. You've got to have immediate open-heart surgery.'

If it's possible for your legs to collapse under you when you are lying in bed, then mine did. I went weak with fear and tears pricked the back of my eyes. I'd pressed the doctors to do the test, and now that it showed what I'd always suspected, the news was shattering. Just the sound of the words 'open-heart surgery' sent waves of shock and disbelief washing over me. Heart surgery was something that happened to other people, not to me. I was frightened to death but at least now I knew the problem and it could be dealt with.

After I'd recovered from the initial shock, my thoughts turned to the girls' holiday. They'd been looking forward to this African trip for months, I couldn't let them down. I pushed my luck with the doctor. 'Can you do this in three weeks when I get back from Africa?'

'No.' He was very firm. 'You don't understand. You can't even move from this bed. Tomorrow morning you've got to have a quintuple bypass operation.'

On my way home in the car twenty minutes later, after checking myself out of the hospital to the howling protests of the surgeon, I started to reflect on what had happened. I was a heart patient and it wasn't a certainty that by tomorrow lunch-time I'd still be a *live* heart patient.

Just outside Croydon, on my route home, there's a tiny pocket of countryside with a lovely valley running through it. I stopped the car and sat there, quiet and absolutely still, staring out at the rolling hills, trying to make sense of what was happening.

The girls. What would become of the girls, if anything went wrong during the operation? What would they do? How would they manage without me? I'd be all right because I'd be dead. But they would be left to go through that awful grieving that comes with losing someone you love.

It wasn't a thought to dwell on. It was too unbearable, and anyway there were practical matters to be dealt with. Like my will, for instance. The debt! How much would go to Jackie and how much to Kat? Who was going to get my collection of *Archers* memorabilia? And what was going to happen to Florence, my darling fur coat that I'd worn in LA winter and summer all through the Seventies, and was now lying in state in the vaults of the Beverly Hills Hotel? Spurred on by these important matters, I gunned the Roller into action and belted home.

That night, we sat round the kitchen table and wept.

Chapter Thirty-five

AFTER THE HEART OPERATION I DON'T KNOW IF I WAS TRYING TO prove to myself that I wasn't mortal but I went totally and utterly berserk. Not only was I the full-time managing director of the Faith company, I was still co-managing Leo Sayer with Colin Berlin.

On top of all that I then talked myself into doing *Budgie the Musical*. Unfortunately it didn't live up to *Budgie* the TV series and in spite of a modest run in the West End it came and went with little incident. Although it was disappointment to be in a West End flop, its closure came as a bit of a relief in some ways, because as if I didn't already have enough to do I'd agreed to write a financial page for a national newspaper.

Some weeks before *Budgie the Musical* opened I received a call that caused beads of sweat to break out on my forehead: 'David Montgomery, editor of the *News of the World*, is on the phone for you.' While my secretary was sounding mildly amused, my heart bypass operation was threatening to blow asunder.

What the hell did the *News of the World* want with me? What had I done? What had they found out? My mouth went dry and I croaked out a strangled greeting. David Montgomery, probably used to this type of response, quickly reassured me that he wasn't planning on wrecking my life but wanted to offer me lunch. Intrigued, but still not entirely convinced that it wasn't a smoke-screen to expose me as an *Archers* fanatic, I agreed.

'We want you to become City Editor of the *News of the World*,' said David, looking up from his Dover sole.

Jo Bowlby and I looked at each other, our flabbers were gasted. I couldn't believe what I was hearing. I laughed at him. 'But you haven't got any finance in the *News of the World*.'

'I know,' he said. 'But after seeing how you talked about the City on television last night we'd like you to come and say the same things to our readers. [I'd been reviewing business pro-grammes on BBC2 the night before.] We'll give you your own financial page.'

Apart from the financial benefits of a weekly wage, the idea of having my own page in a national newspaper was mind-blowing. Jo and I were so excited at the prospect we agreed that after lunch we'd go back to Wapping and meet David's boss. A short drive later, we found ourselves being ushered into the office of Rupert Murdoch. With the shortest of preliminaries Rupert cut to the chase.

'So, are you gonna do the page, Adam?' he drawled in a soft Australian twang. The way he asked the question, his confidence that I could do the job flattered me. If someone like Rupert Murdoch thought I could be a writer, then who was I to argue?

There was a suggestion from David that any shortfall in my writing ability could be taken care of by one of their staff journalists, but the idea of having my name attached to a page that somebody else had written did not appeal to me one tiny bit. No writer, no matter how skilled, can write for someone else, and even though up to then I'd only ever written 'Best Wishes, Adam Faith', I was going to write this page myself, or not at all.

Over the next couple of weeks word got round what is euphemistically called Fleet Street that I was about to sign up for the *News of the World*. I got bombarded by calls from other news-papers offering me a similar deal to David Montgomery's. Actually, I was quite happy with the *News of the World* and in particular David Montgomery. David knew exactly what ordinary people were about and who I wanted to write for, so I was looking forward to working with him. But, curiosity being what it is, I couldn't resist listening to the other newspapers' offers.

I was particularly tickled by a proposition from Andrew Alexander, financial editor of the *Daily Mail*. Jackie and I had first met him at No. 10 Downing Street when we were invited to one of Mrs Thatcher's patronizing celebrity soirées. It was the first time I'd met the Iron Lady and when it came to my turn to be introduced, she gave me a fixed smile and sweetly said to me, 'Oh Mr Faith I do so love your music, where are you singing at the moment?' I coolly retorted, 'I haven't sung for thirty years.' Totally unfazed, she dismissed me with a turn of her head, and went on to her next victim.

Laughing, Jackie and I scuttled off and joined a group which included Norman Tebbit and Andrew Alexander. Due to a mutual interest in gardening and houses, Jackie and Andrew hit it off immediately, and we'd all become quite friendly since that first meeting at No. 10.

Over lunch at the Grill Room in the Savoy, Andrew tried to persuade me that a whole page was too big a job for a novice and that I should be content with a 300-word column and join him at the *Daily Mail*.

But I didn't want a column, I wanted a whole page. I didn't want to *work* for a City editor I wanted to *be* a City editor. So, after a lot of toing and froing, I'm sure much against his better judgement, Andrew agreed to let me have a whole page.

My offer from the *News of the World* was still on the table and just after the approach from the *Daily Mail* I got a call from Rupert Murdoch. He was planning to buy the *Today* newspaper and put David Montgomery in as editor. The offer to write for the *News of the World* didn't seem quite so attractive any more now I was going to lose David Montgomery. Rupert sympathized with my concern and suggested that we put the whole thing on hold until the new editor had got her feet wet and decided whether she even wanted a financial page.

As it turned out, she didn't, and that left me free to take up the *Daily Mail* offer.

A few weeks after I started the page there were rumblings that Quilter Goodison, my partners in the Faith company, were about to get taken over by one of the big boys in the City.

Before it happened they graciously came to me and offered me the option that I could either go with them or I could look for another partner. I'd enjoyed my time with Quilter's but there was no way I wanted to be a tiny cog in a huge corporate machine. So, between bashing out pearls of financial wisdom to my *Daily Mail* readers, I trailed around the City looking for a new partner.

By now Faith was building a very useful list of clients, including Sebastian Coe and Tessa Sanderson, whose affairs needed special personal attention, so the choice of partner was crucial. I started talking to small merchant banks, but without much enthusiasm. I'd got tired of the stultifying straitjacket mentality of the City and felt I needed somebody with a bit more flair.

And boy, did I get a partner with flair!

Jo Bowlby, who'd now been working with me for over a year, got her brother Tommy to introduce me to the man he worked for, Roger Levitt.

Levitt, a small dark-complexioned man with slicked-back hair and a thin moustache, was the spitting image of Freddie Mercury from Queen. Smoking cigars the size of tree trunks and sporting flashy bow ties, he was a caricature of himself.

When I first met Levitt, every instinct inside me screamed out, 'Run away, now, and don't ever speak to this man again.' He was the absolute antithesis of everything Quilter Goodison stood for, and didn't that say it all? But what a salesman. What a salesman! He was so brilliant at selling that if he'd told Mother Theresa that sin was good for the soul, she probably would have believed him.

Intrigued by his sales pitch, I entered into a series of complicated negotiations with him. Put simply, Levitt would get 50 per cent of my company Faith and I would get the option to buy, for two and a half million pounds, 5 per cent of the Levitt Group. If over the five-year period of our agreement the value of his company increased, so would my options. With big City institutions breaking their necks to get a stake in the Levitt Group at that time, the bubble looked set to grow and grow. Figures of five or six hundred million pounds were being bandied about. In theory, it could have set me up for life with a profit of ten or possibly twenty million pounds.

Even though with all my other activities I was earning over five figures a week, I'm afraid that against my better instincts I succumbed to greed, and shook hands on a deal.

While I was settling in with my new partner I was still faced with the practicalities of getting the page written every week.

My relationship with Andrew Alexander and the *Daily Mail* was, to say the least, at times tempestuous. We started arguing over every little issue and I did my best to sabotage my blossoming journalistic career by letting it drift into an 'old stag, new stag' confrontation. In spite of his advice and support during my early days at the *Daily Mail*, Andrew and I were coming at the City from completely opposite directions, and our working relationship was bound to hit the buffers.

Unfortunately my lack of experience in newspaper politics and the hierarchical structure helped to create a lot of the problems between us. Basically my trouble was that I'd always lived a free and independent life and wasn't used to having a boss who could give me orders. Things came to a head when Andrew rewrote one of my stories, as he was perfectly entitled to do as City editor, and I jumped out of my pram, stamped my foot and had verbal fisticuffs with him over the telephone.

My contract wasn't renewed.

In desperation I tried to recover some ground with the *Daily Mail* by agreeing to do an interview with the Chancellor of the Exchequer's wife, Thérèse Lawson, on Budget Day. Every newspaper in Fleet Street had been desperately trying to get the interview ever since Nigel became Chancellor but had had no luck. Because the Lawsons were friends of mine, the *Daily Mail* thought I might have a better shot at getting it, which turned out to be true.

Due to the urgency of the story, I flew up to Leicestershire in a helicopter and over dinner at the Lawsons' house taped my interview with Thérèse.

As soon as I got home the next morning, Rod Gilchrist, deputy editor of the *Daily Mail*, was on the phone asking me for the tapes so that one of his staff journalists could write the piece for me. But I wasn't having any of that. I was quite happy to allow Rod to send one of his staff reporters down to our house, to put some structure on the piece, but if there was going to be a Thérèse Lawson interview with Adam Faith's name on the bottom, then Adam Faith was going to write it.

After several hours of sweat and toil, trying to make sense of six hours of tape, I sent Rod's journalist packing. Using her structure as a guideline, I sat up all night and finished the 2,500-word interview at six-twenty the next morning. Bleary-eyed from my night's efforts I stumbled into Rod's office to deliver my piece.

It turned out to be a triumph and was syndicated all over the world, making the *Daily Mail* a very nice profit, thank you very much. Two weeks later, despite Rod's genuine assurance that the interview would earn me mountains of brownie points, my P45 was in the post.

What surprised me in the following weeks was how much I missed the page. I missed not having my platform to pontificate on a subject I felt passionate about.

For the next six months I used every ruse, every trick, every ounce of persistence I possessed to get my page back, but all my badgering fell on deaf ears at the *Daily Mail*. So I turned my attention to its sister paper, the *Mail on Sunday*. Stewart Steven, its editor, was tickled by the idea, but had been warned by Andrew Alexander that I was a nightmare to work with and he should stay well away from me.

I persisted, I grovelled, I did everything to try to convince Stewart that his paper would collapse without me. Finally, I beat him into submission, and I think, more out of amusement than cold, professional common sense, he made arrangements for me to meet his financial editor, Clive Woolman. If Clive was comfortable with the idea, I was in. Remarkably, considering that his background in journalism was *The Financial Times*, Clive understood where I was coming from and agreed to let me join his team.

I was back. I had my page again.

I got into the habit of preparing factsheets on some of my articles and, considering it was a financial page, the response from the readers was surprisingly enthusiastic.

The page's greatest success was when Paul Killik, my stock-broking chum who had become my main adviser on the page, suggested that we do an article on Permanent Interest Bearing Shares (PIBS). This sounds boring when you say it, never mind trying to write about it. And as I didn't want to fill my page up with a lot of boring jargon, I put together a factsheet in 'English'. The response was unbelievable – a hundred letters to a City page was considered an avalanche. We got sixteen thousand.

Even today I get people thanking me for recommending PIBS, they've done nothing but go up.

Unfortunately for every 'high' there's normally a 'low'.

Mine came in the form of a campaign to turn the whole of Britain into millionaires. At one of many of Jeffrey Archer's parties I met John Bryant, deputy editor of *The Times*. In another life he'd been the editor of the now defunct newspaper the *Correspondent* and had launched a share scheme proposed by a bloke in the City. Robin Griffiths, a chartist with James Capel who predicted the movements of share prices by studying the charts, claimed that over a ten-year period he could 'turn six thousand pounds into a million'. By the time the *Correspondent* went under, the scheme had proved itself a success. Happy to see the idea revived, John felt that my page would be just the home for it. So did I, I absolutely loved the idea. The notion of being able to turn all my readers into budding pools winners was altogether too tantalizing to resist.

In my usual reserved and cautious manner, I totally, utterly and completely over-hyped the idea when I first announced the scheme in the page. I advised people to do whatever they had to to get their hands on six thousand pounds and stand by for launch date six weeks later.

The response to the announcement of the 'Faith in a Million' scheme caught all of us by surprise. The next week we had over twenty-eight thousand enquiries.

For six weeks I plugged the life out of it. The excitement of the build-up was fantastic and people came up to me all the time, egging me on. It seemed that everybody I met was going to join the scheme and become millionaires. Even Stewart Steven and I had our six thousand ready for the off.

Two days before launch date, at the height of the excitement, the 'proverbial' hit the fan in spades. I was on the M25 heading to Elstree Studios for a day's filming on *Love Hurts*, when the mobile burst into life. Clive Woolman, my boss at the *Mail on Sunday*, was screaming ever so slightly hysterically across the waves at me. He ordered me to come to the paper immediately. Robin Griffiths, our genius chartist, who'd masterminded the scheme, for some inexplicable reason had been forced to pull out.

Shattered by the news, I went into terminal shock, but what could I do? There was no way I could turn the car around: time, tide and a day's filming on *Love Hurts* wait for no man. I could just imagine what Zoë would say if I phoned and said, 'Do you mind postponing our love scene for eight hours whilst I sort out my page?' With Clive still spitting blood down the phone at me I promised that when filming finished I'd scoot straight back to the paper for a council of war.

I was in big-time trouble. Without Robin Griffiths there was no scheme. All that evening and late into the night, I sat with Clive and Stewart, desperately trying to come up with a solution to the fix that we'd been put in. Apart from not relishing the thought of a nine-thousand-egg omelette all over my face, the most disappointing thing for me was that I was going to let down all those budding millionaires.

In a way I suppose it was understandable that the boys in the City got cold feet. It was estimated that by launch date, two days later, there could have been over a hundred thousand people with their six thousand pounds at the ready. The trouble was that with so many people playing the game, we could have been in danger of creating a financial Frankenstein's monster. Our 'Faith in a Million' investment fund threatened to grow so big that it would have disrupted the whole stock market. It would have been like an Ealing comedy without the jokes.

The rest of Fleet Street had a field day. I can't remember exactly what they said about me, but words like 'Financial Cretin' and 'Budgiegate' were bandied about.

The next week I went into the *Mail on Sunday* and offered my resignation. It wasn't only that I'd embarrassed the newspaper – I couldn't stand the criticism. It made me want to find a dark corner to hide in until the shooting stopped. Happily for me, Stewart Steven brushed aside my offer to resign, and loyally stood by me through all the flak that subsequently rained down. I shall be grateful to Stewart for the rest of my life and feel privileged to call him a friend.

Years later I still get people coming up to me and saying, 'What happened to that million pounds you promised us?' But what can I say? I was confident that the scheme would work and as it turned out, with world share markets going on to hit record heights, that optimism wasn't misplaced.

But the 'Pinstripes' thought differently. The idea was altogether too popular for its own good.

Chapter Thirty-six

J ACKIE WAS HEARTBROKEN. I WAS BARELY KEEPING CONTROL. WE were both craning our necks to get a better view of our only child standing forlornly on the steps of the Four Seasons Hotel, Philadelphia. Dwarfed by the towering pillars that stand either side of the entrance, she seemed to grow tinier and more vulnerable as the taxi pulled away.

We had just installed Kat into Penn, America's oldest East Coast Ivy League university and, desperate not to let her see how devastated we were at leaving her on her own, Jack and I put on our bravest faces. With one final pathetic little wave from us our taxi turned the corner, and the second Kat was out of sight, Jack opened up the floodgates.

Six months earlier, Katya had woken up one morning and suddenly decided against spending three years doing political rallies and getting legless every night in an English university; instead, she wanted to go to college in America.

So, Kat and I took a trip to the States and gave their Ivy League colleges the once over. Probably because with its cloistered courtyards and period buildings it most closely resembled an English college, she settled on Penn.

We were lucky, because one of Ravi Tikoo's sons had been a student there. Ravi had very kindly introduced us to the dean of the university – a dead ringer for Jack Nicholson – and after a polite chat and a cup of tea, he offered Katya a place on a History course.

Five days before Kat was due to start her first term, Jackie and I travelled to Philadelphia to help her get settled in. There were all sorts of arrangements to be made, not least her living accommodation. As Kat was on her own in a foreign country, she had decided against getting her own apartment and had opted to live on campus.

Totally dissatisfied with 'horrendous' student accommodation, I moved Kat three times in the first two days. The girls, cringing with embarrassment at my demanding antics, completely disowned me and went on a forty-eight-hour tour of the local coffee houses. Finally, I was satisfied with my (sorry, Kat's) accommodation, and Jack set about making the room habitable.

There was the odd piece of furniture that looked as though it had fallen off the back of a famine relief lorry, but Jackie decided to start from scratch and do a complete 'make-over'. While Jackie toured the furniture showrooms, Kat and I slipped into a discount electrical store to get the essentials: video, answering-machine, TV and, of course, the prerequisite nine-thousand mega-watt stereo-system.

Whilst the store manager was stuffing our car full of the electrical goodies, and I was mentally adding up the damage, an enthusiastic English voice rang out from the other side of the store: 'Hi, are you Adam Faith?' A young lad about Katya's age, looking every bit the student, bounded over waving a piece of paper in my face. I gave him an autograph for his grandma and asked him what he was doing in America. His name was Paul Hayman and it turned out that he was doing a year at Penn on a student exchange programme.

'Oh, what a coincidence,' I said, and called Kat over.

'What hall of residence are you staying in?' Kat asked him.

'Van Pelt,' he answered.

'Really? So am I,' said Kat. 'What floor?'

'Second,' said Paul.

'Me too.'

I jumped in, 'What's your room number?'

'Two, four, two.' Kat and I laughed as he said it – her room was bang opposite.

Still giggling in amazement at the coincidence, I paid for our purchases and offered Paul a lift back to campus.

As we weaved our way through the downtown commuter traffic, I asked Paul where he lived back in England.

'Oh, you'll never have heard of it,' he sighed, as he spread himself across the rear seat. 'It's a little village in Kent called Riverhead.'

I nearly ran the car off the road in surprise. Riverhead was less than two miles from our house. When we'd all recovered from the shock of yet another unlikely coincidence, we got onto the subject of birthdays.

Unbelievably, Paul was born on 19 December 1970, the same day as Katya.

I felt like I'd fallen into the *Twilight Zone*. That type of coincidence could never be written into a movie script, because nobody would believe that it could possibly be true. It was very spooky, but Jackie and I had the comfort of knowing there would be at least one friendly face on campus for Kat.

By the time it came to that dreaded farewell on the steps of the Four Seasons Hotel, Jackie and I were having the gravest doubts that Kat had made the right decision. The campus bordered on one of the most deprived areas in Philadelphia and just hours before we were due to catch our flight, three people were shot dead coming out of a cinema one block from Katya's hall of residence.

Jackie and I argued in the cab, all the way to the airport, about whose fault it was that Kat was in an American university. Jack had always been against the idea, and blamed me for encouraging Kat in the first place. Our kindly taxi driver acting as referee tried to reassure Jackie that Kat would be perfectly safe.

I checked us in, getting suspicious looks from the woman behind the desk, as she kept flicking her eyes up at Jack who was doing a good job of flooding the airport with her waterworks. Settling Jackie down in the departure lounge, with a mug of coffee and a piece of cheesecake the size of a block of flats, I excused myself and headed for the gents.

Up to then, I had somehow managed to keep a grip on myself. But in the relative privacy of the urinals, I suddenly lost control.

I was standing in front of the basin, with my shoulders heaving up and down with misery, I was having terrible trouble keeping my hands still and was in grave danger of spraying the whole lavatory.

The blokes standing either side of me recoiled in horror. Profoundly embarrassed, rivers of tears still cascading down my face, I spluttered my apologies and backed away, remembering just in time, thank God, to make myself decent before stumbling back into the airport terminal.

We stoically kept ourselves in check right up until take off. Then unable to hold back any longer we flung ourselves into each other's arms and bawled our eyes out all the way back to Gatwick.

It was at least five minutes after we'd been in the house before we called Kat to see if she was OK. Unable to get her on the phone, we fretted for four days until we finally made contact. She'd been so busy making friends, she'd completely forgotten to ring us.

Kids! Who'd have them?

One year at Penn was enough for Katya. Finding it difficult to settle in Philadelphia, she applied to change university, and after sitting the entrance exam enrolled at Harvard.

She changed her major from History to Environmental Studies – basically film, video and photography – and settled down to three happy years. In her spare time she took to directing plays, and Jackie and I always made sure at least one of us was at her various opening nights.

My biggest thrill at Harvard came when graduation day arrived. Because Al Gore, the Vice-president of America, was giving the graduation speech, security was massive. Not knowing the ropes at these events, I found myself being pushed by the huge crowds to the back of the seating area.

That was no good to me. I hadn't spent £100,000 over the last four years and flown two-thousand miles to watch my 'two-inch' daughter receive her degree. I wanted to see the expression on Kat's face as she stepped forward for her moment of glory. So I waved my way imperiously through Al Gore's security guards, telling them, with my best David Niven impression, that I was an English professor at the university and urgently needed to talk to one of my students. Miraculously it worked. I pushed my way through the madding crowds, offering congratulations to the parents as I went, and plonked myself down in the front row.

To make sure of recording the big moment, I'd brought every bit of camera equipment I owned. I had more cameras hanging around my neck than a Japanese tourist. To the acute embarrassment of Kat, I proceeded to film everything that moved and, would you believe it, I was so busy hustling and bustling to get pole position, when it came for her turn to walk out in front of the gathered masses I missed the glorious moment. All I ended up with was a wonderful photograph of the back of her head. It did cross my mind to ask them to do a second take, but even my cheek failed me under Katya's baleful stare.

Even though I didn't get a perfect photograph of the 'moment', it's a day I'll cherish for ever and I must admit it wasn't only Katya that I was proud of. I allowed myself to wallow in a touch of self-congratulation. Somehow Jackie and I had completed a task set us twenty-three years before. We'd helped our daughter to get through a major stage of her life.

The only other time Kat had been away from home for a long period was when she took off for a back-packing trip around East Africa. Helly Sykes and a friend of theirs, Charlotte Anderton, also went along.

One of her orders from Head Office (namely us) was to try to get to Tanzania. We'd started a charity the year before to help the Tanzanians save their black rhinos and we wanted Kat to check on the progress of our work.

We'd been going on safari to Africa, Helly included, for some years. On one trip we'd met some scientists in Kenya and they'd invited us to slip over the border into Tanzania and join them at their Seronera research station in the Serengeti. Of course we jumped at the chance of being in the depths of the Bush, out of range of the tourists, and we joined them for a field trip.

One night we were sitting around the camp-fire (for which I bravely risked my life collecting the wood) when the conversation got around to rhinos, and in particular to the increasing scarcity of them.

Apparently the Tanzanian government had a plan to do a census of their rhinos, but because of a lack of funds it was gathering dust on the shelf of some government office. Innocently I enquired how much it would take to put the survey into operation.

'We need to raise about £400,000,' one of the scientists replied.

Before I could open my mouth to wish them luck, I found myself being nominated, by Jackie, Kat and Helly, to do the honours. There was no point in protesting – they'd made up their minds that I was going to raise the money, so that was that.

It wasn't only the girls who made it difficult for me to back out of the promise they'd made on my behalf, it was Africa. Once bitten, you're smitten for life.

That night, wrapped up in my sleeping-bag, I let the sounds of the African Bush wash over me. Lions roaring in the distance, their throaty growls travelling over distances of five miles, warning folk to stay away. Hyenas screeching as they squabbled over some poor unfortunate victim. It was amazing. Crickets clicking their back legs together in a cacophony of sound and insects buzzing around in the light of the crackling fire made the night magical.

Kat and Helly had elected to sleep out in the open, under a blanket of stars, and were busy setting up their camp-beds. Lying next to Jackie in our little tent, I listened to the girls giggling helplessly as they tried to cope with their portable mosquito nets.

Although raising money for rhinos was the last thing I had time for, that wonderfully romantic African night seduced me into believing that it was my *duty* to raise the £400,000 to help save the black rhino.

A few weeks after we got back, we started a charity called the Faith Foundation (yes, I know it was a bit pretentious) and set about raising the money and equipment that was needed.

As it turned out, although I enjoyed the challenge of raising the cash, I soon became disillusioned. Sick of rhino charities fighting each other and jockeying to be the prominent player, I closed down the Faith Foundation and merged its assets, and my efforts, with those of the London Zoological Society.

All through Kat's time at Harvard I was still writing for the *Mail on Sunday* and, because of the page, I was to meet a man who was to become one of my very best friends.

One time, I wanted to do a 'Tycoons Top Ten' share portfolio and asked ten major businessmen to give me their favourite share tip. Apart from James Hanson, Gordon White and Charlie Forte, I'd asked Harry Solomon, the chairman of a huge food company called Hillsdown. Although I'd never met him before, Harry was quite happy to give me a share tip. But when I asked him, along with the other nine contributors, to submit a photograph, he refused point blank – publicity being anathema to him. So, I thanked him for his help and arranged to meet this enigma for lunch a couple of weeks later.

One night Jo Bowlby and I were having Bilinis (Champagne and fresh peach juice) in Harry's Bar, when I felt a tap on my shoulder. I turned round and came face to face with a complete stranger.

'You don't know me,' said the stranger pleasantly, 'but we're having lunch tomorrow.' It was the elusive Harry Solomon.

Our lunch the next day at San Lorenzo's went all too quickly and because we'd got on so well we decided to meet again as soon as Harry got back from his holiday. The next day, Wednesday, he was flying to Barbados for three weeks, but I'd made a new pal and didn't want to wait so long to meet again, so I suggested that I fly to Barbados and have dinner with him at eight o'clock that Thursday evening. Harry laughed and dismissed my ridiculous suggestion as showbiz banter.

The day after Harry and his wife Judy arrived at the Sandy Lane Hotel, unbeknownst to them the girls and I were installed in a suite on the floor above. I got Harry, who had no idea that we were in the hotel, on the blower: 'Hi, Harry, it's Adam Faith. I've got my wife and daughter with me and we'll meet you downstairs in the lobby in five minutes' time.'

Disbelief would not be the word. We all started laughing the moment we saw each other downstairs and never stopped for the whole time we were there. I had only intended to stay a couple of days, but we had such a great time with Harry and Judy that I extended our trip to nearly two weeks. Both Jackie and Kat agree with me that it was the best holiday we have ever had.

And so began a fantastic friendship. Harry is a very special bloke who combines incredible business acumen with a compassionate concern for his fellow man. Through some of my worst moments during the Levitt collapse Harry's support and friendship never wavered. If ever I have a problem now, Harry's the first person I go to for advice and invariably I end up taking it.

Chapter Thirty-seven

I WAS ABOUT TO GET THE MOST EXPENSIVE PHONE CALL OF MY LIFE. Driving down the Mall in December 1990, the mobile jangled into life. It was Clive Woolman, my City editor at the *Mail on Sunday*.

'Have you heard the news about Levitt?' he said.

My heart soared. I'd heard that Roger Levitt had been in advanced talks with a heavyweight Japanese bank to take over his whole company for two hundred million pounds. If the deal went through, it meant that I would be able to cash in my 5 per cent options that I'd now been holding for two years, and retire on the expected ten-million-pound profit. I felt a rush of blind excitement. 'Has he done the deal?'

'No,' Clive grimly replied. 'He's gone bankrupt and the Fraud Squad have moved in.'

Ten million pounds gone, in one phone call.

I struggled to keep control of the car and my senses as it swerved towards the kerb. I pulled the car over and stopped. I was in no fit state to drive after that news. I felt disembodied, light-headed. A voice cool and clear, from somewhere deep at the back of my head, kept repeating, 'Serves you right. Serves you right.' What on earth had stopped me following my instincts? Stupidity and greed, nothing less. I went over and over the horror of what had happened and tried to come to terms with it. How was I going to face people? Here I was, with a money page in a national newspaper, and I'd got caught up in one of the biggest business scandals of the day. Some financial guru.

The collapse of Levitt had been sudden, and although I had my concerns, as unbelievable as it sounds now, I never really saw it coming until it was too late. I'd certainly never thought of Levitt as a crook – any worries I'd had about the Levitt Group had been focused on its chaotic administration. So the fact that the Fraud Squad had been brought in only added to the shock of missing out on my ten million.

Fortunately, as far as I know, none of the clients I, personally, introduced to the Levitt Group lost money. In fact some of them, one in particular whose name it would be too indiscreet to mention, are still benefiting considerably from Roger Levitt's advice. Others, however, lost millions.

My ten million pounds was just paper until I was able to turn it into cash. So, even though it was the most awful shock, all I lost financially was a dream.

Unfortunately another casualty of the Levitt débâcle was my friendship with Michael Winner. Through me, Michael had become a client of the Levitt Group but had subsequently fallen out with Roger because of a commission irregularity. As I was the one who introduced Winner to Levitt, there was no way I was going to be able to dodge the flak flying around from that argument, which was a shame because it's never pleasant to lose a friend.

However, some time later when Jackie had a heart attack, Winner was one of the first people to phone her enquiring after her health.

For months after the 'Fall of the House of Levitt' I walked down the street unable to raise my eyes above pavement level. The terrible press I received embarrassed me so much, I crossed the road if I saw anyone I knew coming towards me. I became so paranoid that I started to believe that even my best friends were avoiding me. I imagined that I could guess what they were thinking. Mud sticks, and it's a hell of a job to get it off once you're splattered with it.

In retrospect, the signs had been there that trouble was brewing, I just chose to close my eyes to them. I curse myself for not acting immediately when my instincts were screaming that something was amiss. Why, oh why, when I started to get worried about the Levitt Group, hadn't I listened to Harry Solomon and John Jay, editor of the *Telegraph*, when they told me to get out?

The crunch came a few days before the crash. A paper-shredder disappeared from my office. Apparently someone from upstairs had taken it off my desk, and had been putting it to use all night long behind the locked doors of the boardroom. Alan Shalet and I decided that it was finally time to part company with Levitt.

As it was coming up to Christmas, I wanted my staff to get their bonuses and I made a fatal mistake of deciding to postpone my resignation until the New Year. After all, what could happen in a couple of weeks?

What do people say? 'Never put off till tomorrow what you can do today.' Well, I sure didn't listen to that and, along with my reputation, everything I'd worked for over the last two years had gone up in smoke.

Love Hurts rose like a phoenix out of the ashes of the Levitt collapse. The idea for the series had first surfaced when I was just finishing *Budgie the Musical*. Alan Field, an agent friend of mine from back in the early Seventies, phoned and asked if he could put a project together for me. I wasn't particularly enthusiastic about the idea because it wasn't long after my heart operation. I was still running my company with Levitt, and writing the page in the *Mail on Sunday*, and I didn't relish taking on anything else. But Alan Field persisted, and the result was a meeting between me, him and two writers: Laurence Marks and Maurice Gran.

As it happened, I'd met the two boys years earlier, when they'd offered me the lead in the television series *Shine On Harvey Moon*. Sitting there in the Savoy, supping tea with them now, I considered myself lucky that they were still talking to me, never mind having a meeting.

Ten days before we'd been due to start filming *Harvey Moon*, I pulled out. It was not long after my car crash and the idea of taking on a major TV role suddenly frightened me to death. My courage failing me, I'd scuttled off to America, and left them in the lurch.

Fortunately, things turned out well for the series. The boys called in Kenneth Cranham, who turned out to be brilliant and helped make the show into a success.

After that initial meeting it was to take two years for *Love Hurts* to become a reality, and as luck would have it, the start date in January 1991 coincided with the Levitt crash. Having a new project to work on helped take my mind off that awful event. I was worried at the time that because of bad publicity of the Levitt débâcle the BBC might want to replace me.

As it turned out, my concerns were unfounded – on the whole, people in show business couldn't be less interested in what goes on in the City. I suppose in that respect I'm a bit of a show-business freak. Zoë Wanamaker once said to me that I was the only person she knew who read the bits of newspapers that other people throw away, namely the financial pages.

It was a relief to be working on something that was successful and there was the bonus of acting with Zoë Wanamaker. Originally, the part of Tessa was to have been played by Patricia Hodge, but she'd pulled out in the fairly early stages of pre-production when she happily found herself pregnant. After weeks of considering practically every actress in England, we were still minus a leading lady. Then one morning Laurence Marks rushed into the production office and pronounced the search over.

'I've found our Tessa,' he shouted triumphantly. He'd been to see a play at the National Theatre the night before, and was raving about the 'wonderful' Zoë Wanamaker.

Guy Slater, the producer of *Love Hurts*, put Zoë and me together for a lunch and after about two and a half seconds we were firm friends. Somewhere in Zoë's upbringing someone had omitted to teach her the word 'Take'. She's a very special girl and a wonderful actress to work with. Over the three years that we were in the series together, hardly a cross word passed between us and because we didn't have an affair in real life there was no baggage, no sulks, no avoiding one another's eyes at breakfast.

When *Love Hurts* was a success, the two people who were the most surprised were Zoë and me. After watching the first week's filming, the writers came to us claiming that we had a huge success in the making. Zoë and I couldn't figure it out at all. As far as we were concerned, we were in a 'nice' little series about an odd couple falling in love. Of course what we hadn't figured into our equation was that *Love Hurts* was about the two most important things in people's lives, namely love and money. My character, Frank Carver, had spent his life trying to earn the money to enjoy the lust, while what he was waiting for was love. Fortunately for him, he found that love with Tessa.

After the initial success of the show it was very disappointing to find that the second series totally changed course. The powers-that-be, in their wisdom, decided that the attention span of the audience could not be sustained by a simple love affair, and that *Love Hurts* needed to be spiced up. Silly escapades, like getting kidnapped in Russia, completely changed the second series and, quite rightly, the viewers who'd got hooked on *Love Hurts* the year before showed their disapproval by deserting the show in droves.

Bitterly disappointed, Zoë and I insisted that if we were to do another series it would have to go back to the original format. By this time we'd got ourselves a different producer and a new team of writers. Laurence and Maurice were in overall control as executive producers.

The first scripts were awaited with great anticipation by Zoë and me. When I read them, I was devastated. It seemed to me that nothing had improved from the second series and after seeing my lawyer, I threatened to pull out of the show.

A damage limitation meeting was immediately called by Laurence and Maurice, and along with our new producer, Zoë and I turned up at a Chinese restaurant in Hampstead ready for the fray. Over chicken chow mein and sweet and sour pork balls, battle commenced. I became the unofficial spokesman for Zoë and myself, and I tore into the writers, voicing our complaints.

It got so bad that at one point I challenged Maurice Gran to a duel with bare hands as weapons. Raging at him like a demented banshee, I demanded that he, 'Come out into the street and fight. If I win,' I ranted 'the series goes my way, if you win, I'll shut up and do as I'm told.'

The rest of the table sat in shocked silence. Zoë's mouth dropped open. I don't think she expected her champion to go this far. Waving my chopsticks in Maurice's face, I continued to threaten him. I drew myself up to my full five foot, five and a half inches, and prepared for war. When will I ever learn? Maurice was much bigger than me.

Thank God Zoë had the good sense to jump between us and put a stop to me making a complete fool of myself. In the event, the meeting collapsed in a heap of laughter at my ridiculous suggestion and we all went our separate ways agreeing on a sensible compromise.

While I was waiting for the third series to start there were some decisions to be made. All through the first two years of *Love Hurts* I was still writing my financial page for the *Mail on Sunday*. Every Thursday and Friday night, the minute filming came to an end, Mickey Towner, my driver, would run me straight to the *Mail on Sunday* offices in Kensington High Street.

While I sat there, all night if necessary, banging away at the word processor, Mickey would ply me with hamburgers, diet Coke and lemon tea, until I was satisfied that the page was fit for publication. Even though I enjoyed the work, it was very hard keeping two full-time jobs going and now with the third series of *Love Hurts* coming up, there was no way I could face it any longer. With great reluctance I said goodbye to the page.

During my time as a 'high-powered' City man I'd picked up a few directorships. To concentrate on my acting career, I decided to complete the clear-out of my extra-curricular activities by resigning as non-executive director of the Savoy Hotel and Melody Radio.

Giles Shepherd, Managing Director of the Savoy, accepted my resignation without hesitation. All my shenanigans with Levitt had probably unsettled him.

Melody Radio was a different matter altogether. Lord Hanson, its chairman, whom I'd known since the early Sixties, refused point blank to accept my resignation, arguing that as I'd been there from the conception I should stay and see the station become a success. It would take more than a bit of financial 'tittle tattle' to shake James Hanson's loyalty to his friends and colleagues.

While all these resignations were flying around, Dave Courtney and I were gorging ourselves on a creative feast. Despite our earlier disagreements, our friendship had repaired itself over the years. He'd been on at me to make a new album and had finally caught me on the right day. *Midnight Postcards* was a mixture of old favourites like 'Squeeze Box' and 'Stuck in the Middle' and new songs written by Dave and me. In spite of a mistimed marketing campaign and a confused song policy, entirely down to Dave and me, *Midnight Postcards* sold close to

50,000 copies. Which, although slightly disappointing, was better than a slap in the face with a wet fish.

The third series of *Love Hurts* was screened, and the viewers appeared to have forgiven us our transgressions. The viewing figures picked up and we debated the possibility of going on with the show but no-one could come up with a viable storyline. It was felt that there were only so many times that Tessa and Frank could 'break up' and 'make up' so, in the end, we all decided that it was probably better to quit while we were ahead.

After glasnost and perestroika hit Russia, it seemed like the whole of the Western commercial world was steaming eastward. All wanting to see what deals there were to be done. So when St Petersburg was chosen as our foreign location for the third series of *Love Hurts*, I was thrilled. Although I'd put business on the back-burner, Russia was too good an opportunity from a business point of view. I looked forward to giving the place the once over.

Unfortunately, it didn't take much more than a cursory glance to know that the combination of the Mafia and the chaotic bureaucracy made it not only impossible but downright danger-ous to do business in Russia. For the whole of the six weeks I was in St Petersburg I'd tried to buy a wonderful apartment on the Nevsky Prospekt, the city's main street, but gave up in frustra-tion.

Europeans were opening businesses and finding themselves at the mercy of thugs who were offering 'protection'. The police were helpless to stop the crime because the crooks were better equipped than they were: the police drove Ladas, the gangs drove Mercedes; the police had handguns, the crooks used semi-automatics.

I wasn't ready to become a character in a real-life *Godfather* movie, so I decided to wait for safer opportunities.

Some time later an article appeared in a newspaper claiming that Russia could no longer provide Cuba with overseas aid. In the same piece, it stated that China wasn't interested in filling the gap left by the Russians. With the American trade embargo get-ting tougher by the minute, Cuba was getting squeezed to death economically.

I rationalized that the only option left to Cuba was to open its doors to capitalism and trade with the rest of the world. So off I trotted to Cuba for a recce. I was bang on. My four days there were enough to tell me that Cuba was bursting with business opportunities for the adventurous.

After setting up a 'consultancy' partnership with a friend in the City, I made plans to return to Cuba for a three-month stay. The idea was to set up a base in Havana and investigate investment opportunities: property, import/export, tourism, hotels, etc.

As luck would have it, the Department of Trade and Industry had a trade delegation going out to Cuba at the same time, and I was invited to join it. Being a member of the delegation was very useful: I was able to make contacts at government level and on the second day a meeting with President Castro was scheduled.

All the members of our trade delegation gathered in the lobby of the Hotel Nationale, fidgeting nervously as we waited for the bus to take us to the Presidential Palace. I don't believe there was one of us that didn't feel excited at the thought of meeting Fidel Castro. He was a legend: he'd run with Che Guevara and his poster had adorned students' rooms in every country in the world; he had outlived Mao Tse Tung, Brezhnev and Kennedy. He was the last revolutionary of his kind and it was a real thrill to be meeting him.

At the palace we were ushered into a small ante-room to await the arrival of El Grande. Not wishing to seem uncool I lingered somewhere near the back of the crowd. The wait seemed like ten years, and the coughs and nervous giggles came more frequently as each minute ticked by. I must admit despite my icy exterior, the old nerves were doing a tap-dance on the stomach muscles.

At last the heavy oak doors burst open and six bodyguards pushed through the opening and spread themselves either side of the doorway. Filling the space behind them was 'The Man'. A piece of living history. He stood silently surveying the room. Fidel knew how to make an entrance – the last time I'd seen something as impressive was in Atlanta at an Elvis Presley concert.

Immediately, we fell silent. Castro, used to making this sort of impact on people, cast an imperial eye over the gathered throng, smiled benevolently and moved into the room. Catching sight of our delegation leader Baroness Young, he extended his huge right hand and welcomed her to the palace. He moved about the room greeting us one by one, and occasionally breaking into loud guffaws of laughter as his interpreter filled him in on some witty aside from one of my fellow delegates.

When it came for my turn to be introduced, he stood towering over me like Nelson's column. He studied me for a moment, then leaned back on his heels as if to get a better look, and slowly his face broke into a broad smile. 'I recognize you,' he said. I flashed him my most condescending, why-wouldn't-you-I'm-so-famous smile, and then proceeded, in front of the whole room, to make a complete twit of myself.

Before I'd left the hotel I'd promised myself faithfully that I wouldn't try to impress 'The Man' with my grasp of Spanish. As I was shaving I gave myself a stiff talking to because even at its best my Spanish left something to be desired, but thirty years on it was downright sad. I'd already nearly caused World War Three by asking a taxi driver to take me straight to his wife's bedroom by the shortest route, when all I had wanted was to go back to my hotel.

But standing in front of Castro I couldn't resist lapsing into the local vernacular. Beaming from ear to ear I smugly glanced round the room to make sure my fellow delegates were watching, and launched into a great diatribe on how happy I was to be in Cuba meeting the great man.

It wasn't so much the confused look on Castro's face as he tried to work out what language I was spouting that disconcerted me, it was that his interpreter was laughing so much he couldn't translate my 'Spanish' into a language his boss could understand.

I never used the native lingo again while I was in Cuba. I found I was on much safer ground using sign language.

I've looked forward to my trips to Cuba over the last couple of years and have got involved in some very interesting projects. Along the way I've also made some very good friends. Including a taxi driver called Hiram, who just so happens to be an English professor as well. But as teachers earn the equivalent of about three pounds a month, touting his cab around Havana is the only way he has of earning the sought-after US dollars. While he waits for a fare, he sits in his Merc reading Shakespeare – in English.

After *Love Hurts*, my first project was a huge tour of the UK with the Bill Naughton play *Alfie*. I'd played Alfie twice before, once in the late Sixties at the Alexander Theatre, Birmingham, and then much later in 1983 with Alan Parker (the film director of *Mississippi Burning* and *Evita*) at the Liverpool Playhouse.

When I had first suggested that we should do *Alfie*, Alan had reservations that I might, at forty-three, be too old to play the part. But, he hadn't read the play. Like most people, his impressions of Alfie were formed through watching the movie where Alfie is portrayed as a young 'Jack the Lad' in the swinging Sixties, bonking his way round London.

In fact, when Bill wrote the piece in the Fifties, he'd written Alfie as a much older man. And although the movie was brilliant and hugely successful, Alfie as a pathetic middle-aged man, too old to change his ways, makes the play a much sadder, bleaker and, in some ways, more powerful piece.

The play went amazingly well, and the Liverpool audiences took us and Alfie to their hearts. On one particular evening I was to experience one of the highlights of my acting career.

There's a fantastic scene in the play where Alfie leaves one of his married girlfriends to get rid of their baby. He had arranged for a backstreet abortionist to take care of the 'problem'. Too scared to face up to his responsibilities, he walks out on the woman and leaves her to abort alone.

It's a particularly harrowing scene, and I always dreaded coming straight back on to do the next speech. Standing in the wings, with the fading screams of the unfortunate woman as she aborts echoing around the theatre, you could cut the atmosphere with a knife. The waves of anger coming off the audience, as they sat there in shocked silence at Alfie's callous behaviour, were palpable.

This particular night, when I went back on to face the resentful silence, a woman's tortured voice broke out from way up in the gods. 'You bastard!' The disembodied voice hung in the silent air for a moment and then, as if the unknown woman's fury had lanced a boil, a shocked gasp of agreement went shuddering through the audience. It was a most amazing expression of emotion. Chilled to the bone I stood there, shamefully thrilled to have touched that woman's emotions so deeply.

ChapterThirty-eight

JACKIE AND ADAM FAITH ANNOUNCED THAT SINCE LAST SEPTEMBER, THEY HAVE DECIDED TO LEAD SEPARATE LIVES. THEY REMAIN CLOSE FRIENDS AND ASK FOR THEIR PRIVACY TO BE RESPECTED. THEY DO NOT PROPOSE TO MAKE ANY FURTHER STATEMENTS.

We'd had no intention of announcing our decision to the rest of the world, but were finally forced to go public because of press claims that Louise Lombard and I were having a relationship.

When Jackie and I made that statement concerning our marriage we expected that to be the end of the matter. But it unleashed a flurry of press activity which imprisoned Jackie inside the house with the blinds drawn.

When the press descend on your home it's like having the whole neighbourhood peering at you from behind their curtains. And my goodness, just one experience of their persistent demands can be very upsetting. The way we as a family have dealt with queries about our private life is by giving exactly the

271

same answer, no matter what the questions or provocation: *'I've got nothing to say.'* When the press understand that you mean it, and that they are not going to wake up next morning to see an exclusive interview in one of their rival papers, they relax and normally leave you alone.

Having worked for a paper, I know that the worst thing that can happen to a reporter is to take a victim's word for a story only to be carpeted by his editor because someone else was given an exclusive. That can't happen in our case because we never give interviews, exclusive or otherwise, about our private lives. Writing this book is the nearest I'll ever get to talking about my private life.

That's not to say that the shallower elements in the press don't persist. When Jackie and I announced our separation, Mickey Towner, my driver, was inundated with bribes to spill the beans on our home life. They wouldn't have got much for their money, we've lived a pretty normal home life. They could have the dramatic exclusive that Jackie does the gardening, by floodlight, until the early hours, that I listen to *The Archers* avidly, or that Isabella, our King Charles spaniel, wet the carpet on 19 August 1993.

When the press were camping at the bottom of the drive, Mickey handled them with good-humoured firmness and deflected all their attempts to bribe him. One Sunday tabloid offered him £25,000 to give them the inside story on the Faiths' home life. With an integrity that's rare these days, Mickey politely told them where to put it.

Mickey has been a wonderful friend to me, Jackie and Katya. Permanently optimistic, he's got a knack of making people feel happy when they are in his company. I don't know what Jackie would have done without him during some of the darker moments of the past two years.

The darkest of those moments came in August 1995.

When a telephone jangles in your ear at three o'clock in the morning, you know it's going to be good news.

Jackie had just had a heart attack and was in an ambulance on her way to the Kent and Sussex Hospital, Tunbridge Wells. Twenty minutes later I drove into Covent Garden to pick up Kat. To save time, I'd asked her to wait on the pavement outside her flat. As I pulled into her road, Kat stood alone in a pool of light that the streetlamp had thrown at her feet. I drew alongside her, she looked desolate, her face pale and drawn, she'd been crying. My heart, already aching at the frightening news, wanted to break at her unhappiness.

We sat in virtual silence all the way to Kent. We were both gripped by a horrible debilitating fear that made us feel physically weak and the thought that we might lose her made us realize just how much she meant to us both.

Thank God, when we got to the hospital we learned that she was all right.

Kat puffed away anxiously at a Marlboro Light as we listened to the doctor tell us that the heart attack was caused by years of heavy smoking and had been triggered by emotional stress. Although Jackie wasn't out of the woods, he didn't anticipate any complications. Kat, overwhelmingly relieved at the good news, ground out her cigarette butt in the ashtray next to her and quickly lit up another.

I've complained about press intrusion but I have to say they were kindness itself during the time that Jackie was in hospital. They enquired with what I like to think was genuine concern about Jack's progress and surprisingly it became a comfort to see their friendly faces when we arrived at the hospital every morning.

It's very difficult to work out your personal problems in the glare of publicity and as with most 'celebrities' the question over what is 'public' and what is 'private' has a special significance. It's not easy to guard your privacy in the UK because our press can be quite ruthless and it's probably one of the reasons that I've always kept Terry Nelhams and Adam Faith separate.

As far as I'm concerned Adam Faith is public property and they can have as much access to him as they want. But Terry Nelhams is my private life, and is no-one's business but my own.

This protective instinct is particularly strong when it comes to my family. They have their own lives to live, and should not be subjected to public scrutiny, just because they happen to be associated with someone in the public eye. It's simply not right!

Apart from my split with Jackie, the last few years have brought about other fundamental changes in my life. Changes of a more philosophical nature. I've started to reassess my priorities. Or more specifically, I've started to ask 'Why?' instead of 'How?' The question has always been concerned with how I can achieve something. How can I become rich? How can I become successful? Never giving myself time to reflect on whether I was actually enjoying life.

My philosophy is best summed up in a story I was told by a wise old Asian lawyer, Sadiq Ghalia. I was ranting on about business, achievement and success, when Sadiq quietened me with a wave of his hand, and told me a tale.

A tourist in Africa was taking an evening stroll along the beach, when in the fading light he came upon a local fisherman sitting on the sand, cooking some fish on a driftwood fire.

He stopped and commented on how wonderful the cooking smelled. 'Sit down and join me,' said the fisherman.

The tourist, embarrassed by his generosity, politely declined his offer.

'No, no,' he said, 'it's your fish. I couldn't possibly impose.'

The fisherman smiled and insisted. 'I've got plenty, you are welcome to share it with me.'

After eating the best fish he'd ever tasted, the tourist stood and before making to leave offered to pay for his meal.

The fisherman would have none of it, insisting that he had plenty to go round.

The tourist thanked the man profusely, and as he went to leave, spotted a dug-out canoe lapping up against the beach in the water. 'Is that your boat?' he asked the fisherman.

'Yes,' the fisherman nodded.

'Well, why don't you let me pay you for the fish I've eaten, and then you will have some money.' The tourist moved for his wallet.

'Why would I need your money?' The fisherman looked puzzled.

The tourist, anxious to give the fisherman a lesson in economics, patiently explained. 'If you sold all the fish you have left over, you could buy a bigger boat with the money.'

'Why would I want to do that?' the fisherman asked.

Determined to make his point, the tourist persevered. 'Because, if you had a bigger boat, you could catch more fish.'

'But why would I want to catch more fish?'

The tourist was now getting impatient. 'Because, if you caught more fish, you could sell what you don't eat and get even more money.'

'But why would I want more money?' The fisherman was even more puzzled.

'Because', said the tourist, trying desperately not to lose his temper, 'you could buy an even bigger boat, and catch even more fish.'

'Why would I want to buy a bigger boat and catch more fish?'

The tourist, sure by now that the fisherman was being obtuse just for the sake of it, made it his mission to introduce the fisherman to the law of economics.

'BECAUSE if you bought a bigger boat, you could hire someone to go out and catch the fish for you.' Surely, thought the tourist, it's finally going to sink in.

The fisherman looked up. 'But why would I want someone to catch my fish for me?'

'BECAUSE', the tourist by now was ready to pull his hair out in frustration, 'if you hired someone else to catch your fish for you, you could sit on the beach and eat fish all day.'

The fisherman leaned back on his elbows, shook his head and grinned. 'But that's what I'm doing anyway.'

Jackie had been telling me much the same for years. 'You spend your whole life looking for something you already have,' she'd tell me when I was chasing my tail over yet another piece of nonsense.

I suppose it's true, I just didn't care to take notice of the advice.

The British tour of *Alfie* finished in Cardiff in August 1994 and two days later I started rehearsing with an entirely new cast, only this time it was in Los Angeles.

Melanie Green, my old assistant from the Fortnum & Mason days, who was now living in LA managing actors like Amanda Payes and David Duchovny, had been to England to see the play and persuaded me to give *Alfie* an airing at The Tiffany, a small ninety-nine-seat theatre on Sunset Boulevard.

I was a bit concerned about how I would approach the play in The Tiffany, it being so small, so as Katya was experienced in directing in limited spaces at Harvard University, I asked her to break into her semester and come to LA and direct *Alfie* for me.

Despite reservations from everyone except me, it was a fantastic experience being directed by my own daughter. Although they never expressed it openly, I'm sure the cast were worried about nepotism, but after the first day's rehearsals they could see that Kat was there because she was good. She took the play to a depth and sensitivity that I'd never dreamt of getting back in England, and we went on to enjoy critical success.

Alfie had given me success in both England and America but I grew to resent the effect it had on my emotional state of mind. For over a year I spilled my emotional guts out on stage every night. At first I'd been able to recover my emotions after each performance, but as the tour went on, the residue of unhappiness built up to a point where it never left me.

Unfortunately, I'm one of those actors who can't take a part off like an overcoat once the show's over. I don't *act* a part, I *live* it. Which may be good for the creative soul, but it plays havoc with your emotional well-being.

At times, I'd be walking down a busy street somewhere, in broad daylight, and suddenly find myself, for no reason, bursting into tears. I knew I was behaving irrationally but I couldn't help myself. It got to be quite scary. It felt like I was losing my mind to a force that was taking me over, and there seemed to be nothing I could do to stop it happening.

By the time I got to America, my emotional state was in terminal decline. Being in LA didn't help. It's an unhappy, soulless place at the best of times, and it's the last place you need to be if you are the least bit emotionally rocky. Nobody in LA has the time of day for anyone that might prove to be a negative force in their maniacal quest for fame and fortune. Fortunately for me I had Katya and Melanie keeping an eye on the key to the medicine cabinet, and I got through the experience. But it was a close-run thing at times.

Playing Alfie had got my depression to such a chronic pitch, I couldn't leave the house without feeling paranoid. I'd pray for a phone call to tell me that the theatre had burned down and I wouldn't need to do the show that night. Because we only worked Thursday to Sunday I had three days to hide myself away. Unshaven, unwashed I'd lie in the darkened bedroom, wallowing

276

in self-pity for days on end, seriously considering that a quick leap over the Niagara Falls without a barrel looked a viable option to doing one more performance of *Alfie*.

At one point I got so desperate that I even considered turning to religion for comfort. But that thought was short-lived, organized religion being a bit of an anathema to me. I did toy with the idea of Buddhism – Buddhists seem such happy contented souls – but I turned away from it, in fear of my obsessive nature. Knowing me, before you could say 'Dalai Lama' I'd find myself sitting on top of a mountain in Tibet with a shaved head, wearing an orange nightdress.

But something did happen in LA that proved to be my nemesis. Playing Alfie in front of an audience that was so close I could read their emotions in their eyes, I had to be completely open, and in revealing Alfie's sensitivities I exposed the raw ends of my own. All my life I'd hidden my true feelings for fear of getting them damaged, but now that I couldn't hide them I realized it didn't matter. It was OK to be me.

I felt a freedom I'd never experienced before. I was free of my own fears.

This new perspective on life has come with a feeling of confidence which I've never had before, and I'm sure that this change is largely due to the public's reaction to *Love Hurts*.

I've always felt a warmth from the British public, but since *Love Hurts* there's been a significant change in their attitude. We've become closer, as if I've lived in a village for thirty years and the locals have at last decided that I'm an OK bloke and can become one of them after all.

Another surprise that has emerged from the last couple of years is that at last I'm not afraid of being alone and I'm even starting to enjoy my own company. Will I start getting bored of myself and feel the need to have a permanent relationship in my life? Who knows? At the moment I'm quite happy to enjoy female company when it's there, and concentrate the majority of my efforts on my work.

I've always been anxious about the future and it's made me approach my career as if today is the last time I'll ever work. Petrified of missing opportunities, I seem to have spent my life rushing to catch the tube before the doors close.

But now at last, with my new-found confidence, I'm happy to

sit back and see what fate turns up.

Of course, with the typical irony of life, now that I've stopped worrying about the future offers are piling in from all over the place and I'm already trying to work out how I can squeeze three years' work into one.

'What about the future?' is probably the question I get asked the most. 'What is there that you haven't done that you'd like to try?' Well, as I have probably been one of the most incredibly blessed people on earth and have been privileged to 'play' all my life, it's hard to come up with something I haven't tried, so I've usually settled for this answer:

'I'd like to do everything all over again. Only, *better*.'

Index

Note: The abbreviation AF is used for Adam Faith (Terence Nelhams-Wright).